HOLLYWOOD'S OTHER BLACKLIST

HOLLYWOOD'S OTHER BLACKLIST

Union Struggles in the Studio System

MIKE NIELSEN AND GENE MAILES

BFI PUBLISHING

First published in 1995 by the
British Film Institute
21 Stephen Street
London W1P 2LN

The British Film Institute exists to promote
appreciation, enjoyment, protection and development of
moving image culture in and throughout the whole of
the United Kingdom. Its activities include the
National Film and Television Archive; The National
Film Theatre; The London Film Festival; The Museum of
the Moving Image; the production and distribution of
film and video; funding and support for regional
activities; Library and Information Services; Stills,
Posters and Designs; Research; Publishing and
Education; and the monthly *Sight and Sound* magazine.

British Library Cataloguing in Publication Data.
A catalogue record for this book is available from the
British Library.

ISBN: 0-85170-508-1
        0-85170-509-X

Cover design by Push
Cover still: The Whistle at Eaton Falls (Robert Siodmak, 1951)

Archive pictures of studio pickets courtesy of Los Angeles Daily News Morgue,
Department of Special Collections, University Research Library, UCLA.

Typeset in 10 pt Plantin Light and 9.5 pt Plantin Semi bold
by D R Bungay Associates, Burghfield, Berks.
Printed in Great Britain by St Edmundsbury Press Ltd,
Bury St Edmunds, Suffolk.

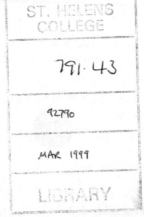

CONTENTS

ACKNOWLEDGMENTS

Gene was blacklisted from Hollywood before I was born. Gene and I would never have met had it not been for the encouragement of Dave Williams and Vincent DiGiorolamo of Santa Cruz, CA and that of Jeff Goodman of Los Angeles. In the early days of my research I had crucial support and help from the Institute of Communications Research at the University of Illinois and in particular from my advisor, Dr. Thomas Guback, whose critical approach to the study of mass communications shaped my ideas on the role of labor in a capitalist economy. Thanks to Dan Citzrom for uttering the words 'oral history' at exactly the right moment. The good people at the UCLA archives helped Gene and I both with our research, holding much of Gene's personal collection of IA Progressives memorabilia and documents until I found them at UCLA in 1984. During the writing of my dissertation which forms the core of my part of this book, I had great help from Mike Budd and especially Clay Steinman in shaping up my ideas about the Hollywood studio system.

Several former motion picture craft workers in California gave me personal interviews in 1984 and I am grateful to all those people for their kindness and hospitality. I would like to thank in particular Frank Barenna and Jerry Kraus. Many thanks to Roy Brewer and Ted Ellsworth for their valuable time. Gene and Laya Mailes were cordial hosts on my visits to their home in Soquel. Gene has done a good job of acknowledging his comrades in arms in the final chapter of the book. It would be presumptuous of me to add to this list.

I received timely financial support from Wesley College and from Florida Atlantic University for my travel expenses to California. Many thanks.

Gene and I will be forever grateful to the publishing division of the BFI for their support and encouragement of this book. In particular, I would like to thank Ed Buscombe, John O. Thompson, David Wilson and Dawn King (who has pulled this final phase together with good humor and enthusiasm).

Finally, saving the deepest debts for last, I thank my kids Hannah and Chris but most of all, I thank my pal/wife Betsy. Sometimes when you see these acknowledgments in books, you read into them that the author is simply apologizing for having taken so much time away from a relationship. There is a bit of that in my thanks to Betsy; however, the truth is that her editing skills and progressive political perspective have both been sewn into the fabric of this book. She has egged me at every stage of this project and without her enthusiasm and patience, this book would never have seen the light of day.

Mike Nielsen, 1995

PROLOGUE

Irv Hentschel was one of the leaders of the IA Progressives and this story is inspired in large part by Gene Mailes' memories of Irv and other friends who stood up to the crime syndicate and the studio bosses and tried to establish honest trade unionism in the Hollywood studios. We have collaborated on this book in order to provide an accurate and fair accounting of the accomplishments and failures of progressive trade unionists working 'below-the-line' in the motion picture industry. Gene was active in the fight from 1939 until his expulsion from the union and the industry in 1946.[1]

We have found it most convenient to keep our accounts separate, and our aim is that they should reinforce each other. Our contributions are distinguished typographically with Gene's account in bold. (M.N.)

The first time I spoke to Irv Hentschel was the night of the riot. I had heard of and read about him, but I didn't know what he really looked like. I was totally unimpressed by him – short, slight, maybe 110 pounds, rather homely. He was frowning into the viewfinder of a camera and there were two husky men there who were guarding him and looking around for any crime syndicate thugs.

It was 1939 and we were in the midst of a union election, trying to set up a democratic trade union for studio workers in Hollywood. We were fighting the International Alliance of Theatrical and Stage Employes [*sic*] (IA), which at that time was under the control of the Chicago crime syndicate of Frank Nitti, the inheritor of the Capone crime syndicate and known as 'The Enforcer'.

Irv was one of the leaders of the dissidents who wanted to restore local control of the union. The elections were being supervised by the National Labor Relations Board (NLRB), and the winning union would have the right to represent several thousand studio workers in negotiations with the studio bosses.

We had been hanging around all day, waiting for some emergency to come up. There were about thirty of us, all told. We were stationed in a vacant lot across the street from where the election was taking place.

At about six in the evening, we got the word that there was some reason to go to the drive-in restaurant on the southeast corner of Beverly and Fairfax. As we approached the drive-in, I noticed that the guys who were with us began to fan out, leaving about four feet between them, in a line facing a group of men sitting at a table. I learned later

that these guys we were approaching were small time hoods brought in from out of town to try to muscle the election in favor of the IA.

When we got close to them, Irv began taking pictures of them. That set them off and they jumped up from the table and began fighting. The biggest guy on our side of the fight led the battle for us. He was one of five guys who had joined us earlier in the day, guys who were well-muscled and looked like the middle-weight boxers. The biggest one of them yanked each one of the IA thugs up, slugged him, and tossed him over his shoulder for the rest of us to take a crack at.

We were playing the part of amateur goons. The American Heritage Dictionary defines 'goon' as 'a thug hired to commit acts of intimidation or violence'. 'Hired' is the key word here. Union goons were usually regular union members who voluntarily protected smaller and more defenseless union members who were on picket lines. A corrupt union such as the IA at that time had to bring in outside goons to try to intimidate the regular working people into playing along with them. Sometimes the leaders of the IA would get studio jobs for these guys to try to cover up the fact that they were there to threaten and beat up people. But they stuck out like a sore thumb. Everyone knew they were mob characters and treated them accordingly.

Irv was standing near me just before we left the drive-in. I asked him if he had actually gotten any pictures. He answered 'Nah!', accompanied by an ugly grimace.

We were in and out very quickly, before the police had time to respond. One of our guys got knocked cold and had to be carried away. We went back to our spot across from the voting place. I was separated from Irv and I really didn't get a chance to talk to him again for more than a year. In later years, it dawned on me what a price this frail man paid for fighting the good fight. During these years, in the 1930s and 1940s, he took a real beating, both physical and psychological. (G.M.)

This is the story of people who worked together to fight corrupt labor unions in the Hollywood motion picture industry. On the one hand, it is an exceptional story of remarkable people. On the other, it is a story of people who have been pushed to the margins of history by their failure to overcome the powers that be.

The story as it is told here is a mixture of academic history and personal recollections. The two authors slowly collided with one another. Independent of each other, we were writing histories of the unionization and corruption of the Hollywood labor force. I was writing an external account, based on trade papers, California labor history books, and an archive of personal memorabilia at the UCLA Special Collections. Gene Mailes wrote his part of the story from personal remembrances and what archival information he could get hold of.

We were both working under the 'Father Dunne' thesis of the events that took place in the 1930s and 1940s in Hollywood. Father Dunne wrote a well-researched report for the Archbishop of Los Angeles in the late 1940s that examined the causes of the famous Hollywood studio strikes of 1945-7. His final report, eventually published by the strikers themselves, was a scathing indictment of both the union leaders and the managers of the studios. In short, Dunne argues that the studio bosses paid off crime syndicate representatives to hold down wages; union leaders stole from the members through special assessments; and union leaders and studio bosses colluded to undermine democratic unionism in Hollywood.

This is a part of Hollywood history that the industry would just as soon forget. It is noteworthy that US producers of feature films have consciously shied away from making films about the studio strikes. The strikes are the 'unspoken thing' among old-time Hollywood folks. The rancor of those events continues to haunt the industry. More importantly, as the chips fell in 1945-7, so they lie today. The winners of that time dynastically picked their successors and today's labor structure in the US film industry is based largely on the deals worked out at that time.

Jurisdictional conflict in the American Federation of Labor was inherent in the concept of unions organized on craft lines and run on the strict idea of protection of the members of a particular craft, in a particular shop. The local unions had no authority to settle jurisdictional questions among themselves, because the various parent national unions had been recognized as having that right. Nothing was going to take a job away from any national union without a fight, regardless of the position of the local union. This is only one of the reasons the American Federation of Labor had not been able to organize basic industry.

This craft structure of the trade union movement worked fairly well for a number of years. However, the AFL unions were never able to organize more than a very small percentage of the total work force. Most of these union officials were what came to be known as 'business unionists'. That is, they were concerned with the day-to-day problems on the job, pay scales and working conditions. By contrast, 'social unionists' had a broader social goal in mind; they felt the need of basic changes in the entire social system.

John Hutchinson, in *The Imperfect Union*, put it very well:

> It does seem from the record that a contrast, however meager in validity, can be drawn between the behavior of the business unionists and those now called 'social unionists' – those of the larger view, committed to the notion of trade unionism as a moral cause, broad in social jurisdiction, demanding in standards and hopefully exemplary in behavior...
>
> Opposition in IATSE to Browne and Bioff was led by men who could qualify as social unionists...
>
> It is hard to avoid the impression that, throughout the history of American labor, the most effective opposition to corruption has come from those for whom the labor movement was more than a service agency.[2]

Of course, there were some union leaders who were outright crooks, in the game for all that they could get. These men were, however, in a very small minority. But mostly there grew up in the American Federation of Labor a strong group of leaders who enjoyed the idea of being union officials. These men were not necessarily the kind that would take bribes.

They simply liked not having to work as hard as the rest of the men they were in contact with, the ordinary working people. Not only that, but they were allowed to call the bosses by their first names and were in turn called by their first names. They enjoyed two-hour lunches. This was called 'the dress suit' bribe. Rank-and-file members called these officials 'pie-card artists'.

There were also some very domineering union leaders whose greatest pleasure lay in making sure that their policies were, without exception, to be accepted as the only way to run a union. These men perfected the means of taking jurisdiction from any other union that was too weak to prevent such raiding. The local unions had no voice in this procedure. The questions were settled on the upper levels. The result of this was that the jurisdiction went from one national union to the other. The man who had been on the job in question was fired and a man from the winning union was put on the job. In this way the winning union received the dues from the man they had put on the job, and the losing union also lost the dues from the man who had been on the job.

When in the early 1920s the idea that craft unionism had begun to break down completely, that this form was no longer adequate, these men fought the idea of industry-wide organizations, i.e. industrial unions. Some of them, a very small minority, believed deeply in the craft set-up. Others saw the industrial union idea as the end of many jobs as union officials. They were right. This started the end of their power in the movement, until the McCarthy era.

The men who led many of the AFL unions were exemplified by the officials of the IA. These men were able to ride out the period of gang control with no misgivings. The mobs could not have done what they did without the help of these basically corrupt officials. When the IA gang members left to go to prison, the entire official family who had helped them maintained their jobs, using the same tactic that the mob had used so successfully – rabid and incessant anti-communism.

Unions have been suppressed as long as recorded history. When I was fourteen years old, I read H. G. Wells' *Outline of History* and I was struck with the idea that there were strikes in ancient Rome. In fact, on two occasions the plebs 'marched right out of Rome, threatening to make a new city higher up the Tiber, and twice this threat proved conclusive.' I was curious about this. I wondered who organized these strikes. Years later, in reading Upton Sinclair's *Cry for Justice*, I learned that there were trade organizations serving in every way as trade unions as far back as ancient Persia.[3]

In the United States we have examples of the arming of private armies of industrial guards with arsenals that were out of proportion to the requirements of normal protection. In addition to this, companies used 'detective agencies' (private secret police) to ferret out union members, with instant firing and blacklisting to follow. The final report of the LaFollette Civil Liberties Committee (1934-5) bore out all the charges against employers throughout the country, made by trade unions and other groups concerned with civil liberties. The report detailed the beatings, firings, blacklisting and murders that had been standard practices for many years. It is hard today for average working people to believe the enormity of reprisals planned and executed by employers against workers who tried to organize unions in the United States. The LaFollette Commission report states that 'The United States has had the bloodiest and most violent labor history of any industrial nation in the world.' The report also described the type of person that went into the business of 'industrial police'. These men were the type that should never have been trusted with weapons – they were a legitimized criminal element in our midst. They were every bit as misfit as today's crack dealers and pimps. Through the efforts of employers to repress unions, these misfits found a place in society in which they could carry on their activities under government sanction at the expense of the civil rights of working people, solely to benefit the employers.[4]

The election of Franklin D. Roosevelt and the consequent New Deal legislation encouraged workers to organize along industrial lines instead of narrow craft lines. This led to a nationwide rush toward union organization. To many industry and financial heads this was seen as the 'revolution' come true. Others saw it as a direct threat to their positions in the United States and the world. They believed that the rush toward workers 'getting together' had to be stopped by any means necessary.

Yet the New Deal also involved the repeal of the Eighteenth Amendment [Prohibition] – now many criminals had to find new jobs. The big gangs had by that time become highly organized businesses and they had to find new sources of income. The labor movement was looked upon as the next field to enter. Not that they had not been in the unions before this time. But now the idea came up to take over unions completely and run them for the vast sums they knew the average employer was willing to pay to union officials to keep wages low and conditions at the lowest cost. There was also the fact that they could assess the members for part of their weekly pay or collect special initiation fees and then pocket the proceeds.

Against this turbulent background, a handful of men, their wives and friends stood up and tried to clean it up. The great tragedy of this was that it seemed that most of the people and forces that should have been with them were against them.

From the perspective of progressive labor unionism, the loss of the Hollywood studio strikes was enormous, and a sign of the purges to come with the passage of the Taft-Hartley legislation of 1947 that drove the militant organizers out of most US labor unions. With the dispersal of progressive union organizers, the remaining labor leaders and business leaders sat down to discuss bread-and-butter issues of keeping wages in line with the spiraling inflation of the costs of goods and services.

What was really lost was the idea of working people educating each other toward building better lives. The labor progressives were acutely aware of the link between education and progress for working people – not just training for jobs, but training for life. The labor progressives wanted US citizens, regardless of their class and status, to take an active role in the economy and government.

In the post-Reagan era such an ideal seems woefully idealist and impractical. We are so very far from that sort of world today. Workers in many strata of the US economy see themselves more as consumers and less as producers. They see their jobs as a means to achieve a certain level of purchasing power and comfort. Through division of labor power, they are terribly abstracted from the production process. Business owners, for their part, view much of their labor force as just so many disposable widgets that they can do with as they please to make their profits. Workers are often laid off solely to make a company more attractive to potential buyers.

A mobilized and militant labor force such as the kind envisioned by the progressives may not be the answer to the current economic woes of the US. Yet if we are to believe the voting statistics and survey results on the topic of US citizens' confidence in the integrity of business and government leaders, we must believe that there is a growing gap between US leaders and US citizens. If there is a phrase that captures the current attitude it would be unhealthy skepticism' – a skepticism born not out of critical thinking but rather out of a general ignorance and fear of our own history, culture and society.

How we have reached this point is a very large story, but the reader can perhaps gain some small insights into the current crisis from the struggles detailed here. Is this story more important than the organizing of the United Mine Workers or the United Automotive Workers? Probably not. Is it worth telling and thinking about? Unquestionably.

Is it correct? As best as we can tell, this account is a fair and accurate telling of the story, although we certainly acknowledge that extremist conservatives with personal knowledge of many of the events depicted here – men such as Roy Brewer or Ronald Reagan – will violently disagree with what is written here. IA International Representative Roy Brewer claimed at the time of the studio strikes in 1945 and 1946 that the disputes were caused by a combination of the greed of Bill Hutcheson, head of the Carpenters' International union and the desire of Communists to subvert the US motion picture industry. He still holds this idea today.

I cannot grant that Brewer was, or is, a man of honor or truth. He played an important role in the Browne–Bioff era of the IA – head of the Grievance Committee at the 1938 IA convention. He worked to reject every grievance against Browne and Bioff. Brewer has claimed in recent years that the mob never touched the IA treasury. In reality, Browne and Bioff had access to special funds, and that is where they ripped off the members, not from the regular union treasury. What difference does it make which fund they tapped into? The whole Executive Board, including Dick Walsh, rubber-stamped this arrangement.

From my own perspective, having studied the subject for over a decade, I don't think Gene Mailes is particularly easy on himself or his friends. He frequently acknowledges how very naive they were. And one of his friends says out loud toward the end of the story that, given all the trouble they had made for the powers in Hollywood, 'It's no wonder they kicked us out. Hell, they *had* to!' He was only half-joking.

Have we left things out? Of course. We did not have access to a great many materials that we know are out there in private collections. But what is here is something that is missing from labor history and certainly missing from the popular histories of the motion picture industry in the United States. It is the progressives' own story told by a man who had intimate involvement in the struggle.

In order to put the story of the IA Progressives in historical perspective, we need to take some time to summarize the initial unionization of the motion picture industry and what happened to the union movement to prompt the establishment of insurgent elements in the unions.

Notes

1. 'Below-the-line' refers to non-supervisory film workers, generally working on an hourly pay scale in the myriad of craft jobs that are necessary for producing a motion picture. These include carpenters, electricians, prop workers, laborers, painters and hundreds more job categories.
2. John Hutchinson, *The Imperfect Union* (New York: E. P. Dutton, 1972), pp. 371-2.
3. H. G. Wells, *The Outline of History* (New York: Macmillan, 1921), third edition pp. 206-7, 391, 435-6, 1003; Upton Sinclair, *The Cry for Justice* (New York: John C. Winston, 1915), p. 431.
4. *Violations of Free Speech and Assembly and Interference with the Rights of Labor,* Hearings before the Subcommittee of the Senate Committee on Labor and Public Welfare, 74th Congress, Second Session. Washington, 1936.

1

INTRODUCTION

Theatrical Roots

The first theatrical unions in the US were formed in the 1890s, around the time of the invention of the motion picture camera and projector. Stage workers formed unions in their communities in response to exploitation by theatrical managers. Shortly after the theatrical stage workers organized and began receiving better wages and conditions, managers of theaters and theatrical production companies turned to motion pictures for increased revenues through lower labor costs. Motion pictures represent the stored labor of theatrical workers: actors, directors and technical stage workers. A single performance before a camera provides a master copy from which hundreds of prints can be duped and distributed at a fraction of the costs involved in sending the same performance out on the road as a touring theatrical company. The unions responded by attempting to organize the workers in the new film industry.[1]

Working conditions for the touring stage mechanics were quite uneven, dependent largely upon the integrity of the manager of the company. By 1890 stage mechanics were complaining of wage cuts, discriminatory work assignments by master mechanics, reduction of crew size after set-up (with the highest paid first to be laid off), intolerably long hours and the stranding of entire companies by defaulting tour managers. The work itself was seasonal and irregular. In some cities, workers who tried to unionize other workers found themselves replaced during strikes by 'scabs' brought in from other cities. The combination of all these problems prompted the stagehands to form a national union.[2]

The roving theatrical companies provided both obstacles and opportunities for union organization. On the one hand, local people competed for jobs with touring mechanics; this undercut the ability of road men to walk out on managers who persisted in unfair practices. But the road men also had the opportunity to talk to the various local groups of stage hands about their mutual plight, typically in back alleys behind the theaters. According to veteran union member Rex Stewart, the traveling mechanics 'would simply look the men of the various locals over as their show traveled about the country, and the good union men were invited to participate in the national organization.'[3]

The formation of a national theatrical workers union marked the culmination of several years of covert organizational efforts. The express purpose of the new organization was to maintain fair wage rates, good working conditions, and job security for its members. The union served as a 'clearing house'

1

for the stage mechanics' many grievances against the theatrical managers. The union put uncooperative employers on an 'unfair list' and prohibited union members from working with these managers. This union would come to be known as the International Alliance of Theatrical and Stage Employes [*sic*] and Motion Picture Machine Operators (alternately referred to as 'IATSE' or the 'IA' in various sources; here, we use the 'IA').[4]

Los Angeles: The Open-Shop City

Prior to the First World War, motion picture production companies were operating in many US cities, including Los Angeles, Chicago, Jacksonville, New Orleans and Philadelphia. But the New York area was clearly the center of film production. The well-established scene shops, theatrical supply shops and skilled theatrical labor pool in New York City played a significant role in the early days of film production in that city and its surrounding suburbs. Yet it was Los Angeles, rather than New York, that became the center of film production for the US. One very important reason for this, overlooked in most film history books, was that Los Angeles offered cheap labor.[5]

In October 1888 *Los Angeles Times* publisher Harrison Gray Otis called together the prominent leaders of business to establish the Los Angeles Chamber of Commerce. This core group established a plan to build Los Angeles into an industrial and agricultural power. Real estate values in the city had fallen sharply in the financial panic of the previous year. Carey McWilliams captures the mood of the time and place in his essay 'The Politics of Utopia':

> For here was a unique situation: a small group of men, under the leadership of Otis, had not merely 'grown up with' a community, in the usual American pattern, they had conjured that community into existence. Having taken over at a moment of great crisis, when the older residents had suffered a failure of nerve, they felt that not only had they 'saved' Los Angeles, but that it belonged to them as a matter of rights. Over the years, this notion became a major obsession with General Otis.[6]

The Los Angeles Chamber of Commerce was battling for survival against its principal West coast competitor, San Francisco. The older, northern Californian community had a significant head start on Los Angeles. San Francisco, the financial hub of the gold rush period in California, had a fine deep water harbor and excellent river routes up to the mineral and timber rich Sierras. From the perspective of the Otis circle of power, the younger city of Los Angeles would have to make its own advantages. To this end, the Los Angeles Chamber's Merchants and Manufacturers' Association (M&M), under Otis' leadership, fought to hold down wages in Los Angeles and thus encourage new businesses to move to the area. In contrast to Los Angeles, San Francisco was long a well-organized union town and wages were comparable to those of most Eastern cities.[7]

Otis decided to set an example for the Los Angeles M&M by 'cleaning up his own house' first. In 1890, the unionized typographers and pressmen of the *Times* attempted to renegotiate wage concessions they had accepted during the financial crisis of 1887-8. Otis, who in fact held a card in one of the unions involved, refused to discuss the matter, forcing the workers to call a strike. Then he immediately brought in strikebreakers from Kansas City. The *Times* continued to publish and led a strident campaign against all unions in Los Angeles.[8]

During the early days of Otis' campaign to destroy unions, the Los Angeles theatrical workers nonetheless formed their first organization. In 1896 this organization became Stagehands' Local 33, chartered by NATSE (the IA's original name). Local 33 became an affiliate of the AFL's municipal labor organization in Los Angeles, known as the Central Labor Council (CLC). In 1908, Los Angeles became one of the first four cities to receive a separate motion picture machine operators' (i.e. projectionists) charter from the IA.

In 1909 members of both the stage and operator locals found themselves on a picket line together with electricians from the International Brotherhood of Electrical Workers (IBEW) and members of Local 47 of the American Federation of Musicians (AFM), protesting the open-shop policies of the Regal Theater. The trouble began when the Regal's manager refused to discharge non-union employees who had replaced striking workers in an earlier dispute. The Central Labor Council (CLC) retaliated by placing the Regal Theater on its unfair list. The CLC hoped that the working classes who attended the theater would support the strike and boycott films shown at the Regal. This multi-union dispute provided a broad base for union solidarity and some much-needed visibility for the CLC in the community. The Los Angeles labor leaders hoped that the Regal Theater strike might provide a clear sign to the community at large that organized labor was determined to resist the campaign of Otis and the Los Angeles Association of Manufacturers and Merchants (M&M) to make Los Angeles a non-union city.[9]

Besides the Regal Theater dispute, unions were battling in several other Los Angeles industries, including the breweries, metal trades and, of course, the newspaper industry. Police jailed union organizers on conspiracy charges, and the city council passed a strong anti-picketing ordinance. The jails overflowed with union pickets. Juries, clearly in sympathy with the unions, let arrested pickets go free as soon as they came to trial. Los Angeles was an industrial battleground with real killings and injuries. The *Times* strike, then a twenty-year-old struggle, reached a peak on the night of 1 October 1910, when union supporters dynamited the *Times* building, resulting in the deaths of twenty workers.[10]

Early Efforts Toward Unionizing the Film Studios

In this period of violent confrontation, Local 33 started organizing in the rapidly expanding motion picture industry in Los Angeles. Workers in the early motion picture industry faced problems not unlike their counterparts in the theatrical industry. They worked very long hours, often more than twelve hours without breaks. There were no special pay rates for overtime or for working on Sundays. Producers simply used workers as much as they wanted and whenever they wanted. Work was irregular and in no way guaranteed. Many studios had a 'family' of core workers who obtained regular employment, but for the most part workers 'panned the gates': that is, they lined up outside the studio gates every morning in hopes of securing a job for that day. This was most commonly known as the 'shape-up'. Foremen blacklisted 'troublemakers' – workers looking for better pay and conditions. Workers had no unemployment compensation, no vacation pay, no sick leave, no pension plan, and no disability benefits.[11]

The drive toward a national theatrical workers' union coincided with the rise of the American Federation of Labor (AFL) and its 'pure and simple' brand of trade unionism (bargaining for better wages and conditions). The impetus for the formation of a national theatrical union originated in New York, the hub of theatrical enterprise.

From the outset, the IA organized along industrial rather than craft lines. This infringed on the jurisdiction of the recently formed International Brotherhood of Electrical Workers (IBEW) and the older United Brotherhood of Carpenters and Joiners (hereafter 'Carpenters'). The nature of theatrical work itself and the peculiar character of the theatrical industry produced a kind of solidarity different from that found in the building trades. Even though the theatrical carpenters pounded nails and cut wood, they were also part of a unique socio-economic formation: show business.

Although the IA's industrial form of organization was beneficial to the theatrical workers (since it allowed various categories of workers to act in unison), it went against the grain of the AFL's Scranton Declaration (1901), which stated that craft (i.e. specific job skills) autonomy was the cornerstone of all organizational efforts. This jurisdictional conflict between industrial and craft union organization was to prove quite detrimental to the effective unionization of the motion picture industry.

From 1914 until 1926 – the year that the major unions and the studios signed the first Studio Basic Agreement – there were numerous instances of the IA fighting with its two major rivals, the IBEW and the Carpenters, for the right to organize workers in the film studios. Management formed its own collective bargaining organization (the Motion Picture Producers Association) and repeatedly managed to play one union off against another to hold down wages, undermine strikes and thwart unionization in general.[12]

IA Local 33 often found itself at odds with its parent organization. As the number of film production companies in Los Angeles grew rapidly, Local 33 was unable to supply the companies with qualified workers. Thus the Los Angeles local allowed IA members from other locals to work in their area of jurisdiction on special permits. These permit workers had neither voice nor vote in Local 33's affairs. The leaders of the stage workers' local wanted to provide jobs for their own members, who were in all probability friends or former co-workers of the leaders of the local. Many union stage workers and film craft workers who emigrated to Los Angeles to work in the new studios found themselves forced to quit their jobs if Local 33 members were in need of jobs. Local 33's insistence on this 'home rule' principle – that a local union controls its own area of jurisdiction without interference from the international office – was resented by the many stage workers in other locals who were losing their jobs because the motion picture industry was displacing the 'live' theatrical industry. It was as if the members of Local 33 were unwilling to share the little wealth that accrued to skilled stage workers as a result of this second phase of the industrial revolution in the theatrical industry.[13]

At the 1915 IA Convention, International President Charles Shay addressed the problem of the home rule law as it applied to motion picture studios, and recommended that it be suspended. Only the delegate from Local 33 raised objections to such a suspension. Shay appointed a full-time business agent from among the ranks of Local 33 whose job it would be to handle only the organization of the motion picture studios. Shay later declared Local 33 in a 'state of emergency', and reorganized the local under new leadership.[14]

The unions should have been a source of strength for the workers; however, both the AFL craft unions and the IA, in order to gain a foothold in the industry, made deals with the producers to cut wage rates for studio work. During and after World War I, a boom period for the US motion picture industry, wage rates in the studios were lower than in the construction industry in Los Angeles.

The migration of film production from the East coast to the West coast accelerated after the war. Workers engaged in the production of motion pictures in New York and New Jersey declined from nearly 5,000 in 1921 to a little more than half that total in 1927; the number of workers in motion picture production in California, however, grew five-fold over the same period.[15]

From 1919 until 1925 there were several instances of union members going out on strike only to find that other unions would supply strike-breakers to the studios. The Building Trades Council (BTC) unions – the Carpenters and IBEW – took the jobs of striking IA workers in 1918 and 1919. In 1921, the IA turned the tables on the BTC unions and crossed their picket lines during a strike.[16]

However, the studio workers, despite the internecine struggles of their unions, were in the process of finding their first collective voice to deal with the arbitrary and capricious management style of the Hollywood moguls and their Wall Street backers. The Carpenters (1921), IBEW (1923), the IA (1924) and the Painters (1925) formed Hollywood studio locals, indicating that the unions were gaining members in the studios. The IA split Local 33, assigning the film workers to a new 'studio mechanics' Local 37. Local 33 maintained jurisdiction over stage work in Los Angeles.

The unionization of the crafts did not come easily, however. The division of labor that had developed in the studios required the coordinated efforts of a variety of crafts: some were quite like normal construction work, but others were more like theatrical work. The typical film production was handled in much the same way as a theatrical production. First, the carpenters and painters constructed and painted sets. Then the grips (roughly equivalent to the 'scene shifters' of the theatrical industry) moved in and erected scaffolding on which to mount follow spots and other lighting instruments. Next, the set electricians would hang and adjust the lights. At some studios the people who hung lights also operated them during the production. At other studios the set electricians who hung the lights moved from stage to stage doing that work only. They did not operate them during production; this crew was called the 'iron gang'. Because of varying daily production demands the producers were unwilling to keep full crews of these grips, painters, carpenters and electricians on the weekly payroll; thus work was 'casual' (irregular). For a majority of film craft workers lay-offs were simply part of their working life.[17]

The absence of job security was a prime reason for workers to seek union representation, but other motives existed as well. One of these had to do with meals. In order to begin filming at 8 a.m. directors often found it necessary to bring in studio electricians as early as 4 a.m. to begin rigging lights. This meant that the electricians ate their breakfasts around three in the morning. Ambitious directors would often drive the crew hard, working them past

5

noon without a meal break. Light operators, perched on high scaffolding and working in the intense heat given off by the arc lamps, would sometimes pass out under such extreme stress and sustain serious injuries. Without union representation workers who objected to such long stretches without food could simply be dismissed. Clearly, the workers saw the value in presenting a collective voice to management.

Open Shop Strategies

The producers had formed an open shop organization in 1917 – the Motion Picture Producers Association – to present a united front in their dealings with the unions. In 1922 they formed a new organization, the Motion Picture Producers and Distributors of America (MPPDA), to deal with several problems facing the industry, among them the scandals linking a few prominent Hollywood actors and executives to prostitution, drug abuse and murders; strained relations between producers and exhibitors; and the creeping unionization of the studios that threatened to expand into the ranks of 'talent' – writers, actors and directors. To deal specifically with labor problems, the MPPDA established a labor relations branch called the Association of Motion Picture Producers (AMPP), with headquarters in Hollywood.

At first it seemed as if the MPPDA and the AMPP were interested in genuine reform for studio labor. In 1924 the first head of the MPPDA, Will Hays, commissioned the Russell Sage Foundation to study alleged abuses in the employment of extras by the motion picture industry. This study led to the establishment in 1925 of the Central Casting Corporation, an extras placement bureau that operated in a supposedly disinterested manner, eliminating favoritism in employment.[18]

In the same year, however, the producers established a placement bureau on Hill Street called the Mutual Alliance of Studio Employees (MASE) to handle the producers' needs for craft workers and technicians. This office was established despite the fact that the unions had plenty of qualified workers on their rolls who could fill the producers' needs. It was a producer-controlled union which supplied workers to several studios. When IA organizers complained about MASE to Fred W. Beetson and Will Hays of the AMPP, they were told that the AMPP had no authority to tell the producers who they could or could not hire and that there was nothing the AMPP could do about the use of non-union labor in the studios.[19]

In the midst of all these tensions, the individual workers in the film industry faced peculiar dilemmas: one problem was deciding which union, if any, they should join. But the most fundamental problem was casualization: the irregular availability of work based on the irregular demand for labor in the industry owing to the nature of the commodity and its marketing patterns. Large-scale productions required a large pool of laborers and extras to be available on short notice. Yet production slumps and simple seasonal marketing strategies led the producers to deny most of their workers full-time, continuous employment.

In time, this led to an unusual division of workers: those inside and those outside the studio gates. The 'insiders' worked nearly every day and were told at the end of the workday when and where to report to the following morning. The 'outsiders' faced the daily 'shape-up' at the studio gates. These outsiders formed informal networks to keep each other informed of where large productions would be taking place on the following day. Those studios reputed to be at work on big productions found their gates crowded with hopeful job-seekers from 7 a.m. onward. As the foremen began to fill the necessary positions, workers would move on to other studios hoping to find work somewhere that day. Some laborers and extras found themselves spending whole days outside the studio gates.[20]

The Studio Basic Agreement

In enforcing intolerable conditions on the workers while simultaneously resurrecting the infamous 'yellow dog' contract (join the company union or lose your job), the MPPDA companies had joined the open shop movement with a vengeance. The National Open Shop Association supported the MPPDA and pledged financial and legal support to the producers in return for a promise that the producers would refuse to bargain with the unions.[21]

The response of much of organized labor to the imposition of the open shop was the short-lived phenomenon of 'progressivism', the conversion of the craft-dominated AFL to an industrial union. One of the factors behind the attempt to shift AFL strategy from craft to industrial orientation was to end the inter-union squabbling that had prevented the organization of many basic industries. However, the conservative AFL leadership, which counted among its core the International President of the Carpenters, William Hutcheson, quickly quashed the movement toward industrial unionism by branding it communist-led.

Hutcheson was not all that interested in fighting communists, so long as they didn't encroach on his own power base. At the root of Hutcheson's and many other union leaders' objections to industrial unionism was the fear that winning representation for all industrial workers would mean far more workers demanding a share of the national wealth. The hierarchy of labor power that put skilled workers on the shoulders of their semi-skilled counterparts was beneficial to the members of the old established trade unions.

Despite the failure of progressivism in the larger labor movement, a certain amount of progressivist spirit must have seeped into the motion picture studio locals in the mid-1920s. According to labor historians Richard and Louis Perry, the movement toward labor unity in the motion picture industry came from the rank and file, not from the international union officials. On 5 February 1925, Carpenters studio Local 1692 signed an agreement with IA Local 37 granting prop-building and miniature sets to Local 37's jurisdiction. The inter-local agreement was worked out on a common-sense basis. Prop-building was naturally connected with the duties of the property workers who belonged to Local 37. The leaders of Carpenters' Local 1692, however, paid dearly for their actions in the following year when Hutcheson, who had sanctioned the talks leading to the inter-local agreement, dissolved Local 1692 and replaced it with newly formed Local 946, under new leadership. The message was clear: local autonomy was to be exercised with extreme caution, if at all.[22] On 1 September 1926, the IA signed new jurisdictional agreements with the IBEW that both unions found acceptable for the time being. This tied a rope around the neck of the MPPDA: the 'divide and conquer' strategy had perhaps outlived its usefulness.

On 20 October 1926, the *New York Times* published a story about a possible strike by some 3,500 members of the IA, IBEW, Carpenters and United Scenic Artists against the MPPDA studios. The producers could probably have weathered the strike by the usual strategy of hiring non-union workers, but the IA threatened a projectionists' boycott of films produced by MPPDA companies, a boycott that would hit during the peak Christmas season. At the core of the unions' demands was the call for producers' recognition of the unions as legitimate bargaining agents for several classes of studio workers. The unions demanded a closed shop, readjustment of wage scales, a standard eight-hour day, six days off with pay per year, and overtime for Sunday work. In response, the producers, through their spokesmen Hays and Beetson, refused to discuss the closed shop, offering instead a welfare program and promises of year-round employment.[23]

On 5 November 1926, the unions issued an ultimatum to the producers: if a closed-shop agreement was not signed by 1 December, the producers' studios and any theaters showing films produced by the MPPDA companies would be shut down by a strike. The IA, the IBEW and the American Federation of Musicians (AFM) offered to waive initiation fees for any studio workers who wanted to join the studio locals. At the last moment, on 29 November, the unions withdrew their demands for a closed shop, called off the strike and, together with the producers, drafted and signed rules of procedure for carrying out negotiations. This was the first Studio Basic Agreement (SBA), the cornerstone of labor relations in Hollywood. The SBA was not a contract *per se*, but rather an agreement to negotiate issues of wages, hours, working conditions and grievances. The producers and the unions set up committees patterned after the industrial committees established in key industries during the First World War to handle labor problems. The rules of the committees gave the right of union negotiation solely to the international representatives, meaning that local business agents, officers and rank and file were denied direct access to the negotiations. The Producers and International Committees each appointed a Secretary with an office in Los Angeles. These Secretaries were to handle grievances by making independent inquiries into the facts of the controversy and then conferring with each other to determine the appropriate remedy. If the Secretaries could not reach a mutually acceptable agreement, they were then to bring the matter to the attention of the full committee.

For the rank and file, this absence of input into the negotiations was part of a larger disenfranchisement. In the US labor movement as a whole, union officials and management both benefited from keeping the workers out of the process. It was a very successful system designed to keep the workers uneducated about their rights and their place in the system of production.

For people working in the studios it was difficult, if not impossible, to have an impact on the terms of the contracts. Local 37, for example, held no local meetings. With negotiations moved to New York, the producers were insulated to a certain extent from fighting with workers on a daily basis about the terms of employment. Now the workers were kept in line by their own union stewards. If workers were upset about conditions or pay, they had to channel their complaints through several layers of bureaucracy. The union officials at the top of the international unions, the ones who negotiated the contracts, had more in common with their counterparts in management than they did with the workers in the studios. Still, it was a start toward collective bargaining.

Joseph P. Kennedy, chief executive of RKO, described the situation: 'What we are trying to do is to maintain an open shop without prejudice to union labor.'[24] Producers told department heads to hold the line below 50 per cent union workers to maintain this open shop. The SBA was, at best, a foundation for the unions to build upon. A new era in Hollywood labor relations had dawned, just in time for the next phase of the industrial revolution in the entertainment industry: sound motion pictures.[25]

Into the Great Depression

Hollywood in the late 1920s was on a financial roller-coaster ride that would plunge into a darkened tunnel in the early 1930s. As in the broader economy, the motion picture industry was full of speculative stock deals in the 1920s. Among the most active speculators were the motion picture executives themselves, who traded in their own companies to manipulate the prices of their stocks.[26]

To attract further Wall Street investment for conversion to sound production and exhibition, the major producers were forced to come to terms with the spiraling overheads of their studios. The producers' 1927 campaign to reduce costs was preceded by the formation of a sophisticated 'company union' for the industry's aesthetic workers – the writers, actors, directors and cinematographers (soon to be renamed 'directors of photography'). This company union, the Academy of Motion Picture Arts and Sciences (AMPAS), was formed in May 1927. Sound motion pictures required the talents of the heavily unionized Broadway actors and writers. AMPAS checked the spread of unionism from the crafts into the talent groups by gaining the cooperation of a large number of prominent screen players, directors and writers, thus bypassing legitimate negotiations with the then rather weak screen talent guilds for writers and actors.[27]

Wages and working conditions for the studio craft workers began a period of steady improvement following the signing of the Studio Basic Agreement (SBA). As the unions began to place more and more people in the studios, the local union offices became much like hiring halls. The IA made a rule for its members: nobody goes in through the 'shape-up' at the gates; all IA members had to go through the local union offices to work in the studios.

Gradually, the IA and the other SBA unions began to recruit new members. A man who worked as an electrician in the studios at this time described the typical sort of recruitment:

> Once you got a steady job and were an IA person in the studios, you would go around and try to get other people to also join the union. You were very careful not to talk to the wrong people, because you could ask some studio electrician or grip to come into the union and he would turn around and tell the boss and you would find yourself out of a job. You would never get back into that studio.[28]

In those days, recruitment was not easy, since there really was not much incentive for workers to join the unions. Studio workers in particular classifications were paid the same rate whether or not they were union members. The studios still maintained their own crews on a full-time basis and depended upon the remaining workers waiting at the gate for their extra help. Seniority at that time was based on how long a worker had worked for a specific studio; thus workers tried to stay with one studio as long as possible. The union activists were walking a tightrope.

By signing the SBA, the producers seemed to be adopting a notably progressive stand in the field of labor relations. However, the real strategy at work was to keep the key people such as cinematographers out of unions to prevent production tie-ups. *Variety* reported that the producers were particularly displeased with the formation of Camera Local 659 (established in 1928), Lab Technicians Local 683 (1929), Film Editors Local and Sound Local 695 (1930) because these workers were considered the most irreplaceable of all production workers in the event of a strike.[29]

For the unions, it was critical to organize the top workers in each special craft. The first cameramen, for example, were critical to the unions because they normally chose the people who worked under them as camera assistants and lighting crew supervisors (key grips). Many cameramen felt that they were more 'artists' than workers and they resisted joining unions. Instead, they became members of a professional association, still in existence today, the American Society of Cinematographers (ASC).

The sound engineers were another case of unions targeting the top workers in a given specialty. Compromise jurisdictional agreements between the IA and the IBEW, arranged in 1925 and leading to the SBA success in 1926, did not cover the issue of sound work in the studios. The 1929 IBEW Convention resolved to get back the jobs that it felt rightly belonged to its members. This resolution set the IA and the IBEW on a collision course. In March 1930, representatives of the two unions met at AFL headquarters in Washington D.C. to attempt to resolve their differences about the motion picture sound jurisdictional questions. But they failed. In September 1930, the IA established Sound Local 695 of Hollywood. This first sound technicians' local immediately began a vigorous campaign to organize the studio sound technicians, beginning with the weaker independent studios.

In 1932, Sound Local 695 set its sights on the major studios, beginning with Columbia Pictures, one of the 'Little Three', (the others were Universal and United Artists) which were large production companies but had no theater holdings. In March 1932, Sound Local 695 had attempted to gain recognition from Columbia. But Columbia rebuffed the union by claiming that under the terms of the SBA, which the company had not signed but under which they considered themselves covered by virtue of joining the MPPDA group, they were unable to recognize Sound Local 695 until the jurisdictional issue between the IA and the IBEW was finally settled. The IA briefly relaxed its major studio campaign in May 1932, satisfied for the time being with a higher wage scale.

The New Deal Arrives

On the night of Roosevelt's inauguration on 4 March 1933, Will Hays of the MPPDA met with several leaders of the major motion picture firms in private session to discuss how to cope with the impending cash crunch to come the following morning, when the banks had their federally mandated holiday.

The companies were in precarious financial condition. The major firms, known as the 'Big Five', had been struggling along with the help of massive revolving credit funds supplied by large Eastern banks. When the bank holiday came, they found themselves short of credit and cash simultaneously; they could not meet their payrolls. The banks were demanding immediate payment of the producers' short-term notes. The producers decided at that meeting to impose salary cuts ranging from 25 per cent to 50 per cent on all employees and managers for a period of eight weeks, retroactive to 4 March.[30]

The SBA was one week from its 15 March renewal date when Will Hays' labor assistant, Pat Casey, asked all unionized craft labor groups for a 20 per cent cut in pay rates for all classifications of workers. The unions unanimously voted on 11 March to reject the producers' wage cut proposals. Other unions with workers in the studios agreed to abide by whatever the SBA unions determined to be the right course of action. The producers relented in their demands for the wage cuts for the craft workers, but a long-time IA sound editor recalled that the producers quietly retaliated against his craft by laying people off between pictures rather than carrying them on the payrolls.[31] *Variety* reported later in the year that the producers took this act of defiance as a declaration of war between themselves and the IA. The producers' retaliation against the IA would come shortly.[32]

Meanwhile the producers held their ground against the talent groups (actors, writers and directors) represented by AMPAS, a move that virtually destroyed the viability of the producers' own company union as a legitimate bargaining agent. Although the producers did impose various salary cuts on the talent groups, most of the major studios restored the cuts before the end of the eight-week period. But the move came too late to buoy the sagging image of AMPAS, which had willingly supported the cuts. In April, some twenty writers, dissatisfied with the handling of the salary cuts and the inability of AMPAS over a six-year period to come up with a standard writers' contract, revived an old branch of the Authors' League: the Screen Writers Guild (SWG). On 12 July 1933, a small group of prominent actors formed the Screen Actors Guild (SAG).[33]

In June 1933, Franklin Roosevelt signed into law the second major piece of legislation dealing with labor unions. The National Industrial Recovery Act established the National Recovery Administration (NRA), a massive program aimed at reforming trade and labor relations practices in industries engaged in interstate commerce. For the two talent guilds, SWG and SAG, the NRA inadvertently lent immediate legitimization when the producers attempted to cut actors' salaries under the terms of a draft version of the NRA code for the motion picture industry, aimed at curbing competitive bidding between the studios for the services of star actors. The company union, AMPAS, supported the producers' draft. This gave the newly formed SAG just the opportunity it needed to discredit AMPAS. After successfully presenting its case to Roosevelt and gaining the needed changes in the NRA code, SAG saw its membership roll swell. The SAG and the SWG were on their way toward recognition by producers.

Beginning in July 1933 under the auspices of the NRA, a series of meetings was held in Washington D.C. for the purpose of establishing an industrial code of fair competition for the motion picture industry. The IA participated in these hearings, representing craft workers in the motion picture theaters, studios and film laboratories. IA officials testified at NRA hearings that out of 14,000 theaters then open in the US, only 4,000 were manned by IA projectionists. This was apparently a severe decline from the number of union theaters in the 1920s.[34]

Under the provisions of the NRA, Roosevelt established the National Labor Board (NLB) in August 1933, which in turn established rules for the conduct of labor relations, such as: 'a majority of workers in any plant were to be allowed to bargain for the whole plant, that secret elections be held to determine bargaining units, and that bona fide efforts be made to secure agreements.'[35] The establishment of the NLB marked the first codification of labor relations in the US. Unfortunately, the terms of the NRA did not grant the NLB the power of enforcement, prompting many labor leaders to dub the NRA a 'national run around'.[36]

The IA Loses Control

On 8 July 1933, IA Sound Local 695 renewed its struggle against the major companies by calling a strike against Columbia, demanding recognition and a specified wage scale. Approximately 400 members of various IA locals walked out of the studios on that Saturday afternoon, halting work on two productions then under way. This brief walk-out was followed by repeated demands by Sound Local 695 that Columbia grant it the right to bargain for Columbia's sound technicians. The studio still refused to bargain with Sound Local 695, again citing their membership in the AMPP and the terms of the SBA as grounds for their refusal. Sound Local 695's business agent issued an ultimatum to the AMPP companies on 20 July demanding the establishment of a standardized wage scale. At that time the AMPP companies were paying the first sound engineers widely varying rates, from $175 per week to as little as $75 per week.[37] AMPP spokesperson Pat Casey issued a statement on behalf of Columbia and the other major studios claiming that 'the studios were caught in the middle of a jurisdictional dispute and if they acceded [to the] soundmen's demands the IBEW would call a strike of their men; therefore producers could do nothing but refuse the demands.'[38]

On 24 July, all IA locals walked out of the eleven AMPP studios in support of Sound Local 695. The studios responded immediately by declaring that the IA had withdrawn from the SBA by virtue of their calling a strike without first polling the members of the affected locals. This technicality allowed the producers to begin hiring IBEW and non-union sound workers to take the place of the striking sound engineers, since the 'jurisdictional dispute' no longer existed between two signatories to the SBA. The producers approached strikers individually with offers of two-year individual contracts without IA representation. The IBEW also approached the striking sound technicians, offering one-year studio contracts for joining their organization.

Despite a large strike fund built up over two years, many members of the IA studio locals began deserting their union, fearing that IBEW and Carpenters members would permanently replace them. Many workers fell back on the strategy, long a practice among studio veterans of labor wars, of maintaining dual cards to avoid having to choose sides in the strike. More than 120 members of Camera Local 695 failed to support the strike in return for lucrative five-year personal contracts negotiated with the AMPP companies by the ASC. One member of the IA at the time of the strike recalled:

> It was a bad time to call a strike; when a man's been out of work for a year, he's going to take the first job that comes along, even though it might be against his conscience to be a strike-breaker. Well, people who had never worked in the business came in, and some of them got pretty good deals. And then, of course, some of the union people gave up and got faint-hearted and gradually went back. And to this day [1971], some never got back. Some were blacklisted. Some of the ringleaders to this day never got back in the industry again. At MGM, some of the people who eventually got back, they still had sort of a black mark against them. And they didn't get promoted. It wasn't good.[39]

It was clearly a bad time for the IA to call the producers' bluff for three reasons: first, the producers had declared in the wake of the bank holiday exigencies following Roosevelt's inauguration in March 1933 that 'the studios must continue production' at all costs to keep the industry afloat. They were surely looking for ways to weaken the most effective labor organization in the studios; secondly, the depression had seriously reduced the IA's ability to call an effective projectionists' boycott. Less than 50 per cent of the theaters employed IA projectionists; and thirdly, as Gene Mailes points out, the leadership of the IA had no experience in leading a successful strike – one in which the strikers would persevere.

As a consequence of all these factors, the IA lost its power struggle with the IBEW and the producers. IA President Elliot's administration tried several legal maneuvers to regain its power in the studios, but these measures proved ineffective and the IA soon found its members jumping to its two rivals.

On 5 August 1933, the SBA was redrawn, reducing the daily rate for most SBA groups from $8.25 per eight-hour day to $7.00 per six-hour day – a 13.5 per cent increase in the hourly rate, but an overall decrease for the workers since many of them worked shifts at two different studios at straight time to pay their bills. This was called 'double-shifting'. The AMPP signed with the IBEW for all sound and electrical work. Grip and property work was reassigned from IA Local 37 to the Carpenters Local 946. According to *Variety*, the inexperienced workers caused a great deal of chaos and frustration in the studios at first. The situation in the labs was particularly acute and producers were holding their daily negatives for fear that incompetent lab workers would ruin their prints. But as strikers deserted the strike and returned to work, they helped train the new people.[40]

In the course of the next few months the rolls of the IA studio locals dropped precipitously: Camera Local 659 dropped from several hundred members to just 62; Local 37 dropped from a few thousand members down to 40. According to Hugh Lovell and Tasile Carter's *Collective Bargaining in the Motion Picture Industry,* the IA's overall membership in the studios dropped from 9,000 to 200.[41] A meeting of unemployed studio workers was called to form a new union, the Society of Motion Picture Employees, made up of workers who had lost their jobs in the strike. Workers who were already members of other unions were encouraged to join the new organization, but little came of this effort.[42]

Throughout these events the AMPP strategy worked exceptionally well. Their 'blameless' stance was predicated on the issue of an alleged jurisdictional fight between the IA and IBEW over which union had the right to represent the sound technicians. Yet, at the time of the strike, Sound Local 695 could claim over 600 *bona fide* working members, while the IBEW had only one-tenth of that number.[43] *Variety* reported that 'two months before the strike producers are said to have had a tacit agreement to fight the IATSE to a finish regardless of the cost and to break the strength of the individual and combined locals.'[44] The IBEW claimed that the AFL had granted them jurisdiction over film sound technicians, but the AFL records from that period offer no evidence of such a ruling by the AFL. The claim to legitimacy under AFL fiat was nothing more than a ruse aimed at covering up what was surely yet another 'backroom' deal worked out between the unions – in this case the IBEW and the Carpenters – and the producers.

At the request of the IA, the newly formed NLB intervened and obtained a settlement that ended the strike on 23 August 1933. In a clarification of the settlement, the National Labor Board stated 'that employees be taken back without prejudice, strikers to be given preference before new employees are taken on, and that they may retain membership in their organization, it being understood that this involves no change in the industrial relations policy of the motion picture industry.'[45] But the NLB did not enforce the settlement between the contending unions and the producers. NLB representative Leo Wolman claimed that despite the seeming support for jobs to be given back to the strikers, the settlement 'in no way abrogates any contracts between the producers and the IBEW'.[46]

Thus it could be argued that, despite the seemingly progressive attitude of the Roosevelt administration toward labor, New Deal programs such as the NRA and the NLB gave management free and easy access to governmental officials. The 1933 Hollywood studio strike clearly demonstrated the need for an effective national policy on the handling of labor disputes, but such a policy was still four years from enactment. Thus, as 1933 drew to a close, the tranquillity that had characterized the few years following the signing of the SBA was decisively shattered. The industry was entering a fifteen-year period of nearly continuous labor strife.

The Industry Rebounds

From the depths of the depression Hollywood began a rapid ascent into relative prosperity in the middle and late 1930s. As the New Deal employment and relief programs began to spread federal funds among the jobless, movie attendance increased.

From 24 July 1933 until 8 December 1936 the studios operated without interference from labor unions. The studios used workers from several local AFL affiliates, but were effectively open shops; the producers still reserved the right to hire anyone for any classification of work without regard to union membership. The IA's sound technicians of Sound Local 695 and the camera crew workers of Camera Local 695 were transferred into studio electricians' Local 40 IBEW. The property workers and stage carpenters of IA Local 37 were transferred into Carpenters Local 946 following the 1933 strike. The leaders of IA Local 37 sent a letter of protest to William Green of the American Federation of Labor (AFL) shortly after the transition to Carpenters' control, asking, 'What can be the result of any superstructure built upon such a shifting foundation?'[47] Green was not likely to answer this query, since the International President of the Carpenters, Big Bill Hutcheson, was Green's friend and fellow 'old guard' AFL Executive Committee member.

For Green, it didn't really matter which AFL union held jurisdiction. The dues that had previously been paid into the IA's treasury were now being paid into the Carpenters'. Carpenters Local 946 was a 'local' union in name only: effective control rested with Hutcheson. Local members were not permitted to strike, nor were they granted input into the negotiations with the producers. At the 1936 bargaining sessions for the Studio Basic Agreement (SBA), the Carpenters did not receive the 10 per cent increase granted to the other unions involved in the SBA negotiations.

In addition to the Carpenters and the IBEW, the Teamsters were also granted recognition during this period, and the American Federation of Musicians (AFM) maintained a stormy but continuing relationship with the producers. But none of the four crafts was granted a closed shop. Although many studio workers maintained dual cards in the IA and either the Carpenters or the IBEW, there was little reason for any workers to maintain a union card beyond support for the principle of collective bargaining or perhaps to gain employment outside the studios during slack periods. The vast majority of workers in the studios, including the talent groups, were without collective bargaining rights in the studios. Under the auspices of the NRA, work was distributed to a larger percentage of studio workers, although casualization (irregular work) continued at an alarming rate. The US Census of Manufactures reported a range of employment in the studios in 1934 from a low of 7,880 in May to a high of 13,734 in September, owing to the traditional seasonal patterns of production that had plagued the industry since its earliest days of feature film production.[48]

The Mob Moves in

The IA began its return to power by purging itself of the failed leadership of William Elliot. Elliot had made several key mistakes in his handling of the studio strike and in his role as chief IA negotiator in the drafting of the NRA Codes for the exhibition branch of the motion picture industry.

Variety reported in August 1933 that the 'Chicago gang' was certainly going to replace Elliot at the upcoming 1934 IA Convention.[49] Hit hard by the end of prohibition, the Chicago crime syndicate 'family' of Al Capone was in the market for new rackets that it could exploit. The depression had also cut into money the Capone gang made from prostitution and gambling. They wanted to diversify their activities to insure their investment, and kept an eye open for potential union racket schemes. They did not have to look far. Willie Bioff, a small-time hoodlum who had done his share of pimping and bootlegging, was about to give them the opening they needed. His good friend George Browne happened to be the head of IA Stagehands Local 2 in Chicago. Browne and Bioff conspired to establish a protection scheme to extort money from theater owners.[50]

In early 1934, Browne approached Barney Balaban of Publix Theaters of Chicago regarding the restoration of wage cuts for stagehands that had taken place at the height of the 1933 financial crisis. Balaban offered Brown $150 per week to forget about the agreement to restore wages to their previous level. Browne consulted with his friend Bioff, who responded that he didn't think that was anywhere near enough money and that he would talk to Balaban. In subsequent bargaining sessions a flat price of $20,000 was worked out between Bioff and Balaban's attorney Leo Spitz. Browne and Bioff pocketed the $20,000, declared by Balaban for tax purposes as a charitable donation to a soup kitchen that Browne had established for out-of-work members of Local 2.

The two friends celebrated their conquest at the gambling resort of Nick Dean (alias Nick Circella), one of Bioff's associates from his days of bootlegging in Chicago. Nick Circella was also a member of the Capone crime syndicate, then headed by Frank Nitti. A few days after their celebration, Browne and Bioff were approached by Nitti's associates and informed that Nitti wanted a 50 per cent cut of whatever action it was they had. With the strength of the Chicago crime syndicate behind them, the two men laid bigger plans.

The potential for gaining control of the entire motion picture crafts labor force was within the grasp of the Chicago crime syndicate. To this end, a series of syndicate meetings was held to discuss how George Browne could be elected International President of the IA at the union's 1934 biennial convention in Louisville. They wanted to avoid a repeat of the past, when Browne had failed to defeat Elliot in 1932 because of opposition from big Eastern locals, such as Local 1 and Local 306 of New York. A who's who of crime family members from New York, New Jersey and Chicago attended these meetings and pledged support to the effort. Nitti assured Browne of additional support from Cleveland and St. Louis. Browne was about to be thrust into the forefront of labor relations – not just of the entertainment industry, but of the labor movement as a whole.

Harry Sherman of New York projectionists' Local 306 was also at the convention, accompanied by New York syndicate 'hit man' Louis Lepke Buchalter. Sherman later testified as a government witness in federal trials involving labor racketeering that he hired Buchalter as protection against the head of the Chicago projectionists' Local 110, Tommy Malloy, but it is clear that Sherman was acting as an agent for the syndicate in bringing Buchalter to the convention.[51] Former IA President Canavan, contemplating a return to power, had been campaigning for several months to gain support for his candidacy, but both he and Elliot were discouraged from running by the not so subtle techniques of Nitti and company. Browne ran unopposed.

The first real test of Browne's authority came in July 1934, when members of New York projectionists' Local 306 attempted to unseat Harry Sherman and his executive board cohorts. The insurgent members wanted an honest accounting of more than $1 million of the local's funds that they believed Sherman and his friends had misappropriated. Browne took control of the local: he banned local meetings, seized its finances and records, and appointed International Vice-President Harlan Holmden of Cleveland as trustee of the union. Browne stepped directly into negotiations for contracts between Local 306 and the New York theaters owned by the majors. The contract negotiations were held under regional NRA supervision, but Browne failed to get wage increases or changes in conditions for the New York projectionists.

Meanwhile, trouble was breaking out in Chicago. Tommy Malloy had come to power in IA Projectionists' Local 110 in a blaze of gunfire in 1916, when he and IBEW gunmen dueled from automobiles in the streets of Chicago to see which union would control the projectionists in Chicago's theaters. Malloy was under federal investigation for alleged labor racketeering. He had been taking kickbacks from projectionists to insure their continued employment.[52] And there was the yet undiscovered business of payoffs from theater owners to hold down wages and to prevent strikes. The potential for Malloy to 'squeal' seemed too great for Nitti and company, who were laying bigger plans. If Malloy testified against Browne, Bioff and the Capone syndicate, then all the hard work of putting Browne in power would have been wasted. Malloy's Packard was riddled with machine-gun fire while he was on his way to work on Lake Shore Drive in Chicago on the morning of 4 February 1935. One week later, following one of the largest funeral processions in Chicago history – some 300 cars – Browne took control of Malloy's Local 110 and placed Holmden in charge of this local as well as Local 306. Browne immediately 'corrected abuses' that had been part of Malloy's tenure by removing permit-holding projectionists from the booths and replacing them with unemployed members of his own Stagehands Local 2. Prudently sidestepping the issue of whether the kickbacks were eliminated (they were not), Browne blandly reported to the 1936 Convention: 'I am happy to say that the membership of Local No. 110 cooperated in a whole-hearted way, and I was pleased to note that this organization had settled down to a proper business management.'[53]

After the seizure of the New York and Chicago projectionists' locals, a blitzkrieg was launched against locals in several other cities, including St. Louis, Kansas City, Pittsburgh and Newark. Not surprisingly, after the Malloy shooting, the affected locals raised few objections to the takeovers. In each case Browne put his own personal representatives in charge of the affairs of these locals under IA constitutional provisions regarding 'emergency cases'.[54] Local meetings and voting by the rank and file were suspended. With absolute control over these key cities, Browne and the Nitti syndicate were ready to begin cashing in their power for dollars.

To regain control of jobs in the studios, Browne and the IA Executive Board initiated an assessment of 2 per cent of gross wages to be levied from 15 July 1935 against all working members.[55] Shortly afterwards Browne held elections in New York City for new officers for Local 306. But the union remained effectively in his control. As a gesture of strength, Browne ordered a strike against New York Loew's and RKO theaters to recoup wage cuts made during the darkest days of the industry in 1932 and 1933. Browne, Bioff, and Nick Circella of the Nitti gang then met with Nicholas Schenck, President of Loew's, and Leslie Thompson of RKO. The strike was ended: they signed a seven-year contract that included a no-strike clause. Browne and Bioff walked away from the bargaining table with $150,000, two-thirds of which went back to the Nitti mob in Chicago via Circella. This one deal meant as much as $1 million in savings to the majors' theater chains. Loew's and RKO later settled out of court with Local 306 for over $100,000 in back wages, tacitly admitting the benefit they derived from the collusion.[56]

For Browne, the leader of a relatively small union of mostly irregularly employed workers, the stage was now set for his greatest triumph. Nicholas Schenck and Barney Balaban were well aware of the character of the men with whom they were dealing, and the presence of well-known gangster Circella at bargaining sessions certainly dispelled any doubts they might have had. Schenck and Balaban knew also that the union was run by 'reasonable' men who would be willing to make deals to hold down wages and prevent strikes.

But most importantly for the producers, they saw in George Browne the opportunity to hold the line against genuine collective bargaining. Their old divide and conquer strategy had been placed in jeopardy by the passage of the National Labor Relations Act (more commonly referred to as the Wagner Act) on 5 July 1935. The new act was similar to the previous New Deal legislation aimed at legitimizing workers' rights to collective bargaining; however, the new law had the necessary legal teeth to enforce its rulings.

The producers knew that their industry was about to turn the corner and begin to show a profit: box-office revenues were steadily improving. But the same New Deal that put money in the pockets of the masses of unemployed and under-employed people now expected the motion picture moguls to pay their fair share of this new prosperity. Granting workers the right to choose their own unions might undermine the tight oligarchical relations between the producers and the international union leaders that had thus far characterized the industry. The producers feared that their studios would be 'overrun' by angry hordes of newly organized labor groups demanding a larger share of these profits. They knew, as well, that the Communist Party had formed a studio workers' organization and was in the process of trying to recruit unorganized workers. Through the MPPDA, the major producers had steamrollered their terms through the old National Recovery Administration (NRA) Code Committee; the new labor law embodied in the Wagner Act, however, was specifically aimed at correcting the weakness of the previous labor boards set up under the NRA. It would be difficult for the producers to ignore arrests and fines for contempt of a circuit court judge.

The producers were worried not only about existing unions but also about new unions and conditions that might take root under the new law. The vast majority of workers in the motion picture industry, as well as in the US economy as a whole, were as yet without union representation. In the general US labor force, the craft orientation of the AFL had helped to keep a majority of workers from obtaining union representation. Teamsters' President Dan Tobin referred to workers in mass production industries as 'rubbish'.[57] But the newly formed Committee of Industrial Organizations (soon to become the Congress of Industrial Organizations or CIO), led by John Lewis of the United Mine Workers, took a new tack toward the organization of so-called unskilled workers as well as white-collar workers. Would the CIO move into the motion picture industry to aid not only the lower paid unorganized workers (particularly in the film labs and exchanges), but also the struggling talent guilds as well? How could the producers deal with such an unruly 'rabble'?

Browne and his associates offered the producers a deal: a phony strike would be called as a pretense for granting the IA complete control over the key workers in the industry. Under continuous threat of a projectionists' boycott, the producers could 'capitulate' to any demands of the IA. Any troublesome groups of workers could thus be safely corralled into what amounted to a company union. It was an ingenious strategy, and the tactics used to carry it out were equally inventive. Two weeks after the deal was struck ending the New York projectionists' walk-out, *Variety* published a small story about an IBEW camera crew heading east in an airplane taking aerial footage for the Paramount film *13 Hours in the Air*. The item mentioned that the last stop on the crew's journey would be within the jurisdiction of IA International Photographers' Local 644 at Newark Airport, where the IBEW camera crew would be required to show their IA cards. If they failed to produce the cards, George Browne would order the projectionists in Paramount's theaters to walk off their jobs.[58]

The script was played out flawlessly. The theaters in Chicago, St. Louis and points in between were packed with the usual Saturday night crowds on 30 November 1935 when the projectionists simply left the booths for fifteen to thirty minutes, demanding that all IBEW electrical maintenance workers be immediately dismissed and that IA members replace them. Then the projectionists returned to the booths and finished the night's shows. The following morning, IA pickets were stationed in front of the theaters and the projectionists failed to report for work. Only through the 'personal intercession' of Barney Balaban was George Browne persuaded to call off the strike for the time being. IBEW maintenance workers with twenty years experience were fired. An emergency conference between Browne and the studio heads was called for the following weekend.[59] This shadow boxing routine fooled the national press well enough. The producers were said to have been 'forced to accede to Browne's demands.'[60]

Variety reported that on the following weekend the producers granted the IA '100% jurisdiction' in the studios (as if union jurisdiction were a matter of the producers' perogative) over all technical personnel with the exception of the sound technicians. Thus the IA was granted the first closed shop agreement in the history of the industry. The disposition of the sound engineers would be the subject of later arbitration between the IA and the IBEW. The theater maintenance workers' jobs were returned to IBEW. *Variety* perhaps unwittingly contributed to the smoke-screen effect by reporting that the IA had made its move because Browne was convinced that the IBEW was about to take over the projection booths throughout the country. Unnamed sources cited by *Variety* said that the IBEW conceded so readily to the IA because the parent body, AFL, was afraid that Browne would move his organization into the CIO.[61]

Perhaps both of these suppositions were valid. But with hindsight, one can see that the producers had found a way to force their restless workers into a union controlled by men who were willing to stop strikes and to trade workers' wages in return for payoffs. Also, the producers could now blame the 'excessive demands' of the unions for any future unpleasantness involving worker layoffs or the recurrent problem of casualization. In fact, as if on cue from the producers, *Variety* mentioned in its 1935 Christmas issue that despite a long-time practice of allowing certain department heads and unit producers the right to maintain a core group of workers between assignments, the studio executives now no longer allowed such production 'families' to exist.[62]

On 2 January 1936 notices were posted at the major studios and labs informing all grips, electricians, stage carpenters, property workers, camera crew members (with the exception of first camera operators) and lab technicians that they must rejoin their respective IA locals within the next few weeks in order to maintain their jobs. The IBEW and the Carpenters were allowed to maintain the same jobs (primarily permanent construction work) they had prior to the 1933 strike. The producers had granted a closed shop to all three craft unions: the Carpenters, the IBEW and the IA.[63] Technically, the unions did not act as hiring halls. Producers were still able to draw from the available union labor pools as they saw fit. The unions had the power, however, to blacklist any uncooperative workers by refusing to grant a card or by revoking a current member's card.

At the 1936 IA Convention, Browne declared to the delegates:

On my visits to the West Coast, subsequent to the final settlement, I was amazed at the rise in the morale of the members at present employed, and which more than compensated for any physical or material expenditure in consummating the adjustment. That they are infinitely grateful for the sacrifice and cooperation extended on every hand goes without saying. I have absolute confidence that their future conduct will not alone justify the means, but that in time they will form a representative unit of the Alliance, which will warrant only the highest admiration and respect.[64]

There was, to be sure, an air of optimism in the early successes of Browne. In other remarks at the convention, Browne addressed the 'past', 'present' and 'future' with the verve of a Patton:

We must build a protective wall around our organization, with each local representing the individual blocks in the structure. By blending genuine materials of loyalty and devotion in the composition of these blocks, we can make penetration exceedingly difficult. Then, as we progress and add new strength, we will automatically be reinforcing our position, rendering it impregnable and adequate to withstand or repel any attempted invasions.[65]

On the surface, Browne presented the image of a genuine militant, but beneath the discourse and the easy victories, he was using his position to embezzle assessments levied on his members and to exchange bargaining favors for payoffs from the producers.

By early February 1936, *Variety* reported that Browne might pull the IA out of the AFL into the just-forming CIO, and that he was definitely laying plans to organize the entire amusement industry 'from cellar to ceiling'.[66] This implied that the IA wanted to take control of all workers in the motion picture industry, including the actors, writers and directors. By the end of January, many of the labor groups that had not yet gained recognition from the producers had formed a rather loose-knit mutual support organization, the Federated Motion Picture Crafts (FMPC). This organization included the art directors, technical directors, sound engineers, set designers, costume designers, lab engineers, and the small group of crafts organized under the Painters, including the studio painters, scenic artists, make-up artists and hair stylists. This first incarnation of the FMPC did not amount to much, but it did establish the groundwork for a reformed version of the organization that would have a brief but powerful impact on the studio labor scene in the following year.[67]

On 25 April 1936, the heads of the studios and International unions that were signatories to the SBA met in New York City to discuss wages and conditions for the coming contract year. The Studio Utility Employees (SUE) and the Screen Actors Guild (SAG) sent representatives to New York, but Browne blocked their participation in the talks. This conveniently let the producers off the hook. Meanwhile Browne and Bioff, with their ever-present syndicate overseer Circella, met in a private session with Leo Spitz, who was then head of RKO, and Nicholas Schenck of Loew's. A deal was struck in which the four largest studios (Fox, Warners, MGM and Paramount) would each pay Browne and Bioff $50,000 per year to keep wages down and to prevent strikes. The two smaller studios (RKO and Columbia) were each allowed to pay only $20,000 per year. Over the course of the next year the major studios covered up the $200,000 total by juggling their books.[68]

To insure absolute control over the studio locals, Browne and his Executive Board declared the studio locals 'in a state of emergency' on 10 July 1936. Local meetings and elections were banned; Browne put his own representatives in charge of each local and placed 'lot checkers' in each studio.[69] Their duties ostensibly involved 'maintaining IATSE jurisdiction', but they also acted as stool pigeons for Bioff and Browne, and collected 2 per cent assessments against studio workers' gross earnings. With such men representing the interests of studio workers, there was no effective avenue of appeal for IA workers who felt cheated by the union or the producers. 'Troublemakers' were blacklisted by their own union.

It was truly an upbeat time for the producers: profits and production were approaching levels not reached since 1929. Bioff and Browne were in control of some 12,000 workers. This rigid and collusive control would save the producers substantial sums over the next four years of Browne's regime. In a tax hearing on the estate of Frank Nitti in 1949, studio executives admitted under oath that their deals with Browne and Bioff saved the studios approximately $15 million.[70]

In addition, the producers now had in Willie Bioff their strongest and most cunning ally ever in their battle against granting recognition to the talent guilds and the numerous other labor groups. For the time being the producers, through their able labor representative Pat Casey, were able to use the labyrinth of inter-union and producer-union agreements to thwart legitimate collective bargaining. There was also a hope that the Wagner Act might be ruled unconstitutional: a number of legal challenges to the law had been filed with the US Supreme Court. This was the same Supreme Court that had ruled the National Industrial Recovery Act unconstitutional. If the Wagner Act met the same fate, the producers could maintain open shop conditions for any group of workers in the studios.

Notes

1. A good explanation of the changes in the theatrical industry in the 1890s can be found in Jack Poggi, *Theater in America: the Impact of Economic Forces* (Ithaca, NY: Cornell University Press, 1968).
2. The early history of IATSE can be found in International Alliance of Theatrical and Stage Employees and Moving Picture Machine Operators of the United States and Canada, *Combined Convention Proceedings*, vol. (Newark, NJ: Musicians' Press, 1926); Robert O. Baker, *Theatrical Stage Employees* (Lawrence, KS, 1933; self-published dissertation); John Russell Cauble, 'A Study of the International Alliance of Theatrical Stage Employees and Moving Picture Machine Operators of the United States and Canada' (Los Angeles: University of California, 1964; unpublished Master's thesis), pp. 9-30; and Germain Quinn, *Fifty Years Backstage* (Minneapolis, 1926; self-published memoirs).
3. Cauble, 'A Study of the International Alliance', p.30.
4. On the subject of the early history of the IATSE, again, the best source is the *Combined Convention Proceedings*, vol. 1, of the IATSE.
5. The most forthright statement on the subject of the move of production to Los Angeles may have come from an early motion picture entrepreneur, Benjamin Hampton: 'The cost of lumber was low and the wages of the carpenters and other mechanics was (*sic*) 25 to 50 per cent less than in New York'. Benjamin Hampton, *A History of the Movies* (New York: Covici Friede, 1931), p. 115.
6. Carey McWilliams in Erskine Caldwell (ed.) *Southern California Country* (New York: Duell, Sloan & Pearce, 1946), pp. 274-5.
7. Grace H. Stimson, *The Rise of the Labor Movement in Los Angeles* (Berkeley: University of California Press, 1955).
8. Ibid., p. 331.
9. Ibid., p. 332.
10. McWilliams in *Southern California Country*, p. 280.
11. This description of the early days of workers standing outside the gates is based largely on interviews with retired film workers by Michael Nielsen in the summer of 1984 in Los Angeles. Frank Barenna, a retired electrician, called the daily routine 'panning the gate'. Gene Mailes recalls that it was known as the 'shape-up'.
12. The best descriptions of early union jurisdictional struggles and how they served the needs of the producers can be found in Richard and Louis Perry, *A History of the Los Angeles Labor Movement* (Berkeley: University of California Press, 1963), pp. 320-5; Hugh Lovell and Tasile Carter, *Collective Bargaining in the Motion Picture Industry; A Struggle for Stability* (Berkeley: University of California Press, 1955), p. 15; and Murray Ross, *Stars and Strikes* (New York: Columbia University Press, 1941), pp. 5-11. They are collectively analyzed and elaborated on in Michael Nielsen, 'Motion Picture Craft Workers and Craft Unions in Hollywood: The Studio Era' (Urbana, IL, 1985; unpublished dissertation), pp. 51-101.
13. For the struggle between the International office of IATSE and IATSE Local 33 in Los Angeles, see IATSE, *Combined Convention Proceedings*, vol. 1, pp. 536, 540, 558 and 579. On the subject of stagehands losing jobs with the decline of the live theatrical industry, see *Variety*, 14 April 1914, p. 10: 'Mushroom growth of movies and closing of shows galore have given stage employees something to worry about...the flopping of legitimate stage houses to pictures has thrown several hundred union stage hands out of work.'
14. IATSE, *Combined Convention Proceedings*, vol. 1, pp. 536, 540, 558.
15. US Bureau of Census, Census of Manufacturers (Washington DC: 1921, 1927).
16. Perry, *A History of the Los Angeles Labor Movement*, pp. 322-4.

17. I am indebted to Frank Barenna, former studio electrician, for his description of the work and conditions of work for studio electricians. Interviewed, 1984, Los Angeles.
18. Perry, *A History of the Los Angeles Labor Movement*, p. 343.
19. Ibid., pp. 324-5; see also IATSE, *Combined Convention Proceedings*, vol. 2, pp. 15-16.
20. Interview, Frank Barenna, 1984.
21. IATSE, *Combined Convention Proceedings*, vol. 2, p. 16.
22. Ibid., p. 14.
23. *New York Times*, 20 October 1926, p. 27.
24. Joseph P. Kennedy, *The Story of Films* (Chicago: A.W. Shaw Co., 1927), p. 24.
25. The statement of the percentage of union workers to be employed by the studios is from Steve Newman. Testimony given in the IATSE trial of Gene Mailes, et al., Los Angeles, 10 March 1946, p. 151.
26. Gertrude Jobes, *Motion Picture Empire* (Hamden, CT: Archon, 1966), p. 277.
27. Ross, *Stars and Strikes*, pp. 27-8.
28. Interview, Frank Barenna, 1984.
29. *Variety*, 5 November 1930, p. 12.
30. *Variety*, 14 March 1933, p. 4.
31. Milo Lory, American Film Institute Oral History Collection, p. 36.
32. *Variety*, 3 October 1933, p. 11.
33. Lovell and Carter, p. 36.
34. IATSE, *Combined Convention Proceedings*, vol. 2, p. 191.
35. Joseph Rayback, *A History of the American Labor Movement* (New York: Free Press, 1966), p. 330.
36. Ibid.
37. *Variety*, 11 July 1933, p. 4.
38. *Variety*, 25 July 1933, p. 27.
39. Lory, p. 37.
40. *Variety*, 8 August 1932, p. 3.
41. Lovell and Carter, *Collective Bargaining*, p. 17.
42. *Variety*, 17 October 1933, p. 2.
43. Lovell and Carter, *Collective Bargaining*, p. 17.
44. *Variety*, 3 October 1933, p. 11.
45. *Nation*, 20 September 1933, p. 326.
46. *Variety*, 29 August 1933, pp. 5, 56.
47. *Variety*, 6 November 1933, p. 6.
48. Employment figures from *Variety*, 9 October 1934, p. 2.
49. *Variety*, 22 August 1933, p. 7.
50. The Browne and Bioff story is chronicled in a number of books and stories, including Jobes, *Motion Picture Empire*; Hank Messick, *The Beauties and the Beasts* (publisher and date unknown) especially pp. 89-92; George H. Dunne, *Hollywood Labor Dispute: A Study in Immorality* (Los Angeles: Conference Publishing, 1950).
51. *Variety*, 8 December 1943, p. 16.
52. *New York Times*, 6 May 1933, p. 8.
53. IATSE, *Combined Convention Proceedings*, vol. 2, p. 223.
54. Ibid., pp. 222-3.
55. Ibid.
56. *Variety*, 2 June 1943, p. 14.
57. Rayback, *A History of the American Labor Movement*, p. 348.
58. *Variety*, 2 November 1935, p. 4.
59. *Variety*, 4 December 1935, pp. 5, 23.
60. *New York Times*, 9 December 1935, p. 25.
61. *Variety*, 11 December 1935, pp. 5, 12.
62. *Variety*, 25 December 1935, pp. 5, 52.

63. *Variety*, 8 January 1936, p. 7.
64. IATSE, *Combined Convention Proceedings*, vol. 2, p. 326.
65. Ibid.
66. *Variety*, 5 February 1936, p. 2.
67. *Variety*, 22 January 1936, p. 7.
68. Dunne, *Hollywood Labor Dispute*, pp. 15-17.
69. IATSE, *Combined Convention Proceedings*, vol. 2, pp. 304, 326.
70. Thirteen Tax Court of United States Reports, Estate of Frank Nitti, Petitioner v. Commissioner of Internal Revenue, Respondent, Docket nos. 8840, 8841, 8842, promulgated 30 November 1949, pp. 858-69.

2

BROWNE AND BIOFF

Signs of Life: The Federated Motion Picture Crafts
Early in 1937, the CIO formed the United Theatrical and Motion Picture
Workers of America to organize all workers not yet covered by union contracts in the studios, labs, exchanges and theaters. In March, this organization
pulled together the remains of a failed campaign of the previous year and
launched an offensive to organize the lab workers at the New Jersey plant of
Consolidated Film Incorporated (CFI). In Hollywood, Painters Local 644,
not a party to the Studio Basic Agreement, was demanding local recognition
and a substantial wage increase from the producers.[1] George Browne responded by reinstituting the 2 per cent assessment against all IA members
earnings to build up a 'war chest', i.e. a strike fund. The IA General Executive
Board placed this money 'at the International President's disposal.'[2]

Browne countered the CIO offensive at the CFI plant by reactivating the long-
dormant IA East coast lab workers' union, Local 669. By mid-April, the IA had
organized a majority of workers at the New York labs of Warners and De Luxe,
and had signed closed shop agreements with those firms as well as with CFI.[3]
Browne chose this time as well to organize the 'girls' in the film exchanges, creating 'B' locals. *Variety* noted the strategic significance of the IA's control of the
exchanges: 'Once a film exchange local is started in operation in territories where
there are many non-union projectionists working, exhibitors may be forced to
install union operators in their booths or have their service cut off.'[4]

Not all unions in the motion picture industry, however, were as successful
as the IA had been in 1936 and 1937. The producers had simply refused to
bargain with the Screen Actors Guild (SAG) and the Screen Writers Guild
(SWG) for over two years when the Supreme Court upheld the constitution-
ality of the Wagner Act on 12 April 1937. The producers issued a public statement claiming that the motion picture production industry was not
interstate commerce because a vast majority of the production took place
within the state of California.[5] Thus the workers in the production branch of
the industry would not be covered by the Wagner Act, which applied only to
industries engaged in interstate commerce. Although the producers' own
lawyers indicated that the tactic would not succeed, the producers used this
legal ruse to block recognition of SWG for over a year. The producers would
have used the same trick against SAG, but that struggle was about to reach a
suitably dramatic climax.[6]

Immediately after the Supreme Court's decision upholding the constitu-
tionality of the Wagner Act, Charles Lessing of Painters Local 644 reformed

the Federated Motion Picture Crafts (FMPC) to present a collective demand for recognition for each of the following studio craft locals: painters, scenic artists, hair dressers, make-up artists, laborers, costumers, draftspersons, plumbers, engineers, boilermakers, blacksmiths, machinists, linoleum workers, sheet metal workers and culinary workers. By far the largest single group solidly within the FMPC were the laborers, organized as Studio Utility Employees (SUE), an affiliate of the Hod Carriers, Builders and Common Laborers of America. These utility workers did any sort of manual labor that lay outside the jurisdiction of the other unions. They were among the hardest working and lowest paid of all wage earners in the film production industry. Although Warners had granted the utility workers a boost to 75 cents per hour in January 1937, the other studios were paying only 62 cents per hour, with no minimum guarantees of work per day and no overtime payments.[7]

The Carpenters studio Local 946 was tentatively affiliated with the FMPC. The failure of their international representatives to get wage increases for the studio Carpenters at the 1936 SBA negotiations had upset a large number of rank and file members of the local. These studio carpenters felt that this failure was evidence of negligence by the Carpenters' international office. The FMPC's policy of bargaining autonomy for studio locals seemed to offer a chance for the disgruntled elements of Local 946 to reopen talks with the producers on a local level.[8] The Screen Actors Guild also had tentative ties to the FMPC, but there was no firm commitment from the actors to support the other FMPC unions in the event of a strike. FMPC Executive Secretary Charles Lessing was convinced that SAG would vote to support the strike in light of the fact that it was Browne and the producers who had specifically blocked SAG from participation in the most recent SBA talks in New York.[9]

Painters Local 644 and SUE Local 724 voted on 24 and 25 April respectively, to strike for recognition. Nine hundred of the SUE members signed cards pledging not to join any other organizations. Willie Bioff issued a public statement offering any SUE members 'Class B' grip memberships and guaranteeing them an increase from 62 cents per hour to 82H cents per hour. Joseph Marshall, the International President of the laborers' union, threatened to bring in pickets from around the country to block the IA from continuing its raiding on Local 724 SUE. On the eve of the impending FMPC strike, there was a potential for the walkout of some 16,000 workers.[10]

On 30 April, the producers' labor representative, Pat Casey, hastily called a meeting one hour before the 6 p.m. deadline to try to head off the strike. According to *Variety*, Lessing and the other leaders of the FMPC walked out after 'one minute' of talking to Casey. At 6 p.m. only the Painters and SUE members walked off their jobs at the major studios.[11]

As FMPC workers were leaving the lots, Bioff's men offered them free IA cards. Several workers accepted the cards, but the vast majority of SUE and Painters members walked out and stayed out for several weeks. The issuing of cards to crafts that had formerly failed to gain producer recognition amounted to a *de facto* expansion of the IA's jurisdiction. The remaining labor groups in the FMPC adopted a wait-and-see attitude; they were afraid of the combined power of the producers and Bioff.[12]

SAG called a mass meeting of its members on 2 May, at Hollywood Legion Stadium; but the SAG leadership did not call for an immediate strike vote, choosing instead to poll their members over the next week by written ballot. Resolutions were adopted at the meeting by some 2,500 actors, forbidding actors from taking the place of striking make-up artists and hair stylists. The issue of crossing picket lines was left to the discretion of each member. This represented an abandonment of the FMPC strikers, since the actors were well aware that most of them were just as replaceable as the lowliest janitor. A star such as Jimmy Cagney could go fishing on his boat for a while, but the SAG Junior Guild members – extras and bit players – could not afford such a luxury during the depression. A producers' blacklist of strike supporters seemed quite likely.[13]

The picketing began peacefully on the following Monday morning. One of the picket captains for the FMPC was Herb Sorrell, who established his reputation during this strike as a resourceful and physically aggressive leader. Sorrell was destined to assume leadership of the studio painters and eventually to lead the largest strikes in Hollywood history from 1945 until 1947.

The Carpenters' international office ordered the members of Carpenters Local 946 to cross the picket lines. Needless to say, Bioff's tightly controlled IA studio locals had no choice about whether they would cross the lines. Groups of actors and technicians who chose to cross the FMPC lines were not initially harassed, but the strike quickly turned bloody. By the end of the first full week of picketing, Bioff had brought in 'muscle' from Chicago to help move his members through the lines. The producers depended on Johnny Roselli, a syndicate friend of Columbia Pictures' president Harry Cohn, to move cinematographers and their assistants through the lines; Roselli also called Chicago for help from syndicate goons. The Teamsters, under the direction of their West coast representative Dave Beck, also ferried actors and technicians through the lines. When pickets attacked vehicles driven by Teamsters, Beck also brought in 'muscle' from outside the Los Angeles area.[14]

The strike significantly slowed work in the studios. Sorrell countered the 'goon squads' of Bioff and Roselli by enlisting the aid of the Longshoremen of San Pedro and members of Los Angeles automobile, steel, rubber and communications locals of CIO industrial unions. Students from Los Angeles colleges and universities also joined the picket lines. Strike-breakers who had defected from the striking unions were natural targets for the pickets' anger. Vandals did $10,000 damage to a beauty salon operated by the famous Westmore family, prominent make-up artists, who had refused to support the FMPC strike. A Painters' 'flying squad' raided the IA's Hollywood headquarters and beat up five former members of the Painters' Local 644 who had accepted IA cards from Bioff.[15]

By the following weekend SAG had tabulated the votes of its members on the issue of whether to strike for recognition. Ninety-nine per cent of the members voted to give their executive committee the power to issue a strike call in the event of the committee deciding that a strike was the only way to achieve results. The SAG demands were for a 'preferential shop' (based on an as yet unspecified percentage of SAG actors per production), better pay for Junior Guild members, and recognition of SAG as the exclusive bargaining agent for its 6,000 members. In a strategic move to block the actors from possibly forming an alliance with the FMPC, Bioff and IA Vice-President Harlan Holmden intervened on behalf of the actors, informing the producers that the IA would call a 'projectionists' boycott of the producers' films if SAG's

27

demands were not met. The producers caved in to this pressure and opened talks with the actors. SAG President Robert Montgomery praised the efforts of Bioff and Holmden, claiming that the two men deserved much of the credit for the success of SAG's bargaining with the producers.[16]

The triumph of the actors, however, was a rout for the FMPC. The collaboration of SAG, the IA and the producers effectively broke the strike. One by one, the striking or sympathetic groups returned to work. The striking unions failed to secure closed shop conditions; however, after the strikers returned to work, the producers signed contracts with those groups specifying standardized wages and conditions. In this way the FMPC unions achieved partial success. The crushing blow to the FMPC effort came on 21 May, when the SUE voted to return to work at 75 cents per hour (still below the rate paid to the IA's Class B grips) and without the guarantee of a union shop. Once again the IA was praised for its intervention, this time by Joseph Marshall, the international representative of SUE. By now, only the painters, scenic artists, make-up artists and hair stylists remained out on strike. FMPC leader Charles Lessing attempted to bargain directly with L. B. Mayer. Bioff, however, blocked any possible settlement that did not meet his approval by threatening a projectionists' boycott of the films of Mayer or any of the other producers who struck bargains with Lessing. Of course, Bioff in this instance may have been acting as the producers' stooge.[17]

The international body of the Painters studio Local 644, the International Brotherhood of Painters, Paperhangers and Decorators (IBPPD), initially lent strong support to Lessing and the FMPC. Painters' locals throughout the country picketed the theaters of the major studios, urging patrons to boycott them until the strikers achieved a just settlement. IBPPD International President Lindeloff pressed the AFL for support for the strikers and asked the AFL Executive Committee to condemn the IA's raiding of the AFL studio locals. After it was abundantly clear that the FMPC would fail to achieve its stated purpose of producers' recognition for the four remaining groups – the studio painters, make-up artists, hair stylists and scenic artists – Joe Clarke, International Vice-President of the IBPPD, attempted to negotiate a 'backdoor' settlement with the producers, a settlement that doubtless involved the participation of Bioff. Clarke worked out an agreement whereby Painters Local 644 would get closed shop status and a 10 per cent pay increase in return for agreeing to relinquish support for the scenic artists, make-up artists and hair stylists. Lessing strategically chose first to poll the make-up artists and hair dressers as to whether they were in favor of being taken over by the IA. The vote was unanimous in opposition to any alliance with the IA. At a meeting of Painters Local 644 on the following night, Lessing and Clarke presented their divergent opinions on the agreement worked out by Clarke. An overwhelming majority of painters chose to continue the strike, despite the fact that the FMPC strike fund was depleted. But the vote was more a show of defiance than anything else.[18] By 14 June the remaining FMPC groups agreed to return to work under the following terms: 1. immediate return to work, in the same job status as of 4 April 1937; 2. start negotiations on wage and working conditions adjustments within six days; 3. terms not negotiated within thirty days to be submitted for arbitration; 4. 100 per cent union shop effective as of 1 July; 5. all persons employed in strikers' places to be discharged unless they qualified to hold jobs and eligible for union member-ship.[19] This agreement led to a closed shop for the Painters Local 644 – the first local union to be granted such status – and a 15 per cent pay increase.

In July 1937, immediately after the settlement of the FMPC strike, Bioff had decided that he wanted the 'good life' of southern California. He wanted to buy a ranch in the San Fernando Valley, having accumulated a substantial nest egg from his share of the producers' payoffs and the embezzlement of the IA's special assessment fund. But Bioff's nest egg was all in cash. He could not simply walk into a bank with a stash of dollars and buy a ranch. Bioff asked his friend Joe Schenck, head of the MPPDA and president of 20th Century-Fox, for a brief $100,000 loan in a money-laundering scheme aimed at covering up the true source of his wealth. As it turned out, it was this comparatively innocent transaction that tripped up Bioff.[20]

Ted Ellsworth, who was later one of the leading voices in the costumers' local union, recalled that Bioff's technique for persuading the costumers to join the IA was simple and direct. He asked Bert Offord, then business agent for the costumers, whether he wanted to bring his group into the IA. When Offord expressed hesitation, Bioff placed a gun on his desk and told Bert to 'think it over.' The costumers joined the IA. In September 1937, Bioff negoti-ated substantial wage increases for the costumers and make-up artists.[21]

The FMPC strike was aided and abetted by one organization that was within the IA during this time. This militant cadre of IA studio workers was known as the '37 White Rats' who vocally objected to the studio labor policies of Browne and Bioff. This group had demanded a return to local autonomy for Local 37 and forwarded a resolution to the AFL Executive Board calling on the AFL to support the FMPC locals and 'to order IATSE to close out all permits, Class B cards, and other subterfuges [sic] issued to workers since the inception of the strike.'[22] The 37 White Rats were, in fact, the nucleus of the 'IA Progressives'. This group, under the leadership of Jeff Kibre and Irv Hentschel, attempted to reform the corrupt labor unions in Hollywood. The struggle of the IA Progressives, under their various pseudonyms, went on for the next fifteen years. Here is where we pick up Gene Mailes' story:

I had started to work in the studios in January 1937, as a greensman, or as it was later called, 'Landscape Set Dresser'. Though I was not actu-ally experienced in union affairs, I was quite aware of union history. In the theatrical world I was aware of what a difference unions or guilds could make in working conditions. My parents were stage actors and I had heard of their being stranded in various towns throughout the East and Midwest and having to wire home for money to return home to New York. No company money. My mother was stranded three times while touring with a play called Sky Farm. Also I remember hearing about the IA, during the Actor's Equity Strike in New York in 1918. The weak fight that the actors and actresses were able to put up was about to fold when the IA honored their picket line and that won the actors' strike. The IA had once been a union, before the Chicago crime syndi-cate led by Frank Nitti took it over in 1934.

In Hollywood, an organization was formed in 1937 to fight the dictato-rial control of the union by the 'mob'. They were called the 'IA

Progressives' and they were doing all the right things to advance the fight for the advantages to be expected from a union. IA Local 37 was controlled by the International and meetings were not allowed. There was no negotiation committee, and no job stewards were allowed to police the contract for the membership. It was all run by the home office.

Irv Hentschel was the secretary of the IA Progressives. Jeff Kibre was Chairman. I never really got to know Jeff. He was a graduate of the University of California at Los Angeles, an extremely intelligent, decent and gifted man. When the chips were down, he stood up to be counted.

Before working in Hollywood, Irv Hentschel worked in the pay-roll office of a Baltimore railroad terminal. He was quite frail. The most that he ever weighed was one hundred and twenty pounds. He and Helen had been married a short time and he was trying to make more money. He looked around the office and saw that his chance of working his way up to a higher position was to be patient and wait for, probably, years. He had noticed that the bigger checks went to the union members and that the more highly skilled men got the biggest pay checks.

He went to several machine shops and cabinet shops and thought about his size and the pay scales. He found that he liked both crafts equally. Most of the heavy lifting in machine shops was done by electric hoist and carts. He also noted that the more highly skilled machinist made more than the cabinet makers. He went to the public library and took out books on both trades. He studied both of them in night school for a year and then started looking for a job as a machinist. He had a pleasant and appealing personality, made friends easily and learned quickly. It was during the Depression, when there were many new ideas for social change being discussed openly. Irv jumped into the arguments and discussions with both feet. He joined the International Association of Machinists and went regularly to meetings. He caught sight of what a union could mean in the way of job improvement, pay scales and benefit to the country at large. Many of his friends were interested in the idea of a basic change in the social system under which we were living. Friends suggested books for him to read, such as the autobiography of Lincoln Steffins. Also, they suggested that Irv read books on American history, and labor history, as well as cultural subjects. He and Helen were stepping into a new, different and exciting life.

As time went on he took more and more part in union affairs. Finally one night a couple of friends suggested that he might like to join the Communist Party. He knew these men well; they were intelligent and active in various fields. After talking it over with Helen for couple of weeks, he asked his friends to submit his name to the local unit of the Party. He was accepted and was soon recognized as being very intelligent and was sent to a Communist Party Labor School. He told me, 'I am Party-educated.' He had a high school education and he used phrases such as 'I says to him' and 'He says to me.' Yet with this new direction his life was taking and his obvious intelligence and quick-study ability, he impressed all who knew him. When we sat down to write a letter, a bulletin or a handbill, he did the typing and most of the make-up. They were always in perfect English, no spelling errors.

Irv had two jobs as Secretary of the IA Progressives. One was to be the Nuts and Bolts organizer – to organize the neighborhood meetings – and, two, to keep up the membership lists of all who belonged to the IA Progressives. Added to this was the file of the contributors, which was kept secret. These were mostly from the talent guilds.

As with many other crimes, the 'mob' rule of the IA did not receive the attention from the public authorities that it deserved. There was no public awareness of the crime or its enormity. Through rumors and bits of information we began to be aware that there was something very wrong with this union which had won the contract we had with the studios. Jeff [Kibre] was in contact with some of the people in Chicago, mostly members of the Newspaper Guild, but he was able to learn very little at first.

At this point, I was more an observer than a real activist in the Progressives. I attended meetings, but I mostly listened. With time, I began to ask questions from the floor, or to offer an idea. It wasn't until the summer of 1939 that I really joined the fight. But once I jumped in, it was an all-out commitment to reform the union.

The IA Progressives became involved in meetings over the question of year-round employment and the long periods of unemployment and tried to generate interest around that issue. They were only partially success-ful. They issued letters that raised questions about general conditions regarding work. Some attention was given in the local press and radio, but little came of this. Something spectacular was needed. The FMPC strike offered this possibility.

The leaders of the IA immediately started to organize scab unions to take the jobs of the striking unions. Again it was the same old problem of a union displacing present workers with other men, new on the job. The fact that the men who were being displaced had families and were part of the community mattered not at all.

When anyone objected to the IA's tactics, the IA's leaders cried 'Communists!' That was always the weapon the mobs used against any threat to their control. One by one, the other unions allied with the Painters in the FMPC strike withered under the pressure and went back to work, either as individuals or as organizations. One of the FMPC unions was the independent Laborers' union. A scab union was formed by the IA with Zeal Fairbanks appointed by Willie Bioff as Business Agent of this alleged union. That was Mr Fairbanks' first leg up in the hierarchy of the IA leadership. Later, Fairbanks was to become an IA International Executive Board member. A great guy, Fairbanks.

It was during this strike that Herb Sorrell began to attract attention. He was elected Picket Captain; also he became, by general consent, unofficial head of the goon squad that beat up strike-breakers. In both jobs he became fairly proficient. He was very willing to fight.

It must be pointed out that some people think that striking unionists should have let the mobs attack them and not make any response to defend themselves. The bona fide reason for union goon squads is for the protection of the striking workers. After the LaFollette Committee Report the legitimacy of this view was granted. Union members out on strike were entitled to protection; if the local police did not grant protection, they were entitled to do it themselves. It seemed that IA goons were never arrested. The Las Vegas casinos were stripped of their 'guards' during this strike. The boys were working on the Hollywood strike. It was a wonder that there were no casinos robbed during this period. Las Vegas must have been wide open as far as protection was concerned. They were all working as IA goons in Hollywood.

The 1937 strike was a turning point in Hollywood labor negotiations. For the first time a contract was negotiated and signed in Hollywood. The Painters won the best contract in the studios. This was denied by many people in the studios at the time, but it was in this contract that the Painters began to get 'special' rates for different textures of paint. That's where the difference was. It was following this strike that Herb Sorrell was elected to the job of Business Agent for the Hollywood Painters local.

In early September 1937 the brief honeymoon between the IA and SAG ended. SAG issued a six-month suspension to Jane Tallent, a SAG extra who had accepted an IA card from Bioff so that she could work as a make-up artist at Paramount during the FMPC strike. Although Bioff pleaded Tallent's case, the SAG board refused to reinstate her.[23] In retaliation for this seeming lack of gratitude on the part of Montgomery and the other SAG leaders, Bioff and Browne began a direct offensive against the actors' union. Bioff announced on 15 September that the IA intended to take control of all unorganized groups in the studios, including actors, writers, directors, unit managers, assistant directors, first camerapersons, film editors, white collar workers, painters, carpenters, electricians and janitors. By that time, according to *Variety*, Bioff had already issued cards to more than 500 former members of the Carpenters Local 946. IA International Vice-President Harlan Holmden issued a follow-up statement disavowing any intention on the part of his union to take control of the '$5,000 per week person who, in most cases, acts strictly as though he was a company emissary advancing not only his company's own policies and purposes but his own selfish motives.'[24] Holmden claimed that SAG kept a far greater number of extras on its rolls than it could ever hope to place in the studios even in the busiest of times. He also claimed that extras had pleaded for the IA to take care of them, although there is little evidence to support such a claim. The leadership of SAG was convinced that they could afford to laugh off the IA's claim to represent the actors. How could Holmden claim to represent actors when there wasn't a single actor at the time with an IA card? SAG was an AFL affiliate; it didn't seem too likely that AFL President William Green would approve of such a blatant jurisdictional grab by the IA. Behind the scenes SAG leaders began to look for ways to fight off IA encroachments.

The Hentschel-Cohea Case

As a result of the IA's actions during the FMPC strike, the Progressives had plenty of abuses to call attention to. In addition, the members of all IA studio unions received a letter telling us that we had to pay 2 per cent of our salary to the IA General Fund for the protection of the union. Approximately two million dollars was collected, for which there was never an accounting. We did ultimately learn that the future President of the IA, Richard Walsh, received the following from this 2 per cent fund – '$2,392 in 1935; $8,932 in 1936; $6,344 in 1937; $5,700 in 1938; $5,200 in 1938; $3,300 in 1937; $5,700 in 1938; $5,200 in 1939; $2,800 in 1940, on which he paid income tax.'[25]

Irv was working on a prop-miniature job. In the same shop was another man, Chester Cohea, also a prop-maker. Chet was one of those 'They can't do this to me!' guys who are sometimes able to throw a wrench into the machinery. The assessment affair came up and Chet told Irv that he was going to file a case to force the return to him of his 2 per cent. Irv asked if he had a lawyer or any other members of the IA to help him. Chet told him that he had been introduced to a lawyer named Aaron Sapiro, a man who had done a lot of work for Harry Bridges, the leader of the Longshoremen's union. That sounded good to Irv, so he asked Chet if he could meet Mr Sapiro. A meeting was arranged and Irv was taken to Sapiro's office.

During the talk in Sapiro's office Irv thought that this man had mentioned Harry Bridges' name too often to suit him. It sounded a bit phony, so he asked Chet to wait a few days so that he could talk to some others who might be interested, to which Chet agreed. At the next meeting of Irv's Party unit, he took the floor and explained about Chet and Mr Sapiro. The Party always took a dim view of a law case against a union. Irv asked them to wait while he talked further to Chet. So the problem was tabled.

Irv went back to Chet and told him the reasons his friends thought a law case was not a good idea: law cases were usually long and expensive and often a dead issue by the time they were decided by the courts. In addition, Irv asked, who was Sapiro? Did Chet have anyone else with him? Irv again asked him to wait until he found out more about Sapiro, and Chet agreed. There were a few men who agreed with Chet that they should file a case. Everything was put on hold until Irv investigated Mr Sapiro. It was suggested to Irv that he write a letter to Harry Bridges, asking him what Sapiro's connection was with the Longshoremen's union and Bridges.

In due course a letter came back from Bridges. As Irv said, when Harry Bridges writes you a letter, you get a letter that is a letter.[26] Irv's letter follows, with excerpts from Mr Bridges' answer:

Harry Bridges
Pacific Coast Maritime Fed.
San Francisco, Calif.

We are appealing to you for information that will help us obtain real unionism in the Motion Picture Industry. The recent strike [1937 FMPC], having further exposed the racketeering and complete domination of our locals by our officials, has made the rank and file more determined to find a solution of their difficulties. It is only natural that they look to industrial unionism and the CIO.

To that end we have set up a representative committee of crafts employed in the studios, the purpose of which you will find explained in the following letter. This committee, in trying to carry out its objective, has been so far unable to enlist the aid of the CIO representative, Mr Larkin, who has been publicly acknowledged by Mr Brophy as the studio workers' contact man. We feel that the reasons Mr Larkin does not cooperate in this preliminary work, is due to his close association with Aaron Sapiro, a lawyer who claims having been connected with the Seamen.

As rank and file, we feel that Sapiro's intimacy with Louis B. Mayer, his phony proposals to a portion of the late strike committee, his incessant smooth talk, together with unfavorable reports from waterfront workers, constitute grounds for investigation of his background. He is now, through Larkin, trying to involve a group of 11 men in a lawsuit against the IA. If his motives are not OK, he would be in a position to control 7,000 men if successful or even to disrupt the whole scene in favor of the producers.

As studio workers, we feel we are more capable of advising Larkin than Sapiro. Also if Sapiro is a faker it is most important that we expose him immediately. We would appreciate any information of his activities on the waterfront that would help discredit him to Larkin and the workers in particular. Understand the Voice of the Federation has printed some of his actions.

Fraternally yours,
Irv Hentschel

The first numbered paragraph of Harry Bridges' letter in reply reads: '1) Your letter of June 26th received. In my opinion your assumptions, especially in connection with Aaron Sapiro, are correct. Regarding Mr Larkin: He has been working in close contact with W. Dalrymple, who has been up to now in charge of CIO field work in this area.' The letter goes on in this manner for twenty-one paragraphs, each citing some act of Mr Sapiro that was detrimental to the labor unions with which he was involved. A remark that IA officials were concerned about was in the nineteenth paragraph: 'It is entirely possible that a lawsuit against IATSE may be a good method of attack, the point being however a law suit with Sapiro and one without Sapiro are two vastly different things.'

Later, when the corrupt leaders of the IA would expel Irv from their union, they tried to portray this correspondence with Bridges as an act of conspiracy. In point of fact, all that Irv and the other Progressives were interested in was restoring honest leadership to their union. Bridges was engaged in the same sort of struggle with his own parent union, the International Longshoremen's Association, a totally corrupt union run by the New Jersey mob, known as Murder Incorporated. As soon as possible, Harry's branch of the ILA, the Pacific Coast Longshoremen, left the ILA.

The reply from Harry Bridges was what Irv expected. They went to Sapiro's office but he was not in, so they talked with his partner. They told him what they had on their minds. Sapiro's partner asked them to leave a copy of the letters with him so that he could talk to Aaron about it when he came in. Irv had to go and have dinner and then to a meeting, so before going to dinner he went back to Sapiro's office and picked up the originals of the letters. Sapiro was still not there. The meeting that Irv and Chet went to ran later than expected. As they were driving home to the San Fernando Valley they happened to see a newspaper. The headline, in big letters, hailed the case, 'Bridges, Hentschel sued by attorney for $150,000!' The case had been filed before five o'clock. When Irv got home his wife was laughing as he came in the house. She told him that the phone had been ringing all evening, and asked him, 'What have you done now?'

At the next meeting of the Party unit, they initially turned Irv down on helping him with the law case. Irv explained that he thought it was a mistake to back off from Chet, since Chet was going to file a case with or without help. The unit saw that great damage might come if the case was filed with the wrong attorney, so tacit consent was given for Irv to do what he felt was right. The Party would not endorse the case but it did not object to Irv collecting money for it. Irv talked for some time with Chet and finally they agreed that an attorney named Carey McWilliams would be good, if he would take the case.

Carey McWilliams was involved with a vast network of progressive people, both in and out of the state and national governments. Irv called him, briefed him on what they wanted to see him about and was told to come down the next day. They were immediately put at ease with Carey and stayed for a couple of hours telling him the whole story, with Carey occasionally asking questions. Irv was the more knowledgeable of the two and carried the bulk of the talk. Carey told them that he thought that it might be a good case and asked them to leave the documents they had brought with them. When Carey asked this, they all laughed at the memory of the headlines a few days before. They were told by Carey to see if they could get about twenty more men to sign an agreement to appear as complainants.

When they returned in a couple of days, Carey said that he thought it was a very good case and that he would take it on a contingency basis. He also said that he would see if he could generate interest in the case to the point of getting financial help from friends, as well as from political organizations. Several days later Irv was called by Carey, and told to be at his office in a couple of days with several other men and verify the complaint, i.e. sign it. The day after filing the case the story was in all the big newspapers from coast to coast. Filing the Hentschel-Cohea case was the right thing to do.

The rank and file wanted either to join the CIO or to form an independent union embracing a wide coalition of guilds. This put pressure on the studios and the mob-controlled IA leaders to actually do some genuine negotiation toward better wages and conditions. These negotiations were played in the press as the producers cringing under the threats of the IA's power, but it was just play-acting for public consumption.

At the urging of Carey McWilliams, the California State Assembly called for hearings into alleged labor racketeering in the Hollywood motion picture studios. State Assembly Speaker William J. Jones initially refused McWilliams' request to investigate Bioff. But Jones, through his law partner William Neblitt, approached L. B. Mayer and informed him that it would be possible to get the IA out of the studios. Although Mayer showed no interest in such a move (small wonder, considering that the ever-corruptible IA was all that stood between the producers and the militant CIO), word leaked back to Bioff that an investigation was in the works.

Bioff paid Jones and Neblitt $5,000 to quash the investigation. This was easily done, since the state's investigators came directly from the law offices of Neblitt and Jones. Not surprisingly, the Assembly Committee not only gave the IA a clean bill of health, but also actually took McWilliams and the Progressives to task for attempting to use the Assembly to prejudice the outcome of the Progressives' civil suit, pending in the Los Angeles County courts, for an end to the 2 per cent assessments and a return of local autonomy to Local 37.[27] The Progressives were, in Gene Mailes' word, 'thunderstruck' by the Assembly Committee's report.

Still, the pressure applied by the Progressives did have some positive effects. First, Browne lifted the 2 per cent assessments on 9 December 1937. Second, at the end of December, Browne arrived in Los Angeles for the ostensible purpose of polling the members of the IA studio locals on whether they wanted to regain local autonomy.[28] The Progressives were ecstatic until they realized that Browne's appearance on the coast was all show and no substance. Browne made it clear to the studio locals that members in favor of local autonomy were not loyal to the IA. Browne gave members of Local 37 the impression that voting for local autonomy meant that the open shop would be restored to the studios. To insure identification of troublemakers, Browne required a standing vote rather than a secret ballot.

To try to dull the fight for local control, IA President George Browne came out to Hollywood and held a meeting of Local 37 at the American Legion Boxing Stadium, so that the local could vote on the question of local control or continued International control. It was made clear that if the members voted for local control that would be the end of any help from the International; they would get no further cooperation in any way from the IA. A publicity man, Ed Gibbons, was hired by the mob to scream about the 'Reds' trying to make the studio workers into Communist dupes.

One of the tactics of handling the meeting was to build a temporary rostrum very close to the entrance against the western side of the stadium instead of speaking from the boxing ring in the center. In effect, the meeting was run from the back of the hall. Another was to have a bunch of stooges to interrupt anyone who tried to say anything against International control, and also to point out to the President any of the dissenters.

Jeff Kibre tried to ask a question and was interrupted by one of these men, shouting, 'I challenge the right of this Communist to speak to this body!' There was some yelling and the president ignored Kibre. The question had been stated. There was another shout, 'I call for the question!' Someone else shouted, 'I second the call for the question.' Browne called for a voice vote. There was no way of telling how the vote actually went, but Browne called it against local control. Someone else yelled, ' I move this body adjourn!' This was seconded, and after another voice vote the meeting was adjourned. The next day the newspapers declared the great victory of democracy over the villainous Reds.

36

Irv Hentschel later told an the IA trial board that 'at that time the I.A. [international office] had full charge of whether you worked or not, and that was certainly true in my case. They had this power to either put you to work or keep you from working, and that had an effect, in my estimation, on the outcome of that meeting.'[29] Browne later reported to the 1938 IA Convention that less than a hundred members out of nearly 10,000 voted to restore local autonomy to the locals. Browne remarked, 'It only goes to show you how a small minority can almost ruin the conditions of nearly twelve thousand members.'[30]

In all the events from April 1937 to the end of the year the newly formed regional office of the NLRB under Dr Towne Nylander played a largely symbolic role. Labor groups forwarded petitions to Nylander requesting representational elections, but the mechanisms for conducting such elections had not yet been established. Besides the talent and craft groups already mentioned, other groups seeking recognition from the producers included writers, directors, unit managers, film editors, script clerks, interior decorators, set designers, artists and illustrators, publicists, agents and art directors.[31] Virtually all of the FMPC had achieved informal recognition by virtue of their contracts with the producers signed during and after the strike; however, the IA absorbed several of the FMPC groups that had sought to remain independent of the Bioff version of the IA – make-up artists, hair dressers and costumers, for example – because of the tardy actions of Nylander in providing elections for those groups.

The aggressive posture of the Progressives forced Browne to remove Bioff from the studios in the first week of January 1938. It was actually Nitti who recalled Bioff; apparently, Nitti wanted things to 'cool off' after the close call of the California Assembly investigation.

Unemployment and Infighting

The usual New Year's report in *Variety* in January 1938 on labor conditions in the motion picture industry noted that the increasing unionization had taken its toll on the costs of production and distribution. In production, wages were up an average of 33 per cent over the previous year; in distribution, the increase was as high as 45 per cent.[32]

Although these statistics seemed to bode well for motion picture industry workers, other statistics indicated a very different condition. A recession in the US economy had prompted a temporary decline in domestic box office receipts. Overseas markets for US films were declining because of the import restrictions imposed by Japan and Nazi Germany. The combined impact of these two factors prompted producers to severely cut back production activities toward the end of 1937.[33]

By early 1938 Painters Local 644 reported an 85 per cent unemployment rate. Jeff Kibre called the first meeting of the Studio Unemployment Conference on 27 January 1938 to discuss possible solutions to the problems facing all workers in the industry. Items discussed at the meeting included the abolition of overtime, the demolition of sets after the completion of every production, and the establishment of a three-day work week.[34] The producers were not terribly interested in equitable distribution of work. They preferred to pay overtime to their most competent or most loyal employees rather than concern themselves with the majority of the studios workers' welfare. The studios all maintained a certain number of people full-time and also kept a 'preferential list' of employees who would be called back to work before any other workers. These preferential workers were essentially 'company men' who did what they were told and offered little resistance to the producers' labor policies.

The IA did not participate in the Studio Unemployment Conference, although the IA Progressives pledged their support. But Kibre's initiative prompted IA Hollywood representative Harold V. Smith to seek improved employment conditions for the 12,000 members of the IA's studio and lab locals. Smith and the producers' representatives, L. B. Mayer and Joseph Schenck, negotiated a spread-work plan. The plan was then submitted to the non-IA labor groups for approval. In effect, the producers had demonstrated to the Painters, Carpenters and IBEW that, despite the absence of Willie Bioff from the Hollywood labor scene, all deals would still have to meet the IA's approval. The plan called for a reduction of the studios' preferential list; a limitation of four days' work per person; and all calls for preferential and other employees (under IA jurisdiction) to come through the IA locals for a minimum period of thirty days.[35]

Most studio workers were dependent on the Browne-appointed leaders of the IA studio locals for their continued employment in the studios. This condition generated a high degree of apathy among the workers. The keynote speech from the 1932 IA convention – 'Work at any price' – had taken a dark turn in the studios in the late 1930s. Although the 2 per cent assessment had been lifted, there was no accounting for nearly $1,500,000 collected by representatives of Browne and Bioff over the course of two years. Local 37 was still under the complete control of Browne-appointed henchmen. All the studio craft unions were interested in placing as many workers as possible in studio jobs in order to maintain their membership rolls. But, as noted earlier, union business agents could and did use their closed shop agreements to maintain control over their members by refusing to allow 'troublemakers' the opportunity to work in the studios.

After Bioff was cleared by the fixed Assembly Committee, Irv was 'let go' by one of the studios and went down to Local 37 headquarters and put his name in the 'out of work' book. He received no calls for work. He found that other men out of work were getting work calls. He then called individual studios and was told at two of them that he was not to be hired by any of them. He was blacklisted.

At this point, all we could do was wait for some kind of break. In due time it came. A phone call came from a newspaperman, with the news that one of the members of the State Assembly committee was a decent sort of man and that another was sore that he wasn't paid off like some of the others. They were both interviewed and on the basis of what they had to say a request from many interested people was made quietly to then Governor Culbert Olson for a committee, to exist just long enough to subpoena the bank records of Willie Bioff and Joseph Schenck. This was done and out popped the $100,000 check from Schenck to Bioff. Again we had the headlines from coast to coast. The fight took off with a vigor that surprised us all. The International office of the IA responded with a bombardment of anti-communist propaganda that was frightening to

many of the members of the union. Several weeks later President Browne and the International Executive Board decided to return partial autonomy to Local 37. This was done not to give way to the membership but in total insincerity, with the intention of taking control back as soon as possible, by any means necessary.

The 1938 convention was coming up and we had to prepare a resolution to be submitted to the Resolutions Committee. There were several meetings to determine the purpose of the resolution. It was decided to put it in the form of a direct charge against the mobs, more or less in the form of an indictment. This was rewritten several times. We did not know how we were going to get this resolution to the floor but we would at least be able to cause them some trouble that they would rather not have to deal with. We strictly followed the constitution as to procedure and form. Of course, we knew that the mob was getting reports on what we were doing.

One of their answers was to have the Los Angeles Police Department raid the home of Jeff Kibre. Jeff objected and was pushed around by the police. He asked to see the search warrant. They didn't have one. They took all of Jeff's letters, files and many of the books that he had in his library. The Los Angeles Police Red Squad operated, to a great extent, outside the law.

Irv told me that he had told Jeff to get his letters and personal papers out of his house, knowing that if his house was raided, by the police or was burglarized by them, his letters would be embarrassing. Everyone near the vortex of the fight was of the opinion that anything that could be done to discredit us would be done. Whenever we thought that something 'just wouldn't be done', that was the next thing that would happen. These papers were not used by the police, they were given to the AFL Los Angeles Central Labor Council, to be used by them to try to discredit the fight against the mobs. They certainly didn't have to give them to the FBI or any Committee of the US Congress; they already had all the names of any Communists in the Party in the Los Angeles area.

The Central Labor Council newspaper spread Jeff's correspondence over their paper, and the regular papers reprinted what they considered the most damaging parts. Of course, the involvement of the mob was never mentioned. Again, we brought up the fact that the AFL was cooperating with the mobs and that the Los Angeles police were helping them to do this. Their theme was that actually the whole thing was a communist plot to blacken the names of these wonderful AFL labor leaders, of whom Browne and Bioff were two of the greatest. Again we realized that everybody who should have been with us was against us. Jeff should have kept his papers somewhere else. His papers and books were ultimately returned.[36]

As the time for the convention approached, we got definite news that the International knew about our resolution. We knew that a delegation was going to be sent from Local 37, but who would be representing the local? On 29 May 1938 Irv received a telegram, followed the next day by this letter:[37]

You have been selected as one of the delegates to represent Local 37 at the 34th Convention of the I.A.T.S.E. and M.P.M.O. to be held in

Cleveland, Ohio, June 6, 1938. Report in person to the undersigned at 501 Taft Building, relative to the usual transportation and convention expenses and other information not later than 12:00 noon, Tuesday, May 31, 1938.

(signed) Lew C. G. Blix, Secretary, Local 37.

It was a set-up. Jeff and Irv knew it, but they felt that they couldn't back down. Irv looked at his clothing to see if he had the necessary union labels on five of them, as the IA Constitution required. He was OK on this point and he went down to the Local 37 office. He was given his delegate's credentials, a one way ticket to Cleveland, Ohio, and $50. He later found that the rest of the delegates were given round-trip tickets and $200 as a bonus and additional money as necessary for expenses. The total amount of cash the others received came to $700. Irv asked when he would get the rest of his money and was told he would get it later. He also learned that this was so that delegates could take their wives.

Our resolution was finished and sent to George Browne:

Dear Sir and Brother
I enclose herewith a copy of a resolution which embodies months of discussion by many members of the Studio Locals of the I.A.T.S.E. for introduction to the Resolutions committee of the current Convention of the Alliance. Our main objective in drawing up this resolution has been to contribute to the best interest of the alliance by a careful evaluation of the past history of the Studio organizations, and, on that basis, presenting a program for materially bettering the organization.

We trust that in presenting this resolution before the Convention you will give it the greatest possible consideration.

Fraternally, (signed) Jeff Kibre, Chairman I.A. PROGRESSIVES.[38]

In Resolution 6, the Progressives cited some of the problems: lack of accountability for the special fund collected via the 2 per cent assessment; lack of examinations to determine if the newly enrolled members of Local 37 were in fact able to perform the work assigned to them; lack of union response to 'stretchouts' and 'speedups' by the producers; a decrease in average yearly wages from $2,400 in 1929 to less than $1,500 in 1937; and absence of cooperation of the IA with its sister AFL unions, particularly in seeking creative solutions to the current unemployment problems. Resolution 6 called for a return of local autonomy and bargaining rights; an effective union steward system; a democratic system for handling employment calls; regular local union meetings; and union officers' salaries limited to the weekly rate for their particular craft.

The officials of the IA have repeatedly tried to say that Irv Hentschel had been sent to the 1938 convention by the Local 37 IA Progressives. That is an outright lie! Irv was a delegate to the convention and was recognized as a delegate by the President on the floor of the convention. Everybody knew the idea behind Irv's being appointed as a delegate.

The official family of the IA thought that Irv was the weakest link in the Progressive chain. They didn't know Irv Hentschel. There was no hesitation on his part whether to go or not.

On the first night of the trip to Cleveland, a meeting was called in the club car. The only item to be discussed was that the whole delegation from the studios – some twenty delegates on that train – was to vote as a block, i.e. to play ball with Bioff and Browne. Whatever the majority of the delegates decided would be the vote of them all. Irv objected that he would not agree to the idea of block voting. That ended the meeting. From then on Irv was isolated, totally, by every other delegate.

Eating on the train was very expensive, and his money was going fast. Representing the two groups, the IA Progressives and the Party, I could never understand his not having plenty of money. Someone should have made sure that he had enough money. In the excitement, this fact was overlooked. He was, however, given the name of a Party contact in Cleveland.

When Irv lined up at the check-in tables at the convention hotel he noticed that there seemed to be a movement away from him. He spoke to a couple of people who seemed to respond for a few minutes, then they in turn edged away from him. After he checked in and received his delegate's badge and room key, he went into the coffee shop and sat next to a couple he had seen standing in the line. They too moved away. From then on until he left Cleveland, no one spoke to him except officers of the union or people he had never seen, threatening to beat him up. He received threatening calls all night long, so that he could not sleep.

That was the start of a very lonely attempt of a very sweet, friendly, intelligent, dedicated man to make contact with other human beings only to meet fear and total rejection from all sides. He felt that there had to be at least one man on the International Executive Board who was aware of what was happening within the IA and to whom he could talk. He was wrong.

The second night, he called the comrade whose name and number he had been given before he left for the convention. The man said that he was expecting Irv's call and arranged to meet him in front of the hotel in half an hour. He picked Irv up and started to drive back to his home. As they were driving, Irv began to tell him about the situation he was facing. The man asked Irv a couple of alarmed questions, then made a 'U' turn in the middle of the block and took Irv back to within a couple of blocks of the hotel and let him out of the car, saying that he had not understood what it meant when Irv called him. Irv said that it was a very lonely two blocks to walk.

On the third day of the convention, Irv was summoned up to the suite occupied by President Browne. Browne, Bioff and several others were there waiting for him. It was immediately obvious to Irv that Bioff, not Browne, was running the IA; Irv had heard about Bioff's contempt for Browne. The argument started when Bioff said, 'Everything is going to be all right!' Irv misunderstood the remark and started to say, 'I'm glad that you are beginning to see things our way ... ' Browne started to call Irv a lot of names, so Irv got sore. Bioff tried to smooth things out, but Browne got madder and continued to call Irv names. All the time Bioff kept repeating that everything was going to be all right, and then Browne would get mad at Bioff. There was general shouting and finally Irv got mad enough to demand that Browne start acting like a gentleman or he would leave the room. At this point Bioff told Browne to leave the room. Browne was unwilling to leave but Bioff ordered him to leave. The shouting quieted down and again Bioff said that now everything was going to be all right, if Irv would just sign this paper saying that he was willing to withdraw Resolution 6. Irv replied that he could not do that unless he was able to take something back to the members of Local 37 that would be of some use in getting the membership some basic advantages.

In a little while there was a knock on the door and Bioff answered it and spoke in a whisper with someone outside. He turned to Irv and said that someone from the FBI was there to question Irv about the resolution that had been sent through the mail. It seemed that, according to the man at the door, some statements were lies and some of it was defamation of character which of course was against the law. Irv looked at Bioff and said that he had thought that postal inspectors always handled things pertaining to the US mail. Bioff slammed the door and turned back to Irv. After a few minutes he offered Irv a good job if he would sign 'this paper.' Irv replied that he didn't think that he would even get cash for the first check for his new job, that the payment on the check would be withheld before he could get to the bank with it. One of the other men in the room said that maybe a ride home in a pine box would do Irv some good. Bioff told him to shut his goddamn mouth. Then he started another line, talking nice, asking Irv if he was enjoying himself as a delegate to the convention. When Irv told him that he was short of money, Bioff acted surprised. He asked Irv why this was; and Irv told him that he had only received $50 for the trip expenses and a one-way ticket, and that he was down to his last few cents and was getting hungry. Again Bioff acted surprised and called one of the men in the room, Harold V. Smith, one of the Chicago boys who had been sent out to Hollywood as a bootlegger and was later appointed as the business agent of the Sound Local, a job that he was able to hold on to for several years until he retired with a nice fat retirement sum. Bioff told Smith to take Irv out and get him a good meal and come back as soon as possible. Smith didn't take Irv to get a good meal, he took him out for a hamburger and a cup of coffee.

The next morning Irv went to the room where the Resolutions Committee was to meet and indicated that he wanted to speak on the resolution. The man to whom he spoke wrote his name down and then looked at his delegate's badge and walked away from him. By now he was used to the silent treatment. He also went to the General Secretary and indicated that he wanted to speak on the resolution when it came up on the floor of the convention.

He had written several letters and telegrams to the Local 37 IA Progressives' office but no one seemed to know or understand what he was going through. He went to his room to try to get some rest. By this time he was tired and discouraged. He picked up his mail and there was a letter from the IA Progressives' office. It was instructions to him as to what to give in the negotiations and what to insist on as the last that we would give. He considered the letter to be completely detached from reality. It was certain that the resolution was going to be voted down, and that he was defeated in his efforts to bring it to the floor of the convention with any backing.

That night he was again summoned to Mr Browne's suite. This time it was just Bioff and Irv alone. Bioff's attitude seemed to have changed and he was downright pleasant. He summoned a waiter and had sandwiches and beer brought in and the waiter kept Irv's glass filled with cold beer. It was wasted. All Irv wanted was enough to keep his throat wet. At his rate of drinking he could drink anyone under the table. As time went on, considering Bioff's questions, Irv began to think that maybe, just maybe, something was going to be given. Bioff was apparently trying to find out what was the IA Progressives' bottom line; but as the hours went on he realized how wrong he had been. Bioff tried to be very nice and he was patient, but nothing was to be given in return for Irv's withdrawal of the resolution. Finally, shortly after three o'clock, Bioff's patience was obviously wearing thin and in a snarl he said, 'Who's paying you off? Somebody is!' This quick turn in Bioff's attitude led to further argument, which turned nasty and vicious. Finally, Bioff told Irv to get the hell out of the room. Irv walked over to the door, opened it and was on the way out when suddenly Bioff rushed at him from behind. He swung Irv around, struck him in the face several times and knocked him down and slammed the door. There were two men in the hallway grinning as Irv picked himself up. One of them said, 'Why don't you get wise to yourself?'

When Irv got to his room, there was a notice that there was a telegram waiting for him at the desk. He cleaned himself up and went to the lobby. The telegram said to drop the resolution and return home. This was in answer to his last telegram; later we learned that a newspaperman had called Jeff Kibre urging that Irv be ordered home while he was still alive. Irv had about a dollar left and no return ticket to Los Angeles. He tried to get some sleep but the phone started to ring again. It was of course just to keep him awake. He put in a call for seven o'clock and tried to get some sleep again. He was close to the end of his ability to function. He finally got some sleep.

When he awoke, he called Bioff's room and told him that he guessed that he finally realized the wisdom of withdrawing Resolution 6. Bioff told him to hurry over and they would tell the Resolutions Committee that he was going to withdraw it. While Irv was on his way to Bioff's room, Bioff found out that the resolution was being considered right then. They went before the Committee and were told that, given that the resolution was already being considered, it could not be withdrawn. Bioff was angered again at Irv's not withdrawing it sooner.

They went out in the hall and near the door they met Harlan Holmden. Holmden went into a diatribe about how they would beat the resolution on the floor of the convention. Both of them gave Irv another verbal beating and told him that no communist would win anything, that they were prepared to beat him into the ground. Holmden's vicious, filthy language poured out again.

Irv felt obliged to stay and to speak on the question, if he could get the floor. Later, I asked him why he thought he should have tried to speak. He said that he considered it part of his job. Even, he felt, if you go down in a heap, it is still necessary to speak for the record.

On the floor of the convention the tables were filling the whole area of the hall at a right angle to the dais, so that all the delegates could see the speakers by turning their heads and not having to turn their chairs around. On the tables were spread the documents pro and con regarding the business about to come up. There were several switches on the side of rostrum connected to the microphones on the rostrum and on the floor of the convention. Whoever stood at the rostrum controlled the ability of anyone to address the convention.

The convention was actually a show put on for some of the more stupid delegates and the more gullible members of the media. The show was run in such a way that one not aware of what was actually happening might think that a very reasonably democratic convention was being conducted for all to see. It was in reality being conducted by the mob's legal staff, headed by Matthew Levy, who did not want any public unpleasantness such as visible beatings or murders.

When the convention was called to order, Irv went in and took his seat at the table. No one spoke a word to him as he sat there. When, finally, the resolution was called, it was read to a drum of noise, talking and catcalls. All the delegates had printed copies of the resolution and it took a long time for it to be read. When President Browne called for discussion, Irv was the only one to rise and ask for the floor. As he started toward one of the microphones, someone tried to trip him. This brought on a lot of laughter. He made it to the microphone and as he started to talk it went dead. He went to the next one and same thing happened. As he went from one microphone to another he was called a series of filthy names and told that he should be strung up 'by the nuts'. Several people tried to trip him as he looked for a live microphone. After these 'delegates' had had their fun, Browne left one microphone on. I am still in awe at Irv's being able to talk at all. The following is from the convention transcript.[39]

Delegate Irwin P. Hentschel, Local No. 37, Hollywood, California was recognized by the Chair. Delegate Hentschel: 'Gentlemen; what you have heard read is an honest conviction of myself and Studio Workers. I have been brought out here as an appointed Delegate, because I was going to be maneuvered into a spot where I would withdraw my objections.

I have had some unpleasant occurrences here at this Convention. I have been ostracized; I have been cajoled; I have been called this and that; I have been called a C.I.O. man. And now when I am near the edge of a nervous collapse I went to the Resolutions Committee yesterday and asked that I personally be able to withdraw that Resolution by the mere fact that I was beaten. ...

Unionism is something besides paying money into an organization for which you supposedly get something in return, but which you don't have an active part in. That organization out there in the Studios of 12,000 members, run by a handful of officials, are [sic] considered in line with the administration.

This is my first appearance before an audience, my first introduction to any official with the exception of one. I do not know your organization, haven't anything to do [with it]; neither do 90 per cent of those men out in Hollywood know the organization.

I have talked to men here; evidently they think the Alliance is a great thing and I do not blame them, for those that have local autonomy and for those that can say and can pass upon certain rulings brought down from above. You democratically put those laws in there – we didn't....

So I think that the Resolution shows that it is a constructive Resolution and that the result of the so-called [autonomy] votes that were taken in Hollywood were not a real opinion. It was an intimidated opinion because they did not want to keep quiet like myself, and furthermore, the thing was presented in such a way that if we voted for local autonomy the International would withdraw all support, chaos would come to us, open shop, and under the circumstances, gentlemen, I do not think that you, as Trade Unionists, would have voted for local autonomy either, but I do say this: we do not ask for an election to wipe officials out, we have nothing personal against the officials; all we do is want to make strong Trade Unionists out of those men out there, so we have a strong Alliance; it is to your benefit to have Trade Unionism, not a dual movement.

If you gentlemen cannot see that it is there, and it can be, men that we live in America [sic], and as President Green very aptly put it the other day: "You cannot take Americans and bang them around like sacks of salt and sacks of sugar," That is what you are doing.

Therefore we ask that the various crafts be taken into consideration and a program worked out, in which way you have local autonomy in a very, very worthy fashion. We do not want it to happen in a month or in two months, but we do want to see the machinery set up whereby sometime when we are capable, when we are able through meetings with each other, that we can advance a program and put it into effect, we want to see that program go into effect.

Gentlemen, after two and one-half years of International supervision your President Browne comes in without any constructive idea or a program as to the return of local autonomy. So we present this plan; we put it up to your Body and believe me, gentlemen, if a plan can be worked out, which I know it can, and it is put into effect in the Studios, you will have one of the strongest organizations that there is in the world in the way of Trade Unionism, because after all, Union men are made – they are not born.'

President Browne: 'I think reference to the President's Report will be ample reply to the Delegate's remarks. A motion is before the house of non-concurrence in the Resolution by the Committee. Any further remarks?' No dissenting voices being heard, recommendation of Committee was unanimously carried; Delegate Hentschel not voting on the question.

Delegate William H. Clendening, Atlantic City, N.J., Local No. 11: 'It is my opinion that this Resolution is a disgrace to the Alliance and should be expunged from the minutes, and I so move.' Motion seconded by Delegate Alexander L. Fell, Camden N.J., Local No. 418.

President Browne: 'This is a matter that has been accorded considerable attention by the Resolutions Committee and it has been decided and agreed that it would be, perhaps, well in view of the attitude taken by these people, this large group of less than 100 out of 12,000 . . . to let this Resolution and the subsequent action taken thereon remain a part of the records of this Alliance. In view of that, I would request that the delegate withdraw the motion.'

Delegate William H. Clendening: 'I withdraw it, Mr President.'

Then Vice-President Holmden launched into a diatribe against the Reds, with no answer to any of the charges contained in the resolution. He read several copies of self-congratulating telegrams from various officials to each other. Listening to them or reading them one would think that the gentlemen of the Syndicate were the greatest of men in the labor movement. Also Holmden read parts of Jeff Kibre's letters, smearing all the Progressives with charges of treason.

After leaving the floor, Irv was sick with worry. He was weak, tired and hungry. Not knowing where to turn next, he sat down in the hotel lobby. He felt that possibly his health and safety depended on his returning home to Helen and his children. He realized that if he didn't do something soon, he would be the only IA member left in town. The convention would be over and all the delegates would leave town and he would be left flat broke with no one to turn to. He had gotten to the point where he didn't care what he did to get home. He decided to do the unexpected.

Irv went to the office of the FBI. This showed, I think, the influence of Carey McWilliams on Irv's thinking. Unlike some rigid thinkers, Carey thought that the FBI and other federal government departments could be troublesome or helpful, depending on the circumstances. Here was a case of one man against a mob-controlled union. Irv had some hope of help in this instance.

At the Cleveland FBI office, Irv told them of being threatened by a person posing as an officer from the FBI, and that according to the constitution of the IA he was entitled to return fare home, having been taken across state lines. The FBI agent listened, asked a few questions and then excused himself. He returned in fifteen minutes to ask Irv to take him to the convention.

At the hotel, the agent showed his credentials and asked for the Chairman of the Finance Committee. When the Chairman of the Committee came out of his office, he asked the agent to come in. Ten minutes later, the agent came out and told Irv that he would soon get his fare home. He was right. There was a bit of scurrying around and the Finance Chairman came out and paid Irv his return fare, the $200 bonus and his unpaid expense money. Irv said that in talking with the agent he had come to like him, aside from the fact that he had so easily forced the money out of the IA. The agent was not in the least judgmental or hostile toward Irv.

Irv went down to the hotel desk and bought travelers checks with all but the necessary cash to get to the railway station. He bought his ticket home and waited until the train to Chicago came. He said that one of the hardest things he ever had to do was to carry his suitcase aboard the train and lift it up above his seat. By the time he got to Chicago and boarded the Santa Fe train to Los Angeles he had calmed down a little and felt like eating. The trip was, except for occasional wonderful views across the plains and the southwest desert, something to be forgotten about. He was buoyed by the thought of seeing Helen and the children. When his mind went back to what had happened at the convention, he went into a terrible depression.

Helen cried when she saw him walking toward her in the Los Angeles station. He had lost ten pounds and looked awful. Friends had driven Helen to the station. On the way home, Helen insisted that they go up to Irv's favorite fishing place, the Fawn Skin campground, on Big Bear Lake. Irv was in no condition to drive, so the friends arranged to drive them up to the campground the next morning.

Irv had built a small camping trailer and a boat for fishing. Early the next morning, two cars and one trailer, with the boat on top, left for the campground. They arrived in the late morning and the friends left as soon as possible, leaving Helen, Irv and the children. Before leaving they had helped get the boat down from the top of the trailer, got them bait and helped get the camping area straightened up. The family had a quiet dinner. They all went for a short walk after dinner, but Irv was still so tied up inside he could hardly talk.

Irv got up early the next morning so that he could get enough fish for them to have fish for breakfast. He had a fitful night's sleep, but he rowed out to a spot where he had always had good luck in fishing. He dropped the anchor and sat there for a couple of minutes and suddenly broke down completely.

Several weeks later a letter appeared in the intra-Party publication criticizing Irv for his handling of Resolution 6. It was plain that Party members had looked on, without offering help. Here, too, perhaps the fact that Irv had turned to the FBI for help made a bad impression on the armchair generals in Los Angeles. Feeling that his usefulness to the Party was at an end, Irv dropped out of the Party. The criticism that had been voiced at the time of the filing of the law case through Carey McWilliams, with this latest misunderstanding about the events at the convention, was too much. Jeff Kibre was enraged at the Party's treatment of Irv, and he tried without success to talk Irv out of quitting the Party.

The article that criticized Irv was a further, devastating blow to him. He was terribly aware of his shortcomings as a delegate under such circumstances. He guessed, rightly or wrongly, that the man who had met him and then backed off from helping him in Cleveland had written it. (He told me that he would have given his right arm for someone to talk with or to relieve him on the phone, so he could have had some sleep, or to loan him some money so he could eat.)

There was a CA hearing [an informal trial] on the subject of Irv's actions at the convention. Irv, so far as I know, did not appear. Here are the conclusions of the report as written by Jeff Kibre:

> 1. That the difference of opinion with respect to the resolution, approach to the IA and so forth, has grown out of a thorough lack of understanding by the comrades in the East, of the role of the IATSE in the motion-picture industry, the problems of the industry and consequently, of our basic line. This lack of understanding is also apparently wedded to the gross underestimation of the motion-picture industry as the foundation of the amusement industry.
> 2. That we affirm our confidence in comrade Irv Hentschel, who is a party member of three years standing in the industry; and further state that Comrade Hentschel, despite numerous mistakes, attempted to the best of his ability to carry out the instructions of the local party organization; and finally, that most of his mistakes were the result of the tremendous pressure and intimidation exerted upon him by the IA officials, plus the lack of proper guidance and counsel in Cleveland.[40]

I have read several times the mistaken idea that Irv was sent to the 1938 convention by the IA Progressves. This is simply not true. He did not 'present' that resolution. He had no authority to present anything. He was appointed by the mob in order to force him to withdraw a resolution that was presented strictly in accordance with the constitution of the IA. It should be remembered that, according to the IA constitution, only one of the sponsors of a resolution can withdraw it from consideration by the convention. They wanted Irv there as a form of show trial.

The 1938 IA convention was notable for more than just the Hentschel incident. On the opening day, Sidney Kent, President of 20th Century-Fox, addressed the convention. This was the first instance of a motion picture executive addressing the delegates. Kent was the 'bag man' for his company in meetings with Browne and Bioff; he and the other executives were paying off Browne and Bioff (and thus the Nitti crime syndicate) to hold down wages and to block strikes. Kent claimed a fraternal tie with the delegates: his father had been a member of the Carpenters' union, and he himself had been apprenticed in the Lincoln, Nebraska local of the Carpenters. Kent further remarked that the absence of local autonomy in the Hollywood studio locals was a logical product of the industry, considering the numerous occasions for filming in distant locations under different IA local jurisdictions. Kent concluded his remarks with a statement that provided a wry counterpoint to the actual state of Hollywood labor relations in 1938:

> I believe that the record that that [sic] industry has compiled, if investigated, would prove that we have had less interruption of employment, less

hard feeling, less recrimination, and have built more good will than any industry that I know of in the country, and boys, that is something that is worth fighting for and protecting.[41]

Particularly ironic was the phrase 'if investigated'. A new investigation was about to take place in California, and labor relations in the motion picture industry were to experience several federal investigations over the next ten years.

Like Kent's speech, Browne's presidential address again hammered against the notion of local autonomy for the studio locals; this time he clearly rewrote the union's history by blaming the 1933 strike (called by International President Elliot) on the studio locals:

These producers were absolutely bitter against our four West Coast Studio Locals on account of the 1933 strike, and would have no part in dealings with them as individual locals, but insisted that they would only make contact with the International and all dealings would have to be handled directly through the International officers.[42]

What Browne left out was that the producers were dealing directly with the International officers because those officers were willing to take payoffs to hold down wages and to prevent strikes. The seizure of the studio locals by declaration of a 'state of emergency' was excused on the same sort of flimsy grounds in his Presidential report.

Aside from the Progressives' resolution, perhaps the most interesting resolution of the 1938 convention was put forward by delegates from a large number of non-studio locals. Resolution 15 condemned National Labor Relations Board support of 'so-called guilds such as the Screen Actors, Screen Playwrights and Screen Writers', because 'the members of these so-called guilds are paid from $250 to $3,500 each week', and because the actors also frequently shared in the profits of productions in which they performed. This bitter resolution called for the NLRB to declassify the talent guilds as labor organizations and for the AFL to revoke the charters of the guilds.[43] The convention as a whole adopted this resolution. One might say that it was an example of 'class struggle, American-style', workers fighting themselves.

The convention also adopted a resolution condemning the production of 'any and all forms of propaganda, whether in the guise of entertainment or otherwise, glorifying any other form of government or its achievements which may tend in any wise to weaken our faith in our democracy.' *Variety* noted that the convention's 'blast' was aimed at 'the so-called "parlor pinks" among film actors who are attempting to influence film production in favor of communistic ideas.'[44]

Browne and Bioff were each presented with gold, lifetime membership cards. Bioff announced that he would be returning to Hollywood shortly to 'organize the film industry 100 per cent', including extras, bit players (both already in SAG), assistant directors (who were already in the Screen Directors Guild), and other labor groups. The new campaign was intended to spread more smoke than light on the Hollywood labor scene. Browne and Bioff were desperately trying to cover their tracks. Perhaps red-baiting and attacks against highly paid actors would do the trick.

Notes

1. *Variety*, 13 January 1937, p. 19; 17 February 1937, p. 31.
2. IATSE, *Combined Convention Proceedings*, vol. 2, pp. 226, 327.
3. *New York Times*, 23 February 1937, p. 10.
4. *Variety*, 3 March 1937, p. 23.
5. *Variety*, 14 April 1937, p. 1.
6. *Variety*, 4 August 1937, p. 7; 6 October 1937, pp. 6, 23.
7. *Variety*, 27 April 1937, pp. 5, 55.
8. Ida Jeter, 'The collapse of the Federation of Motion Picture Crafts: a study of class collaboration', *Journal of the University Film Association*, vol. 31, no. 2, Spring 1979, p. 43.
9. *Variety*, 7 April 1937, pp. 2, 27.
10. *Variety*, 21 April 1937, p. 1.
11. *Variety*, 5 May 1937, p. 3.
12. Ibid.
13. *New York Times*, 2 May 1937, p. 28; 4 May 1937, p. 1; *Variety*, 5 May 1937, pp. 1-2.
14. Hank Messick, *The Beauties and the Beasts* (publisher and date unknown), p. 100; *Variety*, 12 May 1937, p. 2.
15. *Variety*, 5 May 1937, pp. 1-2.
16. *Variety*, 12 May 1937, pp. 1-2.
17. *Variety*, 19 May 1937, p. 2; May 26, 1937, p. 2.
18. *Variety*, 9 June 1937, p. 2.
19. *Variety*, 16 June 1937, p. 23.
20. Malcolm Johnson, *Organized Crime in America*. (Ann Arbor: University of Michigan Press, 1962), p. 204.
21. Interview with Ted Ellsworth, Los Angeles, 1984.
22. *Variety*, 19 May 1937, p. 2.
23. *Variety*, 1 September 1937, p. 4.
24. *Variety*, 29 September 1937, p. 19.
25. United States House of Representatives *Jurisdictional Disputes in the Motion Picture Industry*, Washington, 1948, p. 2072.
26. The text of the letters to and from Bridges can be found in Irv Hentschel, Testimony given in the IATSE proceedings against Robert Ames, *et al.*, Los Angeles, 10 March 1946, pp. 2442-55.
27. *Variety*, 17 November 1937, p. 11.
28. IATSE, *Combined Convention Proceedings*, vol. 2, pp. 331, 334.
29. Hentschel, Testimony given in the IATSE proceedings against Robert Ames, et al., p. 691.
30. IATSE, *Combined Convention Proceedings*, vol. 2, p. 306.
31. *Variety*, 5 January 1938, p. 54.
32. *Variety*, 5 January 1938, p. 44.
33. *Variety*, 5 January 1938, p. 54; 12 January 1938, p. 7; 23 March 1938, p. 4.
34. *Variety*, 26 January 1938, p. 5.
35. *Variety*, 2 March 1938, p. 17.
36. Selected papers of Jeff Kibre are reproduced in IATSE, *Combined Convention Proceedings*, vol. 2, pp. 377-90.
37. Irv Hentschel, Testimony given in the IATSE proceedings against Robert Ames, *et al.*, pp. 2489-90.
38. IATSE, *Combined Convention Proceedings*, vol. 2, p. 336-8
39. Ibid., p. 338.
40. Ibid., p. 382.
41. Ibid., p. 292
42. Ibid., p. 304.
43. Ibid., p. 346.
44. *Variety*, 15 June 1938, p. 16.

Top: Claire McDowell, Gene's mother, an actor
with D. W. Griffith Company
Bottom: Gene in the Marines, 1928

Top: Gene as a boxer while in the Marines, 1928
Bottom: Gene in the Hollywood Hills, 1930

Top: Police read the riot act to strikers at Warner Bros
Bottom: Pickets at Warner Bros running as hoses are turned on them and cars are overturned

Top: Pickets use cars to blockade Columbia Studios entrance
Bottom: Police shove pickets at MGM Studios as strikebreakers pass through in the bus

3

FIGHTING THE MOB

The Progressives Regroup

On 15 June 1938, the Fair Labor Standards Act (also known as the Wages and Hours Law) was signed into law. This law established a minimum wage of 25 cents per hour and a 44-hour work week; the work week was to be reduced to 40 hours over a period of three years. Work more than the regular number of hours was to be paid at overtime rates of time and a half. *Variety* reported that the Wages and Hours Law would have little impact on the motion picture industry. The law, which applied to persons engaged in interstate commerce or in producing goods for interstate commerce, came into effect on 24 October 1938.[1]

Although the minimum wage section of the Act did not affect production workers directly because producers paid a higher hourly rate than the suggested minimum, the clauses on overtime had significant consequences. A substantial number of studio employees were working under contracts that called for a 54-hour or 60-hour week. If the terms of the Wages and Hours Law were to be applied to these workers, producers would be forced to try to regularize production schedules to cut overtime costs. The application of the Wages and Hours Law to the motion picture industry, however, was delayed well into 1940, largely because of the inability of both the federal government and the industry to cope with the burden of classifying over 600 distinct jobs in the industry as to whether they were administrative, professional or technical in character. However, the Wages and Hours Law did have some immediate impact on the motion picture industry: By December 1938, the studios had altered their production schedule to 44-hour work weeks to avoid the possible problem of owing back-pay for overtime payments, in the event that the federal courts decided that the motion picture industry was subject to the new Wages and Hours Law.[2]

Prior to the adoption of these new work schedules, the Conference of Motion Picture Arts and Crafts (an outgrowth of the earlier Studio Unemployment Conference) called a mass meeting in the Hollywood Bowl to discuss some of the same issues that the Progressives had been working on for a few years. A five-point program was offered for the regularization of production in the studios, i.e. the adjustment of the production schedules to eliminate unemployment among studio workers. Among the 3,000 people attending the meeting were an amazing collection of key political and labor figures, including Herbert Biberman (Screen Directors Guild), Herb Sorrell (Painters Local 644), Dudley Nichols (SWG), David Saposs (NLRB Chief

51

Economist) and Sam Yorty (then California State Assembly member and later mayor of Los Angeles). George Browne again balked at cooperation with non-IA groups, preferring to praise the MPPDA, especially its president Joe Schenck 'for his untiring efforts in furthering the laudable program of President Roosevelt to stimulate business and industry that all might have employment.' Browne condemned the 'wailings of so-called progressives' about unemployment among studio workers as a 'smoke screen for their real ulterior motives' i.e. communist propaganda aimed at breeding discontent among American labor.[3]

Meanwhile Browne's accomplice was again under investigation. In August 1938, a grand jury in Sacramento was called to investigate the State Assembly whitewash of the IA in December 1937. Bioff testified under oath that he had received $100,000 as a personal loan and had deposited the money in a Hollywood bank on 25 June 1937. He transferred the funds to a safe deposit box a few days later. IA auditor C. P. Cregan testified that he drafted a $5,000 check to William Neblett, who in turn testified that he received the $5,000 for legal services, the nature of which he refused to disclose on the witness stand. The grand jury probe drew the attention of federal investigators who were curious about the nature of Bioff's sudden wealth. The probe also prompted Browne to again withdraw Bioff from Hollywood. Bioff was allowed to resign from his job and was voted one year's salary by the Executive Board.[4]

IA Progressive leader Jeff Kibre informed federal authorities that the 'loan' was in fact a payoff from the MPPDA via Joe Schenck for Bioff's cooperation during the FMPC strike. *Variety* reported that the Department of Justice was brought into the case 'because of suspicion that certain studio figures and both California and Federal officials were parties to a conspiracy to duck income taxes.'[5]

Kibre also brought charges before the NLRB regional office in Los Angeles that IA leaders and the producers were blocking genuine collective bargaining by holding the SBA talks in New York, far away from rank-and-file input. Kibre claimed that the IA was in fact nothing more than a company union, a charge that brought a quick denial from Joe Schenck. Schenck's 'big lie' strategy seemed to afford the only escape for the producers and the IA at this point. NLRB regional director Towne Nylander ordered a hearing for mid-October to investigate Kibre's charges. Browne quickly returned local autonomy to the studio locals. With the departure of Bioff, Browne placed Harold V. Smith and IA Vice-President Harland Holmden in charge of the IA West coast office.[6]

By the end of October 1938 several petitions for union representation of studio labor groups were on file with Nylander's NLRB office. IA Camera Local 659 filed for representation of all photographic employees, including first camerapersons then under contract via the American Society of Cinematographers (ASC). The Studio Utility Employees (SUE) Local 724 filed for jurisdiction over all studio laborers, hoping to block increasing IA raiding of its ranks. And a host of other smaller independent groups had petitions for representation on file, including the Screen Publicists Guild, the Screen Set Designers, the Society of Motion Picture Art Directors, the Society of Artists and Illustrators, and the Scenic Artists Association, who were fighting Sorrell's Painters Local 644 for control of scenic artists.[7]

52

Certain positive factors complemented this surge of union activity. In the first three months of 1939, studio employment was at pre-Depression levels. This condition relieved the pressure at the jurisdictional border points between the various studio craft unions. The new high employment rate, however, undercut the reform proposals of the Conference of Motion Picture Arts and Crafts, particularly its demand for regularized production schedules. The very slack period of early 1938 was but a dim memory to many workers in the industry.[8]

Browne had returned full autonomy to the IA studio and lab locals. For the first time, IA Camera Local 659 began showing signs of genuine independence from the Browne-Bioff tyranny. Local 659 business agent Herb Aller called for concessions from both sides in the studio situation. He wanted the Progressives to withdraw Kibre's suit against the IA international office; he wanted the IA to return all funds collected under the 2 per cent assessments; and he called for the removal of Harold V. Smith from Hollywood.[9]

The studio labor situation was clouded, however, by battling factions within Local 37. The old guard, led by Smith, was still loyal to Browne and Bioff. Smith began labeling as 'communists' Kibre and his fellow Progressives in Local 37. In early March 1939, the Progressives managed to unseat the Browne-appointed officers of the local by a vote of the rank and file.[10]

An election was held and a slate of men, all backed by the Local 37 IA Progressives, were elected to all offices. The platform on which they ran was in line with all that we had been urging the International union office to pursue since we started. This platform was very conciliatory and well thought out. It voiced the sentiments of the rank and file, yet showed a desire to get along with the rest of the unions and guilds in the picture business. We even made some friendly gestures toward our own parent union, the IA, although we knew that eventually we had to get Browne, Bioff and their stooges out of the picture. We worked out in the open in every way; through letters to the members and handbills, throwaways and talk, we kept the membership involved. We held neighborhood-shop meetings to discuss our platform and hopes for the union. We began to function as a union should.

We knew that the key to any solidarity with the rest of the unions or guilds in the studios was the settlement of jurisdictional disputes. After sweeping the Local 37 elections, we began a program to try to find a way of settling these jurisdictional problems. We contacted the other unions on a strictly informal basis, to get committees together and hold sessions on union problems. We met with the members of local executive boards, men with whom we had been working for years and who in some cases had become friends. We suggested that men with a union background be sent along, with several rank and file in addition, who could contribute ideas on individual cases for settlement of details.

The meetings were open to anyone so that the various headquarters of the unions involved could stay informed as to what we were trying to do. We made it plain that we wanted rank and file members of each union to attend so that they in turn could talk to the men on the jobs who might be affected by any changes. We wanted their input on the subject and we

53

wanted them to clearly understand that we were thinking toward the day when we would all stand together as a unit in the negotiations with the employers. We also invited members of the other IA local unions outside the motion picture business so that they could see that there was an effort being made to get things settled among ourselves.

One of the questions that gave us the most trouble was the position of the Carpenters. Their International office took the position that work on everything made of wood or wood substitutes was claimed by them. In our talks we discussed a trade of some sort with the heads of the Carpenters local. We mutually recognized the problems involved in working out a compromise and agreed to go on to other questions. Bioff and Browne later charged that we were willing to give hundreds of jobs away to our 'enemies' by virtue of holding these discussions with the Carpenters.

We started with the idea that, when a decision was made to change a job from one union to another, a trade had to be made, a one-for-one exchange. When we had a question to ask the International office we didn't hesitate to bring them into the discussions. Our phone bill was high but all reasonable and never for personal calls. We also made sure that all parties at these meetings understood that the discussion were informal and not binding and would be adopted only with the approval of the respective International officials. This was to further show that IA officials would not approve any action on our part to build up a real trade union policy. We were so concerned that we leaned over backward to make sure that the IA, as a trade union, could find no fault.

Joe Carpenter, the Chairman of the Local 37 Board of Governors, was an excellent choice for the job. He was an old union man, an intelligent, patient, decent guy, utterly honest. The rest of the Board were men of the same caliber. The Board was united in their desire to straighten out the problems in the studios.

The new leaders approached the producers' labor representative, Pat Casey, and were assured that they could bargain with him directly. On the advise of attorneys, the newly elected leaders of Local 37 attempted to secure the local's $100,000 treasury in hopes of avoiding seizure of the funds by the International office.[11]

The rank and file of Local 37 was torn between supporting the Progressives, who were after all largely responsible for the lifting of the 2 per cent assessment and the restoration of local autonomy, or supporting the faction still loyal to Browne out of fear of being 'caught off base' if Browne again stepped in with the usual declaration of a 'state of emergency'. The old-timers in the IA's ranks were well aware of the consequences of being 'picked off'. Browne did not give the rank and file of Local 37 much time to mull over the situation. On 17 March, Browne and the IA Executive Board once again declared Local 37 in a state of emergency and seized the offices and records of the local. Browne placed IA International representatives Frank Stickling and John Gatelee in charge of the local.[12]

In spite of our efforts, at two o'clock one night the International officials took over again, in a totally illegal way. Their new constitution was in the way of the mob, so they did not stand on ceremony. Under this constitution the procedure was supposed to act in the following way: an international representative, or a responsible local officer, was to report certain facts to the International president; then the International president was to call and telegraph each of the International Executive Board, explaining the nature of the trouble and ask for permission to take over the local union. The Board members were then to give verbal permission over the phone and formalize the permission by telegraph immediately. This was the 'extreme emergency' procedure – later to be slightly modified but never actually given up. They did not do any of these things. They appeared in court the next morning with an undated document to support their claim that they were justified in taking over Local 37.

We tried to show what a farce this was, but the judge in the case held that the Convention of the IA, the highest tribunal of the union, had approved this procedure; therefore he would not interfere. In short, it was our job, if we didn't like the IA constitution, to work to change it; and meanwhile to see that the International office followed the letter of the constitution. The correct procedure was that the International office had to prove that the local union was out of control and a danger to the interests of the members of the local and the International. The verbal charges against the leaders of Local 37 were that the local was dominated by a bunch of communists, that we had raided the local's treasury; also that we were spending money on parties in the office and that we were conspiring to give away the local's jurisdiction without the permission of the rightful guardians of that jurisdiction, the IA Executive Board. Further, we were running up expensive telephone calls and generally acting in a manner detrimental to the interests of the union. Most of this was not stated in court, but referred to in an oblique manner, to give the impression that the local was actually being protected by the International officials – protected from a bunch of Reds. The charges were made by the mob's press agent, Ed Gibbons, in a paper called 'IATSE Facts'.

Since everything that had been done by the Local 37 Board of Governors had been out in the open, many of the membership were outraged by the take-over. Obviously it was just an excuse to seize control, to oust the local officers, and to identify the opposing activists.

We were tipped off that there was a lot wrong with the technical procedure of the take-over by an informer inside the International office. We had the story checked by friends in New York and, sure enough, it was a crooked story. So the question was how to expose it. Finally, it was decided that a way was to have a suit filed by Herb Sorrell against Joe Carpenter, the head of Local 37. Joe testified that he had borrowed $500 and was unable to pay it back. He was asked how long it might be before he could pay it back. Joe stated that because he was tied up in court he could not pay it back for a long time, if ever. He was then asked if the outcome of this other business could be expedited in some way. His answer to this was that yes, he could pay it back reasonably soon if he could get some information from the American Telephone and Telegraph Company, from Western Union and from the

Management of the Astor Hotel in New York. The subpoenas were granted by the Court.

The traffic managers of A.T.&T. and Western Union and the auditor of the Astor Hotel all testified that no phone calls or telegrams left the hotel, nor were any received by the IA officials in New York or Los Angeles on the night of the move-in on the local offices.

The registry of the Astor Hotel for the night in question showed that the officials of the IA there were George E. Browne and Nick Circella. All the officers named in the list of officers testified again and repeated that they had received the telegrams and phone calls. The judge had to accept the word of these men and we were thrown out of court. The calls and telegrams supposed to have been sent and received were actually sent and received the day after the take-over.

Kibre managed to freeze the local's treasury by obtaining a court order blocking the International from seizing the funds until a full hearing could be held as to the legality of Browne's actions. As in the FMPC battle in 1937, the other studio craft locals lined up in much the same manner, with the Painters Local 644 and SUE Local 724 supporting the Local 37 progressives' battle for autonomy, and the remainder of the AFL locals, under orders from their International offices, supporting the IA's seizure of the local.[13]

Lesson in Inertia: the United Studio Technicians Guild

The fight for autonomy for Local 37 took several strange twists in the six months following the seizure of the local in March 1939. Kibre attempted to force Browne to restore local autonomy by enlisting the aid of Los Angeles County District Attorney, Burton Fitts. Fitts threatened to investigate Browne and Bioff's handling of Local 37's affairs in the hope that he could simply wipe the slate clean by judicial fiat. Meanwhile Browne attempted to clean up the IA's company union image by demanding 10 per cent wage increases for the IA's studio and lab locals. He also demanded that the grand jury investigation initiated by Fitts be called off immediately – a demand that the producers may secretly have shared with Browne in light of the collusive nature of their dealings with the corrupt union. Browne threatened that if his demands were not met, he would issue a strike call to all IA projectionists in the country.[14]

Fitts called a meeting between IA leaders (excluding the Local 37 insurgents) and the producers (represented by Joe Schenck and Eddie Mannix of MGM) to attempt to settle the dispute out of court. Kibre and the other Local 37 autonomy leaders were told to stand by and wait for a phone call from Fitts, at which time they would be allowed to enter the negotiation process. After a wait of several hours, an assistant to Fitts informed Kibre that the IA would not discuss autonomy until the International had held a vote among the captive rank and file to determine whether the members wanted local autonomy.[15]

Meanwhile the long-awaited entrance of the CIO into studio labor struggles occurred in late April. Los Angeles Projectionists' Local 1416 of the CIO threatened to man the booths abandoned by IA projectionists if Browne failed to poll the membership of the IA before calling his projectionists out on strike. By the last week in April, the Hollywood labor situation had reached the attention of the federal government. Kibre received assurances from the US Department of Justice that they were actively investigating the charges of collusion between the producers and the IA. But Browne had been lobbying in Washington, too. He had convinced Senator Martin Dies of Texas to investigate communist labor agitation in the studios. Dies promised a full Senate inquiry by the Fall of 1939.[16]

Kibre advised the members of Local 37 to refuse to pay their second quarter dues to the IA, thus depriving the International of about $100,000 in income. Browne responded by splitting Local 37 into several smaller locals based on craft distinctions. New locals were formed for property workers (Local 44), grips (Local 80), studio projectionists (Local 165), utility workers (Local 727), and studio electricians (Local 728). Members of Local 37 were 'allowed' to transfer into the new locals without initiation fees. Browne appointed the officers of the new locals, thus assuring a compliant leadership of the studio craft locals for the time being.[17]

In early June, IA dissidents formed the United Studio Technicians Guild (USTG) under the leadership of 'long-time gaffer at Columbia Studios', Howard Robertson. The USTG received financial aid from the CIO in order to mount a challenge to Browne via an NLRB representational election. By 5 July, the USTG had gathered enough signatures from studio workers to call for the election. Although the IA had its share of enemies in the studios, a majority of the other AFL groups lent support to the IA in the interest of AFL solidarity. Sorrell's Painters were, of course, on the side of the USTG.[18]

By this time the idea of trying to leave the IA was gaining support. I don't know where it started, probably from several groups. The National CIO was split about the idea, but the California state organization was in favor of it. Several years later I had a long talk with Philip Connelly, the head of the Southern California area CIO. He was sitting at his desk in a big warehouse, south of the center of Los Angeles, in a corner of one of the warehouse floors. There was no door to his office. When I got up to the third or fourth floor, there he was, open to anyone who wanted to talk with him. He told me that he had been against the whole idea of concentrating on the movie industry. For him, the main goal of the CIO was to organize the basic industry belt in the southern and eastern areas of Los Angeles, and then move into organizing the large area that later became the Cities of Commerce and Industry. He described to me how, when they had first rented the building, he and the people who had been with them had climbed to the top of the water tower on the roof and had looked in all directions to the vast area covered by factories of all kinds, from huge steel mills to the slaughter houses and small manufacturing buildings, as far as they could see. All the people with him were convinced that their job was to organize the unorganized in this area. This was the stated purpose of the fledgling CIO. He considered the Hollywood studio fight a distraction that was a big mistake. He said that the California office of the CIO had committed a terrible blunder in trying to get the studio unions to come into the CIO at that time. The effort of organizing the unorganized in basic industry was a thrilling event to anyone interested in the labor movement.

The upper echelons of the intellectuals, including the Left in the motion picture industry, were less than heavy thinkers on this subject. There was some elitism in their encouraging the workers in this 'revolt'. Added to this was narrow sectarianism and just plain dunderhead thinking. The Writers Guild had, following a bitter and stormy fight, managed to defeat the Screen Playwrights, Inc. in a Labor Board election. They had, in effect, seized control from what was in fact a company union. There was, in view of all the defeats that we had suffered, a certain appeal in this idea. However, more research and polling should have been done before any commitment had been made to this move. The conservatism of many of the members of the IA and AFL unions was underestimated. Another factor was the large number of people that the IA had brought out to work in the studios, unqualified for anything but voting 'correctly' and helping to control the members. The forcing of the Labor Board election was really a revolutionary act, and many of the members of the IA were just not ready for the revolution. This tactic of seizing control of the union via the NLRB election was romanticized and not thought through to the possibility of a defeat.

The mob put Ed Gibbons, the press agent for the Syndicate, on the IA payroll. His whole attack on the dissenters was centered on the idea that anyone not happy with the way the officials ran the union was either a communist or a communist dupe. This was drummed into their heads through Gibbons' propaganda leaflets, 'The IATSE Facts'.

The employers were frightened by the prospect of having the West coast Longshoremen's leader, Harry Bridges, as the 'boss' of studio labor. They always thought of a labor leader as a 'boss'. They still did not want a union in their businesses. If they had to have a union, they wanted a conservative one. Even better, they wanted a de facto company union, one that they could control, i.e. the IA. This was what they had, with the Syndicate doing the dirty work.

The feasibility of a NLRB election was put up for discussion before a meeting of the Progressives. It attracted a large crowd. I was sitting too far back in the hall to identify some of the speakers. Irv got up and talked against it. He spoke briefly and to the point. His argument was that he felt that the Progressives were winning the fight, that the national publicity had caused movement toward indictments by the Federal government. We knew that the FBI was gathering evidence, because we were helping them. The liberals in the House and the Senate were helping to push things along; further, the membership of the studio workers was being won over, admittedly not fast enough but solidly.

Another speaker got up and challenged Irv's argument, stating that the time was right to take bold action; that court cases were not the way to organize a union; that Harry Bridges had done it in San Francisco and the whole West coast and that the only way was to organize on solid day-to-day problems; to grasp this opportunity now and gather signatures for a Labor Board election. This was the same position that had been taken by the Party.

Hotheads carried the meeting and the decision was to start gathering the necessary signatures. Later, I heard that some of those present thought that Irv was too struck with 'his case' to see the possibilities in the Labor Board election. The idea was a tactical blunder. It was like taking an army into battle before it was ready in training, equipment and personnel.

In due course the signatures were gathered. The IA's lawyers presented arguments about the appropriate bargaining unit. They wanted the choice to be between the parent body, the IA, and the USTG. This was another way of bringing in the jurisdictional question. If they won the election the International office of the IA would have complete control over the studio locals. Losing the election would mean that the studio locals would be cut out of the right to bargain, totally.

It was at this point that I actively joined the struggle. There was a man, Al Saunders, working with me at one of the studios. Both he and his brother-in-law had told me that he had been working for his father, the head of a big insurance office in New York, and that he had embezzled money from his father's company. As part of the deal to keep Al out of prison, his father had to make up the shortage and Al was to leave the state of New York. At an election of officers of the USTG by voice vote, Al had worked himself into the job of Secretary. When I heard of this I went wild trying to get in touch with somebody that I could trust with the information. Everyone was busy, absent, in an important meeting, not home. I tried Jeff Kibre, Joe Carpenter, Chairman of the Board of Local 37, Howard Robertson, President of the USTG, and even Irv. I was leaving my name around but no one called back in time. I was like a person waiting for a bomb to go off. The next day it went off.

This was taking place during the time when the Harry Bridges deportation hearings were being held. The US Department of Immigration and Naturalization claimed that Bridges had lied when he said on his application for citizenship that he was not then and had never been a member of the Communist Party of the United States. The Immigration Department had so many liars that they thought they had enough to carry it off. Both the Party and Bridges knew all about the old Alien and Sedition Laws of the early 1800s and the mass hysteria after World War I, when aliens were rounded up and deported on the mere fact that they were thought to be revolutionaries, regardless of kind or degree. Knowing this, even if Bridges had wanted to join the Party, which I seriously doubt, the Party interest would have prevented his joining. The Right wanted him tossed out because he was a labor leader who couldn't be bought or scared off. The employers in San Francisco tried both, without success. Bridges wouldn't play ball, so he had to go.

Suddenly Al Saunders disappeared from the USTG office, with something over $200. Some feared for his safety, however, they soon found out where he was. The hearing on the Bridges case was being held on Angel Island, San Francisco Bay. Everyone concerned with the hearing was taken there every morning by boat and brought back every afternoon.

Saunders and a photographer were waiting for Bridges at the dock, and as he came down the gangway Saunders had his hand open for a shake. Bridges recognized a set-up when he saw it and held on to Saunders' hand. When one of Bridges' party saw this, he told him to

59

bring this man back to the Longshoremen's office. Saunders of course went along but the photographer was not invited to join them. Then Bridges told somebody to have someone call the USTG office and get the dope on Saunders being in San Francisco. When they all got back to Bridges' office they knew why he was there. Saunders broke down and told the whole story, even the amount that he was paid for the frame-up, $2,500. Then the police were called and Saunders was examined by doctors and released, with no charges filed.

The next morning Saunders' story was all over the papers across the country. According to the story, Bridges was calling the shots for the USTG and was getting all set to come into the studios and run the whole motion picture industry for the benefit of Soviet Russia.

At this time I had to make a decision affecting my life from then on. I had worked with Saunders for several months, mainly at Columbia Studio. We had talked quite a bit. He was intelligent and quick-witted, not unpleasant to be around. When I was finally able to contact some-one it was after the event. I was told to call the office of Charlie Katz at the law firm of Katz, Gallagher and Margolis, which was handling the legal work for the USTG. He was expecting my call and asked me to come right down to see him. When I got to his office I told him as much as I could remember about Saunders. Then he asked me, 'Will you give us a statement, on the record, which will become a deposition to be used against Saunders and the IA?' I said, 'Yes.' From that time until well into the 1950s, my commitment was total.

This Saunders episode was made the most of by the employers and the mob. The red-baiting by the studios, the mob and the media kept up this line harder than ever. On the day of the election the studios padded their payrolls and then supplied transportation to the polling places at the Gilmore Stadium on Beverly Boulevard near Fairfax Avenue, on the grounds where the CBS Television City now stands.

SAG was a 'wild card' in the studio union scene at the time, largely because of its continuing struggle against IA encroachment. One must remember that in 1938 the IA had set a goal of gaining control of all lower paid actors and extras and had gone so far as to call for the revocation of SAG's AFL charter and for the NLRB to decertify SAG. Another actors' union, the American Federation of Actors (AFA), headed by Ralph Whitehead, saw the struggle between the IA and SAG as a means toward expansion of its own ranks, which at that time were made up of variety show performers. Whitehead actively supported Browne's campaign against SAG, which led SAG to call for the expulsion of AFA from the actors' parent labor organization, the Associated Artists and Actors of America (4-A's). The 4-A's, composed of eleven different performers' unions, complied with SAG's request, prompting Whitehead to seek and to obtain an IA charter from Browne. This was the wedge that Browne had long looked for in his campaign against SAG. Now he could, through threat of a projectionists' strike, strip away the vast majority of SAG's members, leaving that organization with only the most highly paid actors.[19]

SAG began a vigorous campaign to repel the IA. *Variety* reported that SAG was collecting over $1 million as a war chest in the event that the actors were forced to strike the studios to resist Browne and Whitehead. By printing and distributing literature attacking Browne and Bioff, SAG openly lent support to the USTG in their campaign against the IA. In the midst of the IA campaign against the USTG, Browne attempted to negotiate a five-year closed shop agreement with the producers. Again, SAG intervened on behalf of the USTG, forcing the NLRB to block the IA from obtaining any closed shop agreements until after the election.[20]

At this time, SAG leaders also met privately with CIO President John Lewis to discuss moving their organization into the CIO. Lewis rejected the SAG request, preferring to wait to issue a charter after SAG had settled its dispute with the AFA. Murray Ross suggests in *Stars and Strikes* that if Lewis had accepted the actors, the insurgent USTG might well have unseated the IA in the upcoming NLRB election.[21]

SAG appealed to the AFL Executive Board to block the IA from issuing a charter to the AFA, and to remove Whitehead from his post as head of AFA, but the best SAG could obtain from the board was the return of AFA into the 4-A's fold. Throughout the late 1930s, Browne had been an on-off member of the AFL Executive Council, depending on his strategic needs at various points. At the time of the Whitehead controversy, Browne was able to protect Whitehead because of his membership of the AFL Executive Council. SAG realized that Whitehead and Browne were still determined to absorb the extras and bit players. SAG let Browne know that they were quite serious in their intention to sway the USTG – IA election in the former's favor. Browne knew that the actors could probably succeed in this, and he eventually capitulated by signing a 'peace pact' with SAG leaders, in which the IA recognized the independence of SAG and pledged never to raid its ranks again. Browne abandoned support for Whitehead, and SAG returned the favor by switching its allegiance from the USTG to the IA in the NLRB election.[22]

In early September 1939, a newly appointed regional director of the NLRB tossed out Kibre's long-pending Unfair Labor Practice (ULP) charge against the IA on behalf of the Motion Picture Technicians Committee. Two weeks before the September election, Bioff returned to the studio labor scene and began negotiations with the producers; subsequently, Bioff issued a much publicized statement claiming that he had negotiated a 15 – 20 per cent raise for all workers covered by IA contracts with the studios. The USTG filed an Unfair Labor Practice charge against the IA, claiming that the timing of Bioff's bargaining was designed to swing the election in favor of the IA. Bioff then 'voluntarily' withdrew from negotiations until after the elections, but the message had gotten through to the workers. The USTG also filed ULPs, contending that USTG supporters had been intimidated on the lots and that the producers had been assigning lucrative location work only to IA loyalists and not to any workers known to be supporters of the USTG. In a further form of intimidation, Browne's representatives in the studios began preparing charges against some 300 people who were activists in the move to join the USTG.[23]

Not surprisingly, the final vote was 4,460 for the IA and 1,967 for the USTG. Bioff immediately obtained a 10 per cent raise for all IA workers retroactive to 12 August 1939, and obtained a 100 per cent closed shop for all IA studio locals. Workers were given a few weeks to obtain paid-up IA cards. USTG activists tried to regain admittance to their jobs by filing 'nuisance suits' against the IA and the producers with the NLRB. But this strategy was a straw in the wind; Bioff was merciless in his retribution. Known USTG supporters were blacklisted, and many of them never again found work in the studios. A number of workers were granted a 'Thanksgiving Amnesty' in November 1939. To get this amnesty, however, they had to sign a document apologizing to Bioff for the statements that the USTG had made about Bioff during the election.[24] The most militant of the USTG activists were not granted this 'privilege' and continued their fight in civil suits against the IA well into 1940, but to no avail.

The night after the election, we met in our office above the Bar on Cosmo Street, a short block east of Cahuenga Boulevard, in a small apartment. Charlie Katz, who looked as tired as the rest of us, came at the appointed time. He told us that he had been in meetings all day and would be in meetings, it appeared, for several days. He told us, or rather retold us, that the losing side in a Labor Board election had no rights, and it would take some time to come to an agreement, with the mobs and the studios. Both these groups were filled with the idea that they were the winners of a glorious victory and were under no obligation to give anything to us – not jobs or anything else. In both cases the leaders were actually back East and had no connection to us. They just didn't care. Katz had the feeling that both the IA and the studio bosses wanted the whole thing ended and the bad publicity stopped. A committee was elected to get an appointment at Bioff's home.

Two nights later, we were told that the meeting with Willie Bioff was a bust, that he didn't have any real authority to settle anything. Charlie Katz told us to go to the places where we had last worked and see if we could get our jobs back. Many of us took a dim view of this idea because we were going as individuals and we did not approve of this at all.

At the next meeting, a few nights later, Katz had a report to make. An agreement had finally been worked out, the best deal he thought he could get us. There were to be one or two men who would drop out for the good of all concerned. The rest of us were to go down to the IA office and pay our back dues (some of us had not paid our dues to the IA for months), sign an apology for our past actions and accept a term of probation. That was it. The talk that night was loud and long. The idea of apologizing to those bastards was a hard one to swallow. There was further talk of the studios refusing to accept some of the men who had not yet been named. I noticed that neither Jeff Kibre nor Irv Hentschel were present. They had attended none of the post-strike meetings. Apparently they knew they would not be let back into the studios. Other faces were missing as well, men who turned out to be CIO organizers. Some of the men at these meetings actually shed tears of rage and disappointment, just talking and thinking about the members of the IA who didn't have the courage to vote against Browne and Bioff. We were, however, buoyed by the fact that we knew that ultimately we would be proven right in our charges against the mobs and the studios.

The fact that saved the day for most of us turned out to be the Hentschel – Cohea Case. Irv Hentschel and a fellow progressive, Chet

Cohea, on the advice of Carey McWilliams, refused to drop that case unless the expulsions were minimal. Some of the members there that night preferred to go to court on a private case. This turned out to be a mistake. They cut themselves off from any base in the membership. There was a pulling together on the part of many quite powerful elements toward a settlement. It was evident that the studios wanted it over and quieted down. They also knew how the IA had won the election and wanted that forgotten too.

Irv Hentschel and Bob Ames were able to bluff them out on signing the apology. Jeff Kibre went to work as a organizer for the CIO Fishermen's Union, then held a couple of other jobs for the CIO in California, then spent the last decade and a half of his life as lobbyist for the maritime industry unions, where he did an outstanding job. When he died, many government officials with whom he worked, as well as Congressmen and other elected officials, paid tribute to his ability and integrity.

There were two studio locals that had somehow managed to elect progressives to office, without bringing down on themselves the wrath of the International office. The possibility of a few indictments in the offing may have had something to do with this oversight. These two locals were the Laboratory Technicians, Local 683 and the Costumers Local 705. Their backgrounds were similar in that both locals had a high percentage of Jewish workers. The clothing workers and the chemical workers got the message of trade unionism far ahead of most workers, back in the sweat shops of New York City. Their children brought the message with them into the motion picture business, which gave both these crafts a firm foundation in the trade union field.

The victory of the Lab and Costumers locals was not total and there were still the facts that they did not have local control of their contracts and that the IA was still ruled by the mobs acting on behalf of the employers. There was no further action in any of the other locals that had been part of Local 37. The Lab and Costumers workers had not been part of this local.

Willie Bioff's Fall from Power

There is some dispute about who was really responsible for exposing Willie Bioff's criminal background. It seems that most people knew that he was connected to the crime syndicate, that he was a tough guy who used threats of violence to get his way. Some credit Carey McWilliams and Jeff Kibre. Others cite evidence that it was due to the investigations of nationally syndicated columnist Westbrook Pegler, who eventually received a Pulitzer Prize for his writing on the corruption in the IA. One theory has it that former SAG President Robert Montgomery hired an ex-FBI agent to look into Bioff's background, and then leaked the information to Pegler for maximum effect. The first crack in the story revealed that Bioff had somehow managed to evade serving a six-month sentence for pandering in Chicago in 1922, just the tip of the iceberg but at least a start. *Daily Variety* editor Arthur Ungar picked up the cue from Pegler and began daily attacks against Bioff. Willie Bioff's usefulness to the producers and the Chicago crime syndicate was rapidly evaporating.[25]

Almost immediately after granting the 10 per cent increase to the IA which Bioff had negotiated, the producers reversed their position on the raise. Eddie Mannix of MGM issued a statement claiming that the granting of a 10 per cent raise during a period of declining revenues because of war-shrunk foreign markets was tantamount to 'surrender'. On 1 November, Mannix again publicly called on Bioff to give back the raise as a 'signal' to the other studio unions and guilds that the industry was indeed in a state of crisis and that wage increases could only serve to reduce employment. Bioff, who at that time was helping several other AFL studio locals get a similar 10 per cent raise, responded by calling a meeting of all the guilds and craft locals to discuss wage cuts. He claimed that the 'little fellows' (meaning his own rank and file) would give back their raises if the guilds were willing to be the first to give back 10 per cent of their salaries. The Screen Writers Guild (SWG) rejected Bioff's invitation and went so far as to label him 'a scourge on the film industry' and 'a menace to real labor unionism'.[26]

In late November 1939, Bioff negotiated 10 per cent raises for a number of AFL craft groups not affiliated with the IA: machinists, plasterers, laborers (SUE) and building service employees. As part of this settlement, the groups agreed to reopen the contract in February 1940 to decide whether the profitability of the industry justified the wage increases. The producers later passed up the opportunity to reopen talks, indicating that they really weren't in as bad a condition as Mannix had suggested.[27]

At the same time that Bioff negotiated this final labor contract of his Hollywood career, he received a warrant via telegraph for his arrest and extradition to Chicago to complete the sentence for his pandering conviction in 1922. During December 1939 and the first two months of 1940, Bioff fought extradition with the help of IA attorneys. Bioff also received strong support from the Los Angeles Central Labor Council (CLC), largely through the efforts of CLC chairperson J. W. Buzzell. Fighting against Bioff were the leaders of SAG – who withdrew from the CLC to protest the vote of confidence in Bioff – and Arthur Ungar, the editor of *Daily Variety*, the West coast daily version of *Variety* aimed primarily at the motion picture industry.[28]

During these final days of his reign as doyen of the Hollywood labor scene, Bioff claimed that he was in favor of leveling salaries in Hollywood. In an interview with *Saturday Evening Post* writer Florabel Muir, Bioff said: 'You know, the AFL is going more for vertical unions. It's not a bad idea either. It ain't fair for some people in this [business] to be drawing thousands of dollars a week when others can't earn a thousand dollars a year'.[29]

In January 1940, federal authorities indicated that they would try Bioff on income tax evasion charges before he was extradited to Illinois. An investigation revealed that Bioff had under-reported his income for 1936 and 1937 by nearly $200,000 and that he owed at least $80,000 in back taxes. The $200,000 included the $100,000 'loan' from Joe Schenck, which of course raised the possibility that Bioff might be tried for additional charges of labor racketeering. In late January, Bioff demanded that all IA members sign a pledge 'not to resort to legal proceedings against the Alliance [IATSE] for any grievance but to seek remedies within the Alliance, and to be bound by the decisions of its lawful tribunals.' By this time, certain rank and file IA members were in open rebellion against Bioff. Many adopted the producers' line, blaming Bioff for the fact that hundreds of studio craft workers were unemployed. It was his hard line in refusing to give back the 10 per cent increase, they said, that was causing the current high level of unemployment. They further stated that the pledge proposed by Bioff was a violation of their constitutional rights, and they turned the pledge over to Department of Justice investigators.[30]

Bioff was hauled off to Illinois to complete his sentence in the first week of February 1940, the same week in which Martin Dies arrived in Hollywood to initiate a ritual that was to be repeated well into the 1950s. Dies and his investigators were looking for communists in the Hollywood film community. This attack against progressive elements in Hollywood was aimed primarily at talent groups. Dies knew that he could make most political hay out of questioning the loyalty of famous people, such as Humphrey Bogart and Franchot Tone. But it is worth noting that it was George Browne who initially invited Dies to Hollywood and it was Herb Sorrell, a genuine hero of many rank and file workers in the studios, who fired the first volley at Dies, noting that the senator would do better to investigate Bioff than communists.[31]

Low employment levels in the motion picture industry continued throughout 1940. Many workers migrated to better paying and more secure jobs with the burgeoning Southern California defense industry. The IA studio locals were cut off from international support in July when Browne ordered the IA Hollywood office closed. Browne and the other Executive Board members decided to adopt a policy of coercive neglect, hoping that the studio locals would see that they were too weak to bargain effectively with the producers. The locals, however, had decided not to try to negotiate new wage scales in 1940, hoping that improved economic and employment conditions in 1941 would allow them to bargain more effectively with the producers.[32]

The 1940 convention of the IA was held in Louisville, Kentucky, the city where George Browne had made his first successful bid for power. President Browne extolled the dedication of Willie Bioff, portraying him as the victim of 'a merciless series of scurrilous attacks.'[33] The splitting up of Local 37 was excused as expedient owing to the local's 'overly large membership and the many widely separated crafts practiced by those members.'[34] The blacklisted members of Local 37 were characterized as 'disgruntled radicals...who refused to join the newly chartered locals of the I.A.[T.S.E.].' In Browne's closing remarks on Bioff one can detect an almost saintly glow around the then imprisoned gangster:

> Out of the clear sky came rumblings of a Grand Jury investigation authorized by the [California] State Legislature, which was to look into legislative corruption in connection with the previous legislative Capitol Labor hearing. The aforementioned rumblings soon became a matter of fact and shortly thereafter subpoenas were served upon your officers to appear before the California Grand Jury at Sacramento...
>
> It was not hard to see that instead of the Legislature being investigated the I.A.T.S.E was being investigated, and it became apparent that this was another fishing expedition to embarrass my personal representative, William Bioff, who had incurred the everlasting hatred of the open shop

element for forcing the first closed shop in the leading industry in the State of California, namely that of the Motion Picture industry.

William Bioff had done the most remarkable job any man has ever done for labor against terrific odds, but what a price he and his family have had to pay that our members and their families might enjoy a better livelihood in their own pursuit of happiness.[35]

Browne portrayed Bioff as Joe Hill; yet Bioff was clearly a thief and a brutal man, given to waving pistols in people's faces to get his way. In explaining his break-up of Local 37, Browne portrayed the dissidents in Local 37 such as Irv Hentschel as 'vicious radicals' who disregarded the 'duly elected' Lew Blix and who made 'ridiculous accusations' about Bioff to the District Attorney's office in Los Angeles. Browne managed to lump the Local 37 Progressives with the open-shop movement and made the point even more strongly when he placed into the convention record several articles authored by Los Angeles CLC President J. W. Buzzell for a strike newsletter published by the IA – but purporting to be 'Los Angeles Newspaper Headline Articles' – alleging that the Studio Unemployment Conference and other progressive local *ad hoc* organizations were part of the 'CIO-Communist Combine to Blot Out AFL Locals in Hollywood Studios.'[36]

Browne continued the theme of anti-communism that had been used so effectively to obscure the issues in the 1939 USTG challenge. In Browne's remarks the line was blurred between communism and fascism. By Browne's criteria, Progressive Jeff Kibre could scarcely be distinguished from Hitler or the populist radio priest Father Coughlin. Combating disgruntled 'radicals' in the IA, such as Irv Hentschel, was part and parcel of the bloody struggle taking place in Europe at that very time. Browne maintained that communism 'not only exists within the country, but within the ranks of our Organization as well' and that 'our own native patriotism should be sufficient incentive to strive to preserve our Democracy against evil influences.' In all these remarks, Browne mixed the motives of the communists with those of the producers, as if the two groups had somehow conspired to overthrow the IA. Why the communists would want to help Louis B. Mayer or Joe Schenck was never clearly explained.[37]

On the very day that the delegates to the thirty-fifth convention of the IA listened to George Browne's fantastic account of the West coast situation, federal authorities brought charges of income tax evasion against Joe Schenck, claiming that Schenck had defrauded the government of more than $400,000 in taxes. The investigation of Joe Schenck's taxes was a spin-off of the Bioff tax investigation that federal authorities had initiated back in 1938. Federal investigators wanted to know where Joe Schenck had gotten the $100,000 that he had temporarily laundered to enable Bioff to purchase a home in the Los Angeles area. Joe Schenck found himself trapped in a web of lies. He eventually had to admit that he had indeed taken illegal deductions. However, he did not publicly admit that he had made payments to Bioff to stop strikes or to hold down wages. But to reduce his three-year sentence, Schenck privately testified to federal authorities about the payoffs.[38]

Federal authorities stepped up their investigations of labor racketeering in Hollywood, resulting in the eventual indictments of Bioff and George Browne on 23 May 1941. An additional indictment was made against Nick Circella, but Circella was not located until December 1941. His role in the racket was not yet clear; Nitti and the Chicago crime syndicate were not yet implicated in the scheme. In 1943 the full extent of the Nitti syndicate's involvement in the motion picture industry's labor force would finally come to light.[39]

Between his indictment and his eventual trial date, Bioff dealt his last hand at the producers' labor relations gaming table. The Screen Cartoonists Guild (SCG) had obtained a charter from Sorrell's Painters union in 1940. The SCG struck Disney studios on 28 May 1941. Disney was the most adamant open shop advocate of all the producers. He consistently undermined the efforts of his employees to form a genuine union. To give the appearance of fairness, however, he formed company unions and encouraged his workers to join those unions. The strike by the SCG against his studio dragged on for nine weeks. Disney requested Bioff to intervene during the strike. Bioff offered leaders of the SCG a large pay raise and a closed shop contract if they would drop their affiliation with the Painters and join the IA.[40]

The cartoonists refused this offer and stood their ground; they had broad support from other Hollywood unions, including SAG, the International Alliance of Machinists, and IA Lab Technicians Local 683. Eventually, the SCG won a closed shop at Disney as well as at MGM and Schlessinger cartoon studios. The Disney strike actually served to solidify the progressive forces that had been scattered by the defeat of the USTG. In August 1941, the new progressive coalition under the leadership of Herb Sorrell was formally organized as the Conference of Studio Unions (CSU). This organization would lead the final challenge to the IA's domination of the studios in postwar Hollywood.

Browne and Bioff finally came to trial in October 1941, a trial that involved the testimony of Harry Warner, Louis B. Mayer, the producers' labor representative Pat Casey and Nicholas Schenck (Schenck's brother Joe made a brief cameo appearance but never testified). One of the lesser managers of Warners theater chain, James Coston, who apparently had not read the script the executives had prepared for their day in court, offered a devastatingly candid version of a conversation he had with Bioff in mid-1939. According to Coston, Bioff said, 'They can't afford to let me go to jail. I've done too much for the industry in taking care of strikes, etc.'[41] The producers themselves were hardly as frank as Coston, but they did provide a great number of technical details regarding the method of payments to Bioff. The *New York Times* provided this account of Louis B. Mayer explaining how Loew's/MGM covered up its payoffs:

Before July 1937, Mr Mayer said, Loew's had been buying its raw film through J. E. Brulatour from the Eastman Kodak Company. Smith and Aller, Ltd., agent for the du Pont Company, had been seeking this business and Mr [Nicholas] Schenck finally suggested that it be diverted to them if a way could be found to let Bioff share in the sales agency's commission, Mr Mayer said.

This was arranged, the producer went on, and Bioff brought his brother-in-law [Norman Nelson] to act as a sub-agent for the company.[42]

This particular arrangement netted Bioff, and presumably Browne and the Chicago crime syndicate, some $236,474 over a two-year period.[43]

The final accounting of all the payoffs made by producers to Browne and Bioff over six years amounted to over $1 million. Numerous stockholder suits were filed to attempt to recover the money paid to Browne and Bioff, but they were all thrown out of court over the next few years. What the producers were not forced to account for in court was the fact that this so-called extortion scheme actually saved the producers substantial wage increases which, under legitimate collective bargaining, they might have granted to their theater and studio workers. John Cogley, in his *Report on Blacklisting,* reported that the producers saved nearly $14 million through their arrangement with Browne and Bioff.[44]

Browne and Bioff were sentenced to terms of eight and ten years respectively. The IA and the AFL quickly cut their losses. Even before the close of the trial, Browne was defeated in his bid to be re-elected as a member of the AFL Executive Council. Upon his conviction, Browne resigned as President of the IA, and Third Vice-President Richard Walsh replaced him. Walsh had gained his post as part of Browne's slate at the 1934 convention in Louisville. According to Walsh's income tax records for the years that Bioff and Browne were in power, he received a small portion of the 2 per cent assessment in addition to his regular salary and expenses. From that perspective, he was a beneficiary of the Browne – Bioff conspiracy. Certainly, he and his cohorts showed an unthinking and uncaring attitude toward the rank and file, a tendency to put institutional requirements ahead of human needs. Just as in the earlier case of the embezzlement by IA President Charles Shay, the $1,500,000 collected via the 2 per cent assessments was never recovered, nor apparently did Walsh or any other IA Executive Board members ever pay back their cut of the fund.

Joe Schenck served four months and five days for massive income tax violations, perjury and his significant role in the motion picture industry racketeering scheme. None of the other producers suffered materially from participation in the scheme. At the conclusion of the trial, *Variety* ran an editorial noting that the real victims of the scheme were the workers of the industry. While this was a notably courageous stand for a trade paper to take, the characterization of the producers as 'the suckers' in the Bioff payoffs certainly ignored the facts in the case. The producers were the prime beneficiaries of the scheme. *Variety* noted that there was a mixture of joy and caution in the air at the close of the Browne and Bioff trial: 'A fear still seems to prevail that lieutenants of the racketeering pair may have been left around to wreak vengeance on those who voiced opinions.'[45]

In the years following the downfall of Bioff and Browne, the legacy of their tyrannical rule of the IA studio locals haunted the rank and file. Tensions and resentments established over years were not wiped away with the conviction of two men. Bioff had numerous helpers in the studio locals – 'checkers' such as Cappy DuVal – whose real purpose was to collect the 2 per cent assessments and to keep an eye open for candidates for the union's blacklist. These men were still in positions of authority in the studio locals. *Variety* predicted that 'Certain of the more aggressive officials of the locals will fight for a cleanup.'[4]

People like DuVal later tried to deny that they had been put into power in Hollywood by Willie Bioff. But we knew better. Yet, sadly enough, the 'big lie' is sometimes the one that wins the day, as we were to find out in the next several years.

How could the Progressives clean up the corruption? In the wake of such massive abuse of power, the majority of studio workers simply refused to participate in local union meetings. Gene Mailes notes that IATSE Property Workers' Local 44, even with the restoration of local autonomy, could not carry on its monthly business because there were seldom enough members present for a quorum. How could such a politically inert labor force be motivated toward democratic unionism?

In its year-end review of the 1941 labor situation, *Variety* claimed that in the vacuum created by Bioff's second trip to prison in as many years (Bioff had been forced to return to Chicago to serve his sentence on the pandering charge), Herb Sorrell was the 'No. 1 leader' among studio labor groups. As head of the militant Conference of Studio Unions, Sorrell was soon to become the center of the struggle against the duplicity of the producers and the complicity of their 'sweethearts', the leaders of the IA.[47]

Notes

1. On the Wages and Hours Law, see Joseph Rayback, *A History of the American Labor Movement* (New York: Free Press, 1966), p. 360; *Variety*, 8 June 1938.
2. *Variety*, 9 November 1938, pp. 1, 19; 21 December 1938, p. 5.
3. *Variety*, 6 July 1938, pp. 5, 8.
4. *Variety*, 7 September 1938, p. 21; IATSE *Combined Convention Proceedings*, vol. 2, p. 402.
5. *Variety*, 14 September 1938, p. 6.
6. *New York Times*, 8 September 1938, p. 26; 9 September 1938, p. 25; *Variety*, 7 September 1938, p. 21.
7. *Variety*, 26 October 1938, p. 18.
8. *Variety*, 4 January 1939, p. 30.
9. *Variety*, 18 January 1939, p. 17.
10. *Variety*, 1 March 1939, pp. 5, 20.
11. *Variety*, 15 March 1939, p. 5; 3 May 1939, p. 47.
12. *Variety*, 29 March 1939, p. 18.
13. *Variety*, 19 April 1939, pp. 5, 23.
14. Ibid.
15. Ibid.
16. *Variety*, 19 April 1939, pp. 5, 23; 26 April 1939, p. 5.
17. *Variety*, 26 April 1939, p. 5; 24 May 1939, p. 6; 21 June 1939, p. 5.
18. *Variety*, 20 September 1939, p. 5; Murray Ross, 'The C.I.O. loses Hollywood.' *Nation*, 6 October 1939, p. 375.
19. Ross, 'The C.I.O. loses Hollywood', p. 376.
20. *Variety*, 9 August 1939, p. 5.
21. Murray Ross, *Stars and Strikes*, (New York: Columbia University Press, 1941), pp. 198-9.
22. Ross, 'The C.I.O. loses Hollywood', pp. 366-7.
23. Ibid.; *Variety*, 13 September 1939, p. 5.
24. *Variety*, 20 September 1939, pp. 5, 25; 27 September 1939, pp. 5, 20; 14 August 1940, p. 7; Ross, *Stars and Strikes*, p. 201.
25. *Variety*, 12 November 1941; Hugh Lovell and Tasile Carter, *Collective Bargaining in the Motion Picture Industry: A Struggle for Stability* (Berkeley: University of California Press, 1955), p. 20.
26. *Variety*, 1 November 1939, p. 2; 15 November 1939, pp. 2, 24.
27. *Variety*, 29 November 1939, p. 3; 13 March 1940, p. 3.

28. *Variety*, 29 November 1939, pp. 5, 18; 20 December 1939, pp. 5, 11.
29. Florabel Muir, 'All right gentlemen, do we get the money?', *Saturday Evening Post*, 27 January 1940, p. 11.
30. *Variety*, 17 January 1940, pp. 3, 54; 31 January 1940, pp. 5, 54.
31. *Variety*, 14 February 1940, p. 5; 28 February 1940, pp. 1, 21.
32 *Variety*, 18 December 1940, pp. 7, 52; 21 July 1940, pp. 7, 18; 8 January, p. 32.
33. IATSE, *Combined Convention Proceedings,* vol. 2, p. 366.
34. Ibid., p. 367.
35. Ibid., pp. 367-8.
36. Ibid., pp. 377-90.
37. Ibid., p. 372.
38 *Variety*, 5 June 1940, pp. 1, 19.
39. *New York Times*, 24 May 1941, p. 1; *Variety*, 12 November 1941, p. 4.
40. Lovell and Carter, *Collective Bargaining*, p. 21.
41. *Variety*, 5 November 1941, p. 25.
42. *New York Times*, 16 October 1941, p. 23.
43. Ibid.
44. Lovell and Carter, *Collective Bargaining*, p. 21; *Variety*, 26 June 1942, p. 7; *Variety*, 24 March 1943, p. 7; George H. Dunne, *Hollywood Labor Dispute: A Study in Immorality* (Los Angeles: Conference Publishing, 1950), pp. 7-8; John Cogley, *Report on Blacklisting: I, The Movies* (New York: Fund for the Republic, 1956). Cogley's source is sworn depositions of studio executives cited in Thirteen Tax Court of the United States Reports, Estate of Frank Nitti, Petitioner, v. Commissioner of Internal Revenue, Respondent, Docket nos. 8840, 8841, 8842, promulgated 30 November 1949.
45. *Variety*, 12 November 1941, pp. 4-5.
46. *Variety*, 5 January 1942, p. 34.
47. Ibid.

4

DURING THE WAR

An Overview of US Labor during the War

During World War Two, the War Labor Board (WLB) maneuvered labor and management into an armed truce. The WLB established a wage control program known as the Little Steel formula. Under this program, however, wages did not keep pace with the spiraling costs of living. This provoked a number of wartime strikes, particularly in the coal industry. A wide *Variety* of critics condemned these strikes, including the Roosevelt administration, the AFL, the CIO, a majority of their affiliates, and even the US Communist Party (CPUSA). Many groups and individuals considered strikes against industries vital to the defense effort as treasonous acts; President Roosevelt nearly forced conscription of strikers. In *American Labor from Defense to Reconversion,* Joel Seidman noted that the wartime strikes had a noticeably polarizing effect on the US labor movement:

'The growing number of strikes and the publicity given to them, both in the regular press and in the papers published especially for servicemen, had an effect on many men in uniform, who got a distorted impression of the role of unions in the war effort, along with an exaggerated notion of wages received by civilian workers'.[1] In June 1943, the Smith-Connaly Act was enacted over a presidential veto. According to labor historian Joseph Rayback, this explicitly anti-union legislation provided 'for the calling of strikes only after a strike vote was taken by the N.L.R.B during a thirty-day 'cooling off' period; for governmental seizure of any plant where a halt in production threatened the war effort, and for criminal penalties to be imposed on any person who instigated or promoted a strike. In addition it prohibited all union contributions to political campaign funds'.[2]

During the war, the unions suffered a form of institutional identity crisis. They had been established to maintain wage rates and to preserve job security. Federally imposed wage controls seemed to undermine their *raison d'être.* To make matters worse for the unions, Roosevelt invited business executives to become part of the wartime government bureaucracy. This group contrasted sharply with Roosevelt's former New Deal 'Brain Trust' of liberal economists and college professors. By the end of the war these 'drafted' business executives held more influence in government than they had since the better days of the Hoover administration. The motion picture executives were an integral part of this wartime executive draft by virtue of their contributions to the US propaganda effort. Many unions, therefore, felt betrayed by and mistrusted Roosevelt's wartime bureaucracy.[3]

Wartime leaps in productivity generated massive profits. These profits, however, were held in check by special excess-profit taxes. At the close of the war, the business community felt that the appropriate 'spoils of war' should be a lifting of these taxes coupled with a 'consumer revolution' for the workers. There were, however, a couple of snags in this pseudo-revolution. First, reconversion from war-related to peacetime production brought about much unemployment; second, the labor unions now wanted a share in the profits generated by the increased efficiency and productivity of American industry. Many new industries that sprang up during the war could not easily be reconverted to consumer-product manufacturing. This, combined with the return of some twelve million service men and women to civilian life, prompted fears of massive postwar unemployment and social disruption similar to that experienced in the Great Depression.[4]

Still, the top-level labor and management leaders touted the idea of an amicable resolution to the impending conflicts. Eric Johnston, then president of the US Chamber of Commerce and soon to be head of the Motion Picture Association of America (MPAA), along with AFL President William Green and CIO President Phillip Murray, signed a 'Charter for Industrial Peace'. According to Hollywood labor historians Englund and Ceplair; this charter 'looked toward a postwar future devoid of conflict and overflowing with prosperity – a strikeless world of industrial harmony in which labor-management differences were amicably resolved.'[5] Organized labor and the Chamber of Commerce signed this charter on April Fool's Day, 1945, a date that must have had special significance given that the postwar industrial environment was anything but peaceful. Some 4,600 strikes involving about 5 million workers occurred in the twelve months following VJ day. Among the many postwar strikes were the most violent confrontations ever seen in Hollywood. As President Truman gingerly lifted the lid on wages and prices, prices jumped 15 per cent in six months. Food prices climbed an astounding 28 per cent.[6]

Meanwhile, on the US political front, a massive swing to the right was under way. This swing could not be measured strictly in terms of Democratic voters crossing over to vote Republican. Incumbent Democrats were quickly shuffling away from associations with the New Deal because they feared being labeled 'soft on communism'. The 'hot' war had ended, but the 'cold' war continued, producing a noticeable chilling effect on all progressive movements and institutions, particularly in the labor movement.

In Hollywood, the war provided a period of sharp economic upturn. Neither the excess-profit tax imposed on corporations nor the threat of anti-trust actions against the major production-distribution-exhibition firms discouraged Wall Street investment in Hollywood. In January 1942, *Variety* reported that the market price of motion picture stocks was up $29 million during 1941. The major studios benefited financially from the production of military training and propaganda films. For the first two years of the war the Research Council of the Motion Picture Academy of Arts and Sciences, headed by 20th Century-Fox's Darryl Zanuck, channeled a lion's share of the production of government films into the four largest studios: Paramount, 20th Century-Fox, MGM and RKO.[7]

The most critical shortage facing the producers was one of skilled labor. The defense plants of Los Angeles and Orange Counties had begun to lure workers away from the studios as early as 1940. Following the entry of the United States into the war, voluntary enlistment and the conscription of draftees into the armed services aggravated the studio labor shortage. At first, the motion picture producers were aided in their attempt to hold workers in the industry when General Lewis Hershey issued a blanket deferment order for all workers involved in the production phase of the industry. But objections from within and outside the industry to such a scheme led Hershey to rescind the order.[8]

The compromise solution to the problem of labor shortages in the motion picture industry during the war was to substantially increase the work week so that fewer workers could generate greater productivity in return for sizeable overtime payments. The members of the IA film lab technicians Local 683 agreed to lengthen their work week from 36 to 40 hours in December 1942 to avoid bringing in excessive numbers of permit workers. In June 1943, the federal government imposed a mandatory 48-hour work week for all defense industries in Los Angeles County. Just before the federal order, Paramount set a pattern that was to be followed by other studios in which the producers went from the 36-hour week (established during the Depression to spread work) to a 48-hour week with time and one-half paid after 36 hours. The net effect was to give workers 54 hours of pay for 48 hours of work. Workers in the studios were still not given the kind of job security that factory and shipyard workers had; however, a system was established whereby workers who had just finished a particular production were granted 'extended availability certificates' to enable them to go back to work immediately on the next available production in any studio. After the imposition of the 48-hour week there were no further reports in *Variety* of labor shortages in Hollywood. Producers did continue, however, to seek deferments for 'key men' on a case-by-case basis throughout the war. Despite their displeasure with labor shortages, the producers paid out $3 million annually in benefits to the families of permanent employees who joined the armed forces. The families of the service men and women were surveyed and payments were made in cases where the loss of a civilian job created economic hardship.[9]

In general, the labor situation in Hollywood during the war was as peaceful as it had ever been. Although the Little Steel formula held wages in check, conditions were substantially improved for workers; such improvements included the first paid vacations ever granted to studio craft workers. But the problem of local bargaining rights for studio unions persisted. Contract negotiations were still carried out in New York City. To many studio workers, this smelled of 'sell-out'; thus the long-smoldering feuds between the various AFL unions in Hollywood were still not resolved.

Rebuilding the Progressive Base

After the defeat of the USTG, I worked at reforms within Local 44, albeit with little success. The IA Progressives no longer existed as a formal group, but I was not quitting the fight. I attended meetings of the local and when anything seemed important I spoke up or made a motion from the floor. I was constantly looked upon as 'a clear and present danger' by the officers. In a couple of instances, however, I did get a few good points across at meetings. I was appalled at how few members attended meetings. I made a motion that called for an investigation to look into the reasons so few came; a quorum was ten or fifteen members and sometimes there were not even that many, so the meeting was adjourned. At least we were allowed to hold meetings; that was something to work with. The few who were there that night decided that it was a good idea, so they voted for it. The president appointed a committee of three, with a member of the Executive Board of the local as Secretary and me as Chairman. Needless to say the effort was minimal, and the officials of the local swept the issue under the carpet.

I also tried to submit a series of resolutions aimed at revising the Local 44 constitution to allow the various crafts of the local to meet separately and then submit business to a Resolutions Committee for action at the general membership meetings. The local constitution allowed one member to submit resolutions. I wrote them up and submitted them at a meeting. It was obviously a hot potato, so the president allowed them to be submitted for consideration only – a delaying tactic. The resolutions were aimed at laying the ground for getting the form and structure of Local 37 back together. The Local Executive Board met and decided to write to the International office to ask them if I, being on probation, had the right to submit resolutions. Of course the IA office replied 'No!' A resolution was drawn up and passed, requiring twenty members to start any more resolutions.

I had some success in contacting people in the talent guilds. By that I mean the Story Analysts and the Writers Guilds. They were simply contacts, nothing formal. I went through the 1940 IA Convention Proceedings and made a list of the people, in the studio locals who had introduced any progressive resolutions – all of which had been voted down – and contacted them directly. Most of them were in either the Lab or Wardrobe locals. In this manner I built a network of people to at least talk with. Frankly, I was getting nowhere. Making friends, yes, but like Irv Hentschel at the '38 Convention, I needed help.

Finally, one day when I was talking to Norval Crutcher, the Secretary of the Lab Local 683, he said that he would have a talk with Irv and would let me know what he had to say. A couple of days later he told me that he had talked with Irv, and to give him a call.

I went to Irv's home, a few blocks from where Thelma and I lived, in Burbank, just over the hill from Hollywood. Irv was a small man, maybe five feet five inches tall. He weighed about one hundred and twenty pounds. My first impression of him, looking rather unpleasant, had been totally wrong. He was now relaxed and pleasantly at ease. I recognized him immediately as the man I had talked to the night of the 1939 riot. He was in his shop in what was supposed to have been a two-car garage. His shop had everything needed to work with wood, metal or plastics.

We went into the house and I met Helen. She was also small, like Irv, slim and rather plain, but a truly warm person. She and my wife Thelma formed a close friendship in a very short time. They had two children, a boy and a girl, both teenagers. Helen was very cordial to me. Irv got a couple of beers and we went into the living room and sat on a davenport facing the radio and record player. Under these was a shelf filled with what appeared to be thirty-five or forty classical records, heavy with the 'three B's' – Bach, Beethoven and Brahms. The record player and the radio were both put together by Irv, as well as the cabinets they were in. The book shelves, and the coffee table and cabinets were all made by Irv. Everything there except the davenport and easy chairs was made by him.

We reminisced a bit about the riot and the occasion when I had first seen him. We talked about an hour about what I had been trying to do since I joined Local 44 and how I had made contact with other people in various unions and guilds. When I got to the point of asking him if he would come back into the fight, he thought for a couple of seconds and asked, 'Does the fact that I am a communist bother you?' (On the way home it occurred to me that he had not said '...that I am a member of the Communist Party'.) It would not have bothered me at all.

He told me that I had done the right thing in contacting people in the other guilds and unions and that we must do the same thing with all the other unions and guilds. I picked up on the word 'we' and he grinned and said, 'Well, yeah, I guess so'. We chewed the rag for a while then slowly got down to work. Irv said that the first thing to do was to get together a complete list of the membership of Local 44. Jeff Kibre had the membership lists of both the IA Progressives and the USTG, so Irv said that he would call him the next morning and arrange to have me pick them up. I called Jeff later in the day and picked them up in the afternoon. We would have to go through them and pick out the members of Local 44 by craft.

When I was driving home after this meeting with Irv, I felt that at last 'we' would get somewhere in our efforts. Working alone had been fruitless, but now ... I had been surprised at how different Irv had been from the first time I had seen him. Here was a delightful drinking companion, a guide, a counselor and a true friend. And he knew what he was doing.

Jeff let us have the cards without question. There were three boxes, about the size of shoe boxes, filled with 3" x 5" cards. With these boxes, wrapped separately, were about 200 cards. This was the master contributor list! These were the files that Irv had charge of for several years, from the time that the whole fight started to the time of our defeat in the Labor Board election. When I took them to Irv's house that night, we started to go through them and select out the various cards by craft, property-men, prop-miniature men, upholsterers and drapery seamsters, special-effects men and greensmen. We pulled out several hundred cards. This was our base. Our first job was to look up each member of Local 44, then check for the correct phone number in the phone book. The rest of them, such as lamp operators, grips and electricians, we put back in the boxes. This took us a couple of weeks, checking them all.

When we opened the small package of cards, Irv started through them and let out a snort. These cards were coded by activity like the others; but they also had the names of the various people who had contributed to the fund of both the Party and the Local 37 Progressives. Symbols, such as stars and letters and numbers, meant different things and amounts of money contributed. Irv, Bob Ames and I were the only ones to know about this file of cards. We never contacted any of them for anything at all.

It was slow going, trying to pull things back together. Part of our problem was that because of the approaching war there was plenty of work to keep most of the studio workers going most of the time. We continued our name gathering, talking at meetings and generally trying to move things along as best we could. We were able to create some interest in a local election. Irv and I both ran for places on the Local 44 Executive Board. We did rather well but neither of us was elected.

The job fear generated during the USTG campaign was wide and deep. This fear, combined with losing the election, built up a hopelessness on the part of the membership. We were probably seen by many members as losers.

Ted Hansard had been elected to the job of Business Agent of Local 44 when Local 37 had been broken up, following the Labor Board election. He and the Secretary, Del Crawford, had a fight one night and the Secretary filed charges against Hansard. The upshot of this was that the man who had been sent out by the mob to check membership cards for evidence of payment of the 2 per cent assessment was appointed to the job of Business Agent by the Local 44 Executive Board. This man, Cappy DuVal, made a hit by trying to take some of the jurisdiction away from the grips and electrical locals; this in good old AFL fashion – 'Don't organize the unorganized, take jurisdiction from another union'. DuVal's job was one of intimidation. If he caught anyone who had not paid his assessment, he told them he would see that they wouldn't work until they had done so. We called him 'Old 2 per cent' behind his back.

That was the way it was until Irv met Chet Cohea. The men who had become identified with the opposition to the mobs paid their dues and assessments promptly in order not to make it easy to be forced out of the union. Our success was very slow in coming.

Finally we had a large enough mailing list to make it worthwhile to start sending letters to the membership. The list was so complete that the officials of the Local 44 thought that we had paid off one of the clerks in the office. They finally realized that we had been gathering names and addresses for almost a year, and dropped the witch-hunt. We finally had a complete list of the membership. We had assessed ourselves two dollars a week so that we had enough to send out a few editions of our sheet. We called attention to the fact that the mob had still not been indicted and the same people were still running the IA. We did it in language which was legally not in violation of our apologies to Browne and Bioff.

On the first occasion of our literary efforts, I asked Irv if we should send letters to the officers of the local. His answer was, 'Hell, yes! I'm surprised that you ask'. We sent copies of everything to Browne and Bioff. We didn't send them information on everything we were doing, but Irv felt it was right to let them know that we were alive and kicking.

The New Order in the IA

Richard Walsh entered the office of IA International President as a 'reform' candidate. His version of reform was not radical but conciliatory; that is to say, he wanted to mend fences with the rank and file of the locals without admitting that former IA President George Browne had massively abused his executive powers.

Walsh had been a Third Vice-president on the IA Executive Board during Browne's tenure as president, and he was raised to the office of president by a vote of the same Board following Browne's conviction in November 1941. He, along with the other eight members of the Board, approved all the actions of Browne and even spent large sums of the union's money to defend Browne and Bioff in their 1941 trial. Later testimony in Congressional hearings suggests that Walsh and other members of the IA Executive Board took payments and paid income tax on money collected as part of the special 2 per cent fund that was embezzled by Browne. Browne had brought public disgrace to the IA, and at the 1942 IA convention Walsh was faced with the unenviable task of attempting to recuperate the honor and integrity of Browne and his Executive Board by initially portraying Browne as a victim of circumstance:

Inasmuch as our former President had served the International in a wholly satisfactory manner in various official capacities for many years, it must be assumed that he had become the victim of circumstances beyond his control. If he was cognizant of the acts being perpetrated by his appointees, possibly he was left with the alternative of remaining silent or paying the supreme penalty. The difficulty of having to make a choice between the two, with the latter a price beyond recall, should be readily apparent and is a distinct throwback to the adage of self-preservation. Taking the human side, I am certain that it is a decision relished by no one.[10]

Walsh certainly overstated the case for Browne. As noted earlier, the presence of well-known gangsters at the IA convention in Louisville in 1934 would have been enough for reasonable individuals to suspect Browne's intentions and motives. Walsh, however, could not publicly admit that the Board had knowingly ratified the actions of a corrupt president. If he did, he would have to abdicate power to a genuine reform slate. More critically for Walsh and the other incumbents, they might face investigations if their part in the racket came to light.

Under the four-year term approved by the 1938 convention Walsh was entitled to remain as IA President until 1944. But Vincent Jacobi of IA New York stagehands Local 1 circulated a petition among the delegates calling for officer elections at the 1942 convention; this forced Walsh to run for office under less than favorable circumstances. To insure his victory, Walsh's supporters initiated a whisper campaign against Jacobi and another challenger, William Bennett of IA stagehands Local 22, Washington, D.C. They informed delegates from places like Boise, Memphis and Peoria that the Walsh's opponents were 'pro-Jewish' or 'anti-Semitic', or that the opposing slate of candidates, which initially had the support of the West coast locals, represented the special interests of the East and West coasts to the detriment of the rest of the IA.[11]

Several rebellions against the Walsh regime occurred at the 1942 convention. Russell McKnight, President of IA lab technicians Local 683, Hollywood, issued a rousing denunciation of Walsh's whitewashing of Browne.

77

McKnight, along with fellow Local 683 officers Norval Crutcher and John Martin, had tried to limit the absolute powers of the IA presidency at the 1940 convention through two motions dealing with 'emergency cases' and 'assessments'. Pro-Browne delegates had labeled these resolutions as part of 'a Commie movement'. By the 1942 convention, however, rank and file members had begun to resent the dictatorial power of the International office. The entire IA West coast district voted by a margin of three-to-one to reject a convention resolution supporting the 'official family' (Walsh and his fellow members of the IA Executive Board).[12]

Although Walsh and his slate won an overwhelming victory in the election, he resented the defiant attacks from the 'disloyal' elements of the Hollywood locals. The power struggle between the International and the studio locals continued with merely a new set of characters. Walsh and his slate of board members won again in 1944, but Walsh's margin of victory was much slimmer than in 1942. He polled 577 votes against challenger William Bennett's 416.[13]

To understand the new terms of the struggle between the International office and the studio locals, one must remember that back in early December 1941, just three weeks after assuming the presidency, Walsh publicly declared himself in favor of local autonomy for the West coast IA studio locals and in favor of conducting negotiations for studio contracts in Hollywood rather than in New York City. But two weeks later Walsh reversed his decision and convinced the executive boards of the studio locals to move the contract talks to New York, where, Walsh claimed, the studio executives would be more available for consultation. *Variety* praised the new IA President in its 1941 labor wrap-up, declaring Walsh to be 'business-like and above-board', and claiming that he was dedicated to 'zealously respect and protect the local autonomy of [the IA's] many members'. The studio locals sent representatives to New York for contract talks on 4 January 1942. On 18 January the producers and the representatives of the studio locals signed a two-year agreement that was retroactive to July 1941, the expiration date of the previous contract. The new agreement established a number of blanket working conditions which the studio locals had unsuccessfully sought during Bioff's tenure as chief Hollywood IA negotiator; it also included wage increases amounting to 12-15 per cent over the two-year run of the contract.[14]

The rank and file of the IA was pleased with the substantial back pay, wage increases and improved working conditions; however, there proved to be a critical proble with the new contract. When understandably wary members of the studio locals examined the contracts, they discovered that they included cover sheets not discussed in the January meetings. These cover sheets granted the International office of the IA the right to bargain for the studio locals, which was a de facto surrender of local autonomy. Although a few dissident rank and file members objected to the surrender of local autonomy, the leaders of Local 44 (props), Local 80 (grips), Local 165 (studio projectionists) and Local 728 (set electricians) favored the surrender of bargaining rights. George Browne had appointed the leaders of these locals when he split up Local 37 (studio mechanics) into five smaller locals to dilute the power of the troublesome local. These men were loyal to the International office because their jobs depended upon that loyalty more than upon the sentiments of the members. As noted in the previous chapter, the problem of apathy in the studio locals was severe following the corruption and domination of Willie Bioff. A majority of members simply wanted to forget about the IA and to get on with making a living in the film industry.[15]

Not all the Hollywood locals, however, were apathetic or willing to surrender their bargaining rights. The leaders of three of the IA Hollywood locals – Harold V. Smith of Local 695 (sound), Herb Aller of Local 659 (camera) and Russell McKnight of Local 683 (lab technicians) – all rejected the idea of International negotiation of their contracts. And within Local 44, Gene Mailes led dissident members in an attempt to raise objections to the surrender of local autonomy, albeit with only slight success.

The Whitewash Rubs off George Browne

While Walsh was trying to 'reform' the IA, the Browne–Bioff kettle was still on the fire and about to boil over. Instead of being transferred to federal prison, Browne and Bioff had been held in the federal house of detention in New York. *Variety* reported in October 1942 that the Federal Prosecutor, Mathias Correa, was still attempting to discover the people behind the extortion/bribery scheme. One must remember that, in the 1941 trial, Harry Warner had testified that when Bioff asked for a payoff at Christmas 1937, he made special mention of the 'boys back in Chicago'. Correa wanted to know who these 'boys' were.[16]

In early 1943 unknown assailants set fire to the Chicago girlfriend of Browne's and Bioff's felow conspirator Nick Dean. The federal investigation came out into the open. Indictments were handed down in the New York federal court on the morning of 18 March 1943, naming Frank Nitti and seven of his associates on counts of labor racketeering, mail fraud, and conspiracy. Nitti committed suicide the following afternoon rather than face trial. Louis Kaufman, business agent of Newark IA projectionists Local 244, was indicted at the same time on a single count of racketeering. The day before the indictment was handed down, Kaufman was arraigned in Newark on a state charge of accepting bribes to guarantee employment to a projectionist. In late March, George Browne's wife received threatening calls. This prompted federal authorities to move her and the Browne children from their suburban Chicago home to protective custody in a New York hotel room. The trial against the racketeers opened in Chicago, but it was quickly postponed and moved to New York for the protection of witnesses and the indicted gangsters.[17]

The racketeering trial reopened in New York in September 1943. On 26 October 1943, Browne explained that he arranged for Bioff to remain on the IA payroll even after he had been officially withdrawn as his Hollywood representative in January 1938. Browne admitted that he had never even read the Studio Basic Agreement and was not familiar with its terms. Finally, he admitted under oath that he had knowingly aided the Nitti syndicate in the scheme.[18]

Bioff, providing a wealth of information on how the scheme had worked, included this vivid glimpse, quoted in *Variety*, of his astounding cynicism during his reign as Browne's assistant:

Counsel then shifted to former testimony given by Bioff concerning the demands made by the IATSE for two projectionists in each motion picture house in Chicago. Counsel asked Bioff if it was necessary for two men to serve in the same booth. Bioff answered: 'To be honest with you, I never was inside a booth in my life'.[19]

A former regional theater manager of Warners testified that he paid Louis Kaufman, Browne's hand-picked representative in Newark, $20,500 to stop strikes in the Warners' theaters in New Jersey. The manager revealed that the Warners' labor negotiator told him in 1936 that the payoff should be made 'because the Chicago mobsters had taken over the IATSE'. Clearly, anyone with eyes to see and ears to hear in the industry in the late 1930s knew that a crime syndicate was running the IA.[20]

Since the Federal Attorney, Mathias Correa, was more interested in attacking organized crime than in collusive motion picture producers, the defense pursued a more provocative line of questioning than did the prosecution. One of the more interesting exchanges during the trial occurred when defense attorney James D. Murray cross examined Nicholas Schenck of Loew's:

Murray drew from Schenck the fact that he had earned around $250,000 in 1935 on a salary and percentage basis, and then Schenck cracked that he had earned 'plenty anyway for your purposes, because $250,000 yearly is plenty for any man'. At the same time, Schenck was forced to concede that the negotiations over Local 306 resulted in a 10 per cent cut for the members. Murray hinted that the $120,000 thus saved was nearly equal to the $150,000 paid Browne and Bioff.[21]

The defense attorney consistently attempted to prove that the so-called extortion by the Nitti syndicate was in fact bribery by the producers to hold down wages and to stop strikes. Paramount Pictures' general counsel, Austin Keough, who was involved in handling his studio's share of the payoffs, responded to this line of question by stating that the payoffs were ethical business practices, and not in violation of New York state laws. It was not until the tax trial of the estate of Frank Nitti in 1948 that the financial benefits gained by the studios were publicly admitted.

Herb Sorrell represented the studio locals' point of view during the trial, attacking Bioff as the 'producers' man' and Lew Blix as the 'bag-man' for Bioff, the one who collected the assessments from the studio workers. *Variety* reported that Blix, under cross-examination by defense counsel Murray, 'practically admitted being a "stooge" for Willie Bioff during diverse occasions when other of the west coast unions got out of line and were talking strike'.[22]

To the delight of *Variety*, Billy Wilkerson, publisher of the *Hollywood Reporter*, was called to testify during the trial and admitted that he agreed not to print unfavorable stories about Bioff during one of Bioff's periods of trouble on the coast. *Variety* gleefully quoted large portions of Wilkerson's testimony verbatim, and noted that their competitor admitted that he 'wrote and published an article in which he stated that Bioff "is a type of man that the IATSE should be grateful about'.'"[23]

The trial ended with the conviction of Louis Campagna, Paul De Lucia, Johnny Roselli, Louis Kaufman, Frankie Diamond, Phil D'Andrea and Charles Gioe. In the meantime, IA President Walsh cleaned house in Chicago. During the trial, members of IA Chicago projectionists Local 110 filed suit against the Browne-appointed leaders of the local and several Chicago theater chains. They wanted to recover wages lost through deals struck by the officers of the local and the theaters. Shortly after the dissident members filed their suit, their lives were threatened by anonymous callers. Walsh intervened and forced the incumbent officers to resign. He took over the local so that new elections might be held without fear of the kind of reprisals threatened by Nitti's henchmen during previous Local 110 elections.[24] New officers were finally elected in May 1944.

For their cooperation with the federal investigation, Browne and Bioff were granted early releases from their prison sentences; they left federal prison on 28 December 1944, having served less than three years in jail. Browne withdrew from public life and lived quietly with his family in the suburbs of Chicago. He apparently suffered no reprisals for his testimony. Bioff assumed the alias of William Nelson and, after a time, established a new life for himself in Arizona. He became friends with Senator Barry Goldwater and in March 1955 became 'talent director' of the Riviera Hotel and Casino in Las Vegas. With such visibility in a city with well-known crime syndicate connections, Bioff became something of a public embarrassment. On 4 November 1955, he was killed in a truck-bomb explosion in Phoenix.[25]

In January 1945, on prompting from studio Locals 683 and 695, the IA Executive Board issued a general declaration to all members of the IA notifying them that Browne and Bioff had 'betrayed and brought discredit to our great Alliance'. The statement contained an official notice to the effect that no local would be permitted to admit either man to membership nor to associate itself with either man in any capacity whatsoever. The board noted, however, that Browne had achieved an honorable record of gains for members during his tenure.

> In view of such a record, it is not surprising that the delegates to the Convention in Louisville in 1940 voted unanimously to support Browne. It is true at that time rumors were being circulated alleging certain illegal conduct on the part of Browne and his appointees, and that, on the whole, no recognition was given to them either by the delegates or the officers of the IA. The Executive Board, like the delegates to that Convention, did not take such attacks seriously, for before them was this record of achievement that far surpassed our fondest hopes in the dark days of 1934. Employers who pay off labor leaders, we concluded, pay them off for tearing down union conditions, not for building them up as had been done during the past six years.
>
> The Browne–Bioff incident in the life of the IA is closed. It is imperative in the interests of the future of the Alliance that the public be permitted to forget it. IT IS EXPECTED THAT THIS OFFICIAL DECLARATION BY THE EXECUTIVE BOARD WILL END THIS MATTER FOR GOOD.[26]

The government had at last started to move on the indictments of the mobs. We, that is the whole progressive movement in the studios, had considerable backing in some government circles. Such men and women as Senator Wagner, Congressman Marcantonio, Congresswoman Helen Gahagan Douglas and others were keeping the pressure on for move-

ment against our leaders. The only immediate difference it made was that on the day the indictments were handed down Frank Nitti blew his brains out. Browne, Bioff and several of the Syndicate, the Costello Mob and Murder Inc. were jailed. There were what seemed to be well founded rumors about meetings being held in the Tombs of the New York jail. The way that we got it was that seven or eight optometrists went to jail to examine Willie Bioff's eyes. Subsequent investigation of the Tombs' records confirmed this. Then, shortly after this body of men left the Tombs, there was an IA Executive Board Meeting at which Richard Walsh was elected to fill the place just vacated by George E. Browne. From this distance in time it would be difficult to confirm or deny these events. I am satisfied that is the way it happened. It would have been fruitless to bring up anything about it. Their tactic was to attack anyone who didn't go along with them on this. Their way was to tell a lie and then viciously challenge anyone who questioned them on it. A campaign was immediately launched to proclaim Walsh to be the greatest man since George Washington. Of course, the Communist tag was hung on anyone who expressed any doubt on the subject. Nothing in the way of advantage to the employers gained from the period of gang control was surrendered, or demanded. Virtue triumphed again!

Over the time that I was closely associated with Irv [Hentschel], he and I of course exchanged many ideas on throwing the left-over bums out of office. Starting at our first meeting, when we talked of gathering the membership file, my education on the subject of organizing a union began. The following is a compressed account of the main points involved in what is in effect the organizing of an army while fighting at the same time. All the facts of those cards were noted with the permission of the members. Some of the more unpleasant information was left off the cards. The actual mailing list was made from the cards and had only the name address and phone number.

First off, we developed the file for mailing letters or calling people on the phone. These cards had their name, address, telephone number, craft, regular studio for work and any other studios that they worked at when their home studio was not busy, their date of birth, marital status, the name and birth date of their spouses if they were married, the names of any children with the dates of their birth and sex. Then we included any pertinent information that would indicate their interests, hobbies, reading, music etc. The question of the health of the whole family was noted also.

We worked at finding out who was the most respected person in each department in each studio – Republican, Democrat or whatever. Even if we differed in political views, we felt we must judge them in terms of integrity, decency and honor. The person we were looking for was usually one of the best workers. Also, it was important to think about who were the most intelligent. The more intelligent workers were apt to be more open-minded. If he or she does a lot of reading, what is the subject that interests them the most?

On several occasions we went to their homes and took along whatever they liked to drink and talked to them for hours. If their wives or husbands were home, we encouraged them to join us. On one occasion we went to one of the key men on the MGM lot, a Republican. The mobs were entrenched at the MGM studio and were very hard to buck. This clique voted as a block in local union votes. We knew that if we could persuade this one man we could change things at MGM. We answered all his questions and went on to tell him what we had done and why we had done it. He was intelligent and he asked good questions. He listened carefully to our answers and compared them with what someone had said that we had done and compared the two versions.

I mentioned that I had been in the US Marine Corps. He told me that he had been told by a friend that I had been to Moscow to study communism. I had to tell him that the closest I had been to Moscow was the western side of the Great Wall of China, when I was in the Corps. Mrs Smedley Butler, the wife of the commander of the Third Brigade, on duty in Teintsin, had arranged for every man in the brigade who wanted to, to see Peking and the Great Wall.

The poor guy was shocked to hear this since he had trusted the man who told him I was a Moscow-trained communist. He was our friend from then on. They had brains enough to listen to us. We had known before we went to his home that he was a conservative Republican and that he did not look at us in a favorable light. However, we had been told that he was intelligent and respected. That was all we had to know. We stayed until about 10:30 and got up to leave. In his manner toward us we sensed a change toward us and what we had tried to do. He thanked us for coming, and we knew from his tone that he meant it.

When we got about a block away from the man's home, Irv turned to me and said, 'We just cracked MGM'. It turned out that Irv was right. It was our first ray of hope of being able to split the hold that the old-line union politicians had on that studio.

We were concerned about the drinkers and gamblers. If this was a problem, was there anything that we could do to help them? A heavy drinker or gambler might be in debt and vulnerable to financial pressure, therefore subject to possible informing. If they drank on a casual, social basis, we invited them to get-togethers where there was moderate drinking. We let their wives know that their husbands would not be allowed to drive home drunk or get taken in a poker game. We rejected malcontents and racial or religious bigots. We considered whether a husband and wife were getting along. Could they be helped?

We looked for anybody on our list who might allow their homes to be used for small neighborhood meetings. At the meetings we asked questions. We got the members to ask questions, too. At all meetings, of any kind, we always took up a collection. Small amounts, but always. As soon as possible, we elected someone as Chancellor of the Exchequer, all checks signed by two members. We never had more than a small amount of money in the fund, until later when we took up a collection for three of us to attend the 1946 convention of the IA.

We got people involved in writing letters to the members, producing a weekly newssheet, folding and stuffing envelopes, whatever they could handle.

At neighborhood meetings, before leaving, we put the furniture back in place if it was moved for the meeting. We tidied up, emptied ashtrays, washed up any glasses we used. Sometimes we took the trash home with us when the meeting was over. At some meetings, it was just the wives, without their husbands there. One woman who knew this issue would attend these meetings and try to answer their questions. She also would ask the wives what they thought was important.

At all the meetings we asked questions. We got people to talk about what was important to them. We answered their questions as truthfully as we could. We tried as best we could to learn what the members wanted to do in a given situation. I guess that is what really set us apart from the regular union bureaucrats – we listened to the members.

We held backyard barbecues for everyone who wanted to come, kids included. We planned these events carefully – strictly fun, if possible. We got people to bring musical instruments to the parties. Sometimes we got musical groups to come and play at the parties for the price of dinner.

Our ultimate object was to get full control of the union into the hands of the rank and file. This meant that contracts with the employers would be controlled by the local union membership. Finances, both the raising of funds and their disbursing, the same. Every bill would go to the floor of the meeting, before anything was done with them. The members would set policy. The spending of even the smallest amount of money would have to be approved by the members. Any misunderstandings would be settled by the membership assembled.

In 1945 we had a very good chance of unseating 'Old 2 per cent' DuVal from the job of business agent. We were running a very fine man, Jesse Sapp, for that office, as well as trying to make a clean sweep of the Executive Board. All the men that we were backing were not up the standard of Jesse, but they would have been an improvement over the men who had been in office so long. All these men had been in office when we were fighting the Labor Board election – in short they were mainly Browne and Bioff backers. We were able to have the local membership pass a vote-by-mail motion that everybody, including the incumbents, saw as a probable way of getting the incumbents out and new officers in.

We knew that education was the key to changing things in the union. That was another way in which we really differed from the regular union bosses. We wanted people to think and get involved in how the union was run.

Notes

1. Joel Seidman, *American Labor from Defense to Reconversion* (Chicago: University of Chicago Press, 1953), p. 144.
2. Joseph Rayback, *A History of American Labor*, (New York: Free Press, 1966), p. 382.
3. Seidman, *American Labor*, pp. 195-210.
4. Ibid., pp. 215-53.

5. Stephen Englund and Larry Ceplair, *The Inquisition in Hollywood* (New York: Anchor/Doubleday, 1980), p. 215.
6. Seidman, *American Labor,* p. 240.
7. *Variety,* 14 January 1942, p. 1.
8. *Variety,* 11 February 1942, pp. 4, 21; 18 February 1942, p. 20.
9. *Variety,* 23 December 1942, p. 7; 19 May 1943, p. 5; 2 June 1943, p. 5; 7 March 1945, p. 7; 13 June 1945, p. 3.
10. IATSE, *Combined Convention Proceedings,* vol. 2, 1942 Convention (page number missing).
11. Ibid.
12. *Variety,* 3 June 1942, pp. 7, 22.
13. *Variety,* 10 June 1942, p. 18
14. *Variety,* 3 December 1941, p. 6; 5 January 1942, p. 62; 21 January 1942, p. 20.
15. *Variety,* 11 November 1942, p. 19; on the matter of the cover sheets on the contracts, see Gene Mailes, Testimony given in the IATSE proceedings against Robert Ames, et al., Los Angeles, 10 March 1946, pp. 1122-4.
16. *Variety,* 28 October 1942, p. 6.
17. *Variety,* 31 March 1943, p. 25.
18. *Variety,* 27 October 1943, p. 34.
19. *Variety,* 20 October 1943, p. 27.
20. *Variety,* 27 October 1943, p. 34.
21. *Variety,* 3 November 1943, p. 6.
22. *Variety,* 8 December 1943, p. 16.
23. Ibid.
24. *Chicago Sun,* 4 December 1943.
25. Hank Messick, *The Beauties and the Beasts,* (publisher and date unknown), pp. 155-6.
26. IATSE, *Combined Convention Proceedings,* vol. 2, pp. 660-1.

5

POST-WAR BATTLES

The Conference of Studio Unions

While Gene Mailes and Irv Hentschel were working with the other Progressives to reform the IA, and Richard Walsh was trying to bolster its sagging image in the wake of increasingly damning revelations regarding Bioff and Browne, the remnants of the United Studio Technicians Guild (USTG) coalesced around the Painters' Local 644 and Herb Sorrell to form the Conference of Studio Unions (CSU). This group represented what amounted to the last major effort by any substantial organization to unseat the IA and its peculiar brand of sweetheart unionism. (In union slang, a sweetheart union is one that serves the need of the owners and the union bosses to the detriment of the rank and file.) Sorrell became the dominant labor leader in Hollywood after the fall of the Browne–Bioff regime. He adopted the same sort of strategy that his predecessor Charles Lessing had used in the early 1930s: namely, to obtain Painters' local-union charters for any non-IA groups seeking an alternative to IA control. The Screen Cartoonists' Guild (SCG), the Screen Publicists Guild (SPG) and the Story Analysts Guild received local Painters' charters from the International Painters' union. The CSU was not a union itself but rather a federation of studio locals established to preserve local autonomy and to form joint strategies to improve the studio workers' welfare. In purely strategic terms, the CSU was a coalition of unions that wanted to remain independent of the IA; and, in much the same way that the IA counted on its projectionists' locals to achieve its goals, they signed a pact to support one another in the event of a strike by any of the locals. One renegade IA local, lab technicians Local 683, also chose to join the CSU.[1]

By 1943, the Carpenters studio Local 944 and IBEW studio Local 40 had joined the CSU; this significantly swelled the organization's ranks. John Cogley, writing in the aftermath of McCarthyism, presented a multi-faceted view of the CSU:

> A number of groups had a stake in the CSU. The AFL craft unions [Carpenters and IBEW] saw it as a rival to their ancient rival, the IA [TSE]. The Communists saw it as a base for party operations in Hollywood. The studios saw it as an IA rival which could sap IA strength. And Herb Sorrell, its fiery leader, may have seen it as a vehicle for his own ambitions.[2]

In *The Inquisition in Hollywood*, Englund and Ceplair, writing twenty-five years after the McCarthy era, painted a more positive portrait of the CSU:

86

The non-Communist, but militant, democratic, and decentralized Conference of Studio Unions (CSU) had, in the four years since its formation in 1941, organized and tantalized the thousands of Hollywood studio workers who either chafed under the IA's sweetheart unionism or were left unorganized because of it. IATSE had been consistently more sensitive to the needs of the studio executives than to those of its rank and file membership. The only gains that IA members won during these years were in the form of payoffs for anti-labor actions, such as voting against the rival United Studio Technicians' Guild in an NLRB election in 1939, or those required to keep pace with gains won by democratic groups such as the CSU. IA people were readily available as scabs, strikebreakers, and thugs.[3]

These two divergent perspectives on the CSU might initially seem contradictory, but the differences are more of emphasis than of substance. Given the producers' long-running strategy of pitting one union against another, it seems logical that the producers would welcome the emergence of the CSU in the wake of the demise of the Browne–Bioff regime. The producers knew that if the IA and the CSU could somehow be drawn into a major confrontation, the energy thus exerted by the unions would divert their attention from bargaining with the producers.

Also, it seems likely that the Communist Party, having failed to penetrate the studios' labor force via the USTG or the earlier Motion Picture Workers Industrial Union, would welcome the CSU as a crack in the IA union fortress. The 1928 Communist International had issued a call for radicalization of labor through the establishment of dual unions to combat bourgeois business unionism, i.e. the brand of unionism practiced by most AFL international unions. Although there is little evidence to suggest direct ties between the CSU and the CPUSA, the two organizations did in fact collaborate on a number of projects during World War Two, when cooperation between the US and the Soviet Union was at a peak. The CSU endorsed a number of Popular Front campaigns such as the Second Front resolution, International Labor Defense, the Hollywood Democratic Committee and the Joint Anti-Fascist Refugee Committee. But the CSU broke with the CPUSA policy of 'no war time strikes' by calling a walkout in March 1945. The CSU and Herb Sorrell were not lock-stepped with the CPUSA at all. The title of Sorrell's biographical oral history held by the UCLA archives – 'You Don't Choose Your Friends' – indicates his own attitude toward accusations by certain elements in Hollywood that he was a card-carrying Communist. No one could fault Sorrell for his dedication in getting better wages for the unions he represented. *Variety* reported in 1943 that the Painters were at that time the highest paid craft workers in the industry. Sorrell was consistently on the cutting edge of wage negotiations and set the standards that the other studio unions were hard-pressed to match.[4]

Events Leading to the 1945 Studio Strike

The most serious and violent labor confrontations in Hollywood started with a seemingly insignificant dispute over the union representation for seventy-seven set decorators. The set decorators had organized the Society of Motion Picture Interior Decorators (SMPID), and had obtained bargaining recognition from the producers in 1939 in the wake of the Supreme Court's affirmation of the Wagner Act. They attempted to gain affiliation with the IA, but were rejected. Still, they managed to get a contract with the producers in 1939 that ran through 1942 and obtained a five-year renewal of their contract in May 1942. The new contract contained the following clause: 'In the event that a majority of the interior decorators and assistant interior decorators in the employ of the producer should designate a different bargaining representative, the name of each representative shall be inserted herein in lieu of the name of the society or the producer may, at its option, declare the agreement null and void.'[5]

In October 1943, the SMPID voted to affiliate with the drafting artists and illustrators in Painters Local 1421. In addition, Painters' charters had been granted to studio publicists and story analysts. The SMPID, by virtue of its Painters' affiliation, joined the CSU as well. On 6 November 1943, the leaders of Local 1421 notified the producers that they wanted to reopen the contract they had signed in 1942. They wanted to discuss with the producers adjustments in certain provisions of the contract. In the following week, the producers responded in writing that Local 1421 should put their contract revision proposals in writing.

The producers and Local 1421 began negotiations on 30 December 1943, and those talks continued into June 1944. During this time the producers dealt with the Local 1421 Business Agent in regard to grievances and other adjustments. On 25 July 1944, the producers made a surprising move in their negotiations with Local 1421: they requested that Local 1421 present a letter from the SMPID indicating a change from independent status to affiliation with Local 1421. This was the beginning of a series of producers' stalling tactics. In early August 1944, the producers further requested that Painters Local 1421 obtain NLRB approval over the set decorators.

Painters Local 1421 followed up on both requests by the producers. The local filed for certification with the NLRB for representation of the set decorators. At that point, IA property workers' Local 44 filed as an intervener in the Local 1421 petition before the NLRB, noting that at least 10 per cent of the set decorators held cards in Local 44; and they called for an NLRB election. Those decorators who held Local 44 cards did so to work in the prop departments when there was no set decorating work to be done. The entire situation was made even more contentious by the fact that the set decorators were the de facto bosses of the property workers on individual productions. Again, we should remember that the key to organizing the studios was to 'begin at the top', to organize supervisors who had influence over who was hired to work under their supervision. Yet, for whatever reason, the IA had not yet organized the set decorators.

The set decorators and Local 1421 felt that they had been 'set up' by the producers, perhaps with the cooperation of IA Local 44. Local 1421 withdrew its petition for certification with the NLRB, claiming that there was no question as to the proper bargaining agent for the set decorators. In a series of written communications between Local 1421 and the producers, it became clear that the producers intended to block Local 1421 from representing the set decorators.

Clearly, the set decorators had joined Local 1421 to gain the extra bargaining leverage of close affiliation with Sorrell and the CSU. According to John

Cogley in *Report on Blacklisting,* Sorrell was something of a folk hero to studio workers for his forthright opposition to Browne and Bioff and for his unveiled hostility to the remnants of their corrupt regime who continued to hold positions of power in the studio locals.[6] Perhaps the most visible member of the old regime was B. C. 'Cappy' DuVal, a man who had been a 'lot checker' under Bioff, meaning that he was in charge of making sure workers on the lots had IA cards and that they had paid their 2 per cent assessments. It was DuVal who had filed the intervener petition on the behalf of IA Local 44 in Local 1421's attempt to gain NLRB recognition for the set decorators. DuVal had taken this action without consulting the members of Local 44. Veterans of the many struggles of the 1930s in the studios saw the situation as business as usual in studio labor relations: top-down control of the workers. The set decorators clearly wanted to affiliate with the Painters but they were being railroaded into IA Local 44.

On 5 October 1944, the CSU unions, then representing some 7,000 workers, began a strike against the major studios, starting at the MGM lot, to gain recognition for the set decorators. The War Labor Board (WLB) intervened in the dispute after one week, ordering the strikers back to work pending a decision by the Board regarding the set decorators' issue. On 7 December, Local 1421 filed a strike notice with the WLB in accordance with the Smith-Connaly Act. After the thirty-day 'cooling-off' period, the local voted overwhelmingly to strike for recognition. On 17 February 1945, WLB arbitrator Thomas Tongue formally requested the producers to recognize Local 1421 as the legitimate bargaining agent for the set decorators until an NLRB election could be conducted.

The producers responded by asking the WLB to set aside Tongue's decision. It was, of course, in the producers' interests to encourage a jurisdictional dispute. If the unions called their members off the job over a jurisdictional dispute, the producers were not required to bargain with the unions involved, and they were also legally entitled to hire strikebreakers to keep their studios operating. *Variety* reported throughout the war and well into 1946 that the major firms had built up a substantial backlog of films, initially out of fear that production might be curtailed by the War Production Board at any point. The producers used this backlog to great advantage during the ensuing round of strikes.

The producers were determined to break the CSU, and it is highly likely that they had decided that the set decorators offered just the wedge for such a destructive blow. By the producers' standards, CSU leader Herb Sorrell was not a 'reasonable' labor leader. According to Sorrell's oral history, the producers had tried to buy him off several years earlier via Willie Bioff and learned that Sorrell would not play ball.[7] Thus they realized that he must be eliminated. The producers were well aware that they could count on the leaders of the various AFL internationals involved (the IA, the IBEW, the Carpenters and the Painters) to fight among themselves; the old divide and conquer strategy was being dragged out for a final showdown with the studio labor groups. The unions would be forced to expend energy that might, under other circumstances, be used to get higher wages and better conditions for the workers.

By the time of the set decorators' dispute, the largest CSU unions – the IBEW and the Carpenters – had been fighting over several jurisdictional issues with the IA for about three decades. Each of the many ineffective juris-dictional compromises reached by the unions was negotiated under the possi-ble threat of total extinction of the weaker union from the studios. Any peace that did exist between the IA and its rivals had been tentative at best. The unions involved in these recurring disputes had built up a substantial backlog of grievances against one another. The paradoxical 'peace during war' declared by the AFL labor unions only served to raise the level of antagonism.

We were beginning to hear about a dispute between the IA and the Set Decorators Guild, an independent guild. The IA had never tried to organize them. The Set Decorators felt that they could increase their strength if they affiliated with a national union. The unions which seemed logical options were the IA or the Painters, which had formed the Conference of Studio Unions. Accordingly, they appointed a com-mittee to investigate the best move to make. The committee sent letters to both organizations and asked for a meeting with each of them to discuss the question of affiliation.

The meeting with the IA was held. The International was represented by one of their Vice-presidents, Carl Cooper, who was also Business Agent of the IA Stagehands Local 33. Cooper struck us as being a decent enough person, trying to hold on to his union job until his retirement, just another AFL politician. Cooper presented the case for the Set Decorators to join the IA. Among the first questions asked was why the IA had made no effort to help organize the set decorators in the first place. Cooper had no answer to this question. He told the committee that if the Set Decora-tors remained independent the IA would leave them alone, but if they joined the Painters, the IA would fight them.

The Set Decorators decided to join the Painters, affiliated with the Conference of Studio Unions. The necessary signatures were gathered and a petition filed with the NLRB for recognition as the bargaining agent. The IA filed an intervener petition on behalf of Local 44 and the IA. This had never been discussed with the membership of Local 44. The Set Decorators were granted a charter by the Painters Union as Local 1421.

Again, note should be taken of the power plays that were at work here. The International Painters Union was no more interested in democratic local unions than the IA was. Herb Sorrell was attracting attention in the International Painters Union as a possible replacement for Lawrence Lindeloff, the President of the International. Lindeloff was not going to do anything that might make Sorrell look good, and he ultimately 'slit Herb's throat'. Also Lindeloff wanted a means of bargaining away any-thing to the IA, anything that Herb Sorrell and the Conference of Studio Unions saw as an advantage. In short they could have been arranging the CSU jurisdictional claims as a bargaining chip to sell Sorrell down the river. We mentioned this idea to Herb once and Herb discounted it: 'Larry wouldn't do that to me!' Irv Hentschel razzed Herb for this, right then, and later – in private, of course.

If the International President of the Carpenters, William Hutcheson, had been able to regain any jurisdiction previously lost, he would have been very happy too. He was no friend of democratically controlled local unions. If Sorrell was forced out of the labor movement, Walsh, Lindeloff and Hutcheson would all benefit. By looking good, he made them look bad.

The International Brotherhood of Electrical Worker (IBEW) and the Plasterers Union were run the same way. Herb Sorrell was like a child wandering around in a snake pit. Arrayed against him and the Conference of Studio Unions were not just the IA and the employers and the people in the unions who had helped the mobs, but also the US Chamber of Commerce and the Merchants and Manufacturers Association. When the cry went up to fight Communism, he even had the 'super-patriots' and many of the fundamentalist church groups against him. All of this was to the benefit of the studios and the reactionary political forces in the country.

The greatest immediate advantage went to the studios. But in the larger scheme of things, the losses of the CSU halted movements toward greater democracy in unions throughout the country. This series of strikes that started with the Set Decorators' issue continued into 1947. Had the CSU won their encounters it would have had a positive effect on the whole US labor movement.

Herb Sorrell was a very hard man for some people to get along with. He had a strong personality that required attention when he entered a room. In appearance, he was only slightly above average height. Obviously he had been an athlete; in fact, he had been a boxer. He had the overweight look of most athletes when they give up their activity. The marks of boxing were on his face; his nose had been broken and had not been set correctly or had been ignored. He was sure of himself physically and gave the impression of a man quite willing, if necessary, to defend himself with gusto – which he had proved on numerous occasions. He was also a politician with a 'hail fellow well met' manner. In addition he was honest and had the quality of inspiring confidence in others. To some people he seemed hard-headed, which was true to an extent. But he never said stupid things if he was approached correctly. Irv Hentschel and I had some heated arguments with him, but found him to be, when the argument was over, quite reasonable and willing to change his mind if we were able to show him that we were right.

The worst thing that could be done to him was to oppose him in public, at a meeting, and most importantly if the person opposing him showed any annoyance with his not seeing things their way. He was aware that he did not have a great education. Any hint of public reference to this was dead wrong.

The wartime 'No Strike' pledge was the first thing that Sorrell and the Communist Party had a real disagreement about. Irv Hentschel's and my position was that war or no war we should not give up any basic American trade union belief. This in effect was Sorrell's view of it also.

When the producers first indicated that they were going along with the IA again, Sorrell saw the same old game starting over, and he was right. He reacted to it as he had before, willing to fight. However, he should not have lunged at the bait, as several people have said. There was a conspiracy between the IA and the Producers Association to wreck the democratic unions in the business and drive the memberships of the CSU into the IA, acting as a company union. This was not successful when they first tried it in 1945, but the second time, in 1946-47, they did it – they broke the only democratically run unions in the studios.

After several of the War Labor Board hearings, at which the IA and the producers stymied the CSU, some of the members of the local branch of the Communist Party had called Herb Sorrell a 'dumb son of a bitch.' This of course got back to Herb. His friends were intensely loyal to him, and felt that he should know this. This created a split between Sorrell and the Party, and weakened the position of the CSU. Yes, Sorrell was bull-headed. Yes, he was taken in by some of the studio heads, but he was still the closest thing there was in Hollywood to an honest labor leader. Irv Hentschel was right when he said to me, 'It was the job of the Party to have stayed with Herb, to have taken his crap, rather than to isolate him and to allow him to isolate himself.'

When we realized that a fight was being seriously discussed, we decided to try to have the question brought up at a meeting of the Local 44 membership. After all, the attempt to get control of the set decorators was being taken in the name of our local union, so we thought it would be a good idea to let the membership know what they were being involved in. The IA's claim was that the set decorators belonged in Local 44. What was more appropriate than letting the members of that local know what was being said were their wishes? We felt that we already knew the answer to that question. We had been asking the members, not only among our little group, but other members of Local 44 with whom we worked. We also called a lot of the members by phone and talked to them about the set decorators' issue.

I saw our chance when I heard in the minutes of a Local 44 Executive Board meeting that DuVal had filed an intervener petition with the War Labor Board to get control of the set decorators. He did this on behalf of the members of Local 44. I rose to ask about this action, suggesting that it would be right if the question were to be discussed now, on the floor of the meeting. The Local 44 President ruled that the matter was in the hands of the International Office, therefore not debatable. I rose again, to a further question; when did the local membership ask for the jurisdiction of the set decorators? The answer was quick: only the International Office, according to the constitution, could decide such questions as jurisdiction.

We did not appeal any of these decisions of the Chair for fear of losing the vote, thus legalizing the action of the Chairman and the International Officers. This tactic strengthened our hand in letting the membership know that we were trying to get input into what the higher-ups were doing.

All the important questions affecting our lives as studio workers were in the hands of the 'goddamn International'! The union didn't trust its own members and the studios didn't trust their own employees. The employers had things rigged so that the only ones they had to deal with were the same men who had run the IA for the mob. That was an advantage the studio bosses were unwilling to give up. When we think of the studio heads, we must include the financial heads of the industry, in New York. It is unquestionable that these gentlemen were tied in with the power elite of the rest of the country.

The talk of a possible strike over the set decorators was becoming louder. We heard that the set designers, members of the Draftsmen and the Architects Guilds, were going into negotiations with the local studios' head negotiator, Pat Casey. Irv Hentschel called me at work and arranged that we meet at Herb Sorrell's office as soon as possible. We were expecting to see him alone. When we got in we saw that there were about six or seven men there and Sorrell told us that these men were members of the negotiating committee for the set designers who were going to see Pat Casey that afternoon. We were introduced to them, and Irv Hentschel said that we had not meant to butt in on anything and suggested that we come back the next day. Herb would not have it so, and asked us what was on our minds. We told them that we had just heard that a possible strike was pending over their contract, and that we had some information that we were not sure they knew about. We told them that DuVal had been making claims that Local 44 should control the set decorators. We thought that they should know that there was an election coming up in Local 44 and that we had a good chance of forcing DuVal out of office.

Herb started to tell us what they were going to do that afternoon. Irv and I were beginning to feel a bit embarrassed about what we were hearing, especially when we saw the expressions on some of the faces there. Finally one of the men spoke up and wanted to know who we were that we should be told what they were going to do at their meeting. He was right, of course. They did not know who we were. Our purpose in going to them was plainly based on the isolation of the groups of studio workers. Herb Sorrell knew what we were trying to get across, but it drove home to him and to us that the whole of studio labor didn't know what each group was doing. We were right in wanting them to know what we were doing relative to the elections in our local. We had not known that they were going in to bargain that afternoon. The point was made both ways. We wished them good luck and left. In *Variety* a couple of days later we read that they had bargained successfully for a pay raise and some conditions had been adjusted, better than they had expected.

In the first week of February the realization was developing that a fight was coming. We called Herb Sorrell and asked for an appointment. We went to his office the next evening at seven. He was alone. We told him that we had heard there might be a strike over the question of the set decorators. The papers were carrying stories every day that the threat was being made at the War Labor Board hearings. We were not so much concerned about that as we were about some of the things that Herb had allegedly said, remarks quoted in the newspapers. He had been quoted as saying that, if the CSU were successful in the strike, it would tear Local 44 apart. We told him that, if he had said such things (we knew he had), we would do our best to stop him, that we would fight him and the CSU. We put it to him cold turkey: was he willing to say that there was no place in the studios for an industrial, industry-wide union, and was he convinced that the IA could not ultimately be that union? Herb was quiet for what seemed several minutes, then answered, 'No, to both questions.'

We became aware that he was under great stress and was rather lonely. In a rambling way he told us how the IA leadership – he singled out DuVal of Local 44 as representative of the whole bunch – were continually trying to extend the IA jurisdiction by whatever means they could. He was sick and tired of it, as were most of the Local leaders, even in the IA itself. Every time they went up to discuss conditions and pay adjustments DuVal would bring up a jurisdictional question. Herb thought that this was a ploy by the IA International to use DuVal in this manner so that when necessary they could 'blame it on the cat' and withdraw from some of his claims. There were jurisdictional disputes that Local 44 had with several IA locals as well as with the CSU unions and guilds. These disputes were blocking labor peace and would continue to do so unless they were settled, once and for all.

Herb realized that he had been too strong in his language on the Local 44 questions. He had been mad at the wrong people. We reminded him that, before Browne had taken over Local 37, we had been trying to settle these disputes, and we thought the idea was still worth trying. The broadest problem facing studio labor, as Herb saw it, was that the local unions were not in charge of their own contract negotiations and the conduct of their own affairs generally. He was, at last, aware of the fact that the International presidents of the Painters, the Carpenters and all the rest of the regular AFL unions that belonged to the Conference of Studio Unions were not favorable to locally controlled unions such as the CSU member locals. He knew very well that the Painters' International President, Lindeloff, saw him as a threat to his own job. And he knew that the studio heads were in favor of dealing with the parent union's heads. But against this he had a group of local unions and guilds that would fight to preserve their democratic gains. It was not the quietest meeting we ever had held with Herb, but when we parted, late in the evening, it was with friendly handshakes.

We ended up at Irv's home talking far into the night. We felt that the way things were going a terrible and destructive fight was possible over the issue facing studio workers. We were not able to see ahead to what was to happen regarding the national anti-communist hysteria that was being planned against all liberals, though. Again Irv was gloomy about the position of the Communist Party relative to Herb Sorrell and the possible position of the Party on the question of the wartime 'No Strike' pledge. The wartime 'No Strike' issue was exploited by the studios and the IA, acting as though this was the first time there had been a wartime strike. This was not true and they knew it. There had been millions of workers out on various strikes during the war, in industries much more vital to the war effort than the motion picture industry.

We never dreamed that the Party position would be 'We all must do whatever is necessary to bring the strike to a speedy end.' This translated as 'Go in and be a scab.' We saw that the pledge was being used to keep wages down and to discredit the militant leaders in the labor movement throughout the country, and that at the same time the employers on the national level were doing their best to disarm the unions of any powers granted by the laws passed during Roosevelt's presidency.

The studio heads were standing fast with the people who had operated with the mobs against the membership of the IA. This should be overlooked? Disregarded? We would do this when the studios started to deal honestly with their own employees. They were not going to give up a single advantage that had accrued to them as a result of their association with the three largest criminal gangs in the country, for what they could make out of it. They later testified that they had saved approximately $15 million in wages by bargaining with the mobs.

If the CSU was forced out on strike, what would be our position? We knew that it was an effort to get the democratic unions out of the studios, to destroy them. IA President Walsh was already threatening to make IA members cross the picket lines and to take the jobs of striking workers. The purpose of the studios standing with the IA was to keep a strike-breaking force present.

Irv Hentschel would frequently come back to the idea that the American Communist Party, as well as the European Communist Parties, had taken their cue from the rise of nationalist sentiments in the Soviet Union. After the collapse of the United Front and the defeat of the Spanish Republic, the Third International was a thing of the past. The Soviet Union, in playing this game was thus turning inward and the idealism of the Third International was being replaced within the Soviet Union with the same ambitions as all of the politicians in the rest of the world – expansion and/or preservation of world empires.

We discussed the efforts of Local 37 to settle the jurisdictional disputes. The centralism of power in the AFL had been like an inexorable force, choking off the democratic process. Had it been naive of us to think that the AFL union could or would have allowed a membership of any local union to have settled any dispute between themselves and another union? These unions had become fiefdoms governed by men who jealously guarded their positions, rights and privileges from the encroachments of any other unions or individuals. The hell of this was that when the International union held the jurisdiction of a job and it went from one union to another, the man on the job did not go with the change of unions. The man who had been doing the work was fired and another man was brought in to do the work. All unions usually have men on the 'out-of-work book', so the change of job went to a new man being brought in. Had the authority rested with the local unions, the adjustment could have been that the man could just change locals and keep his job. That was what we had in mind when Local 37 tried to work it out back in 1939.

The Strike Begins

On 9 March, Irv called me at the Fox studio and said that he had just received a call telling him that a strike was possible for Monday the 12th. I asked him if it was a rumor or definite. He said that it seemed pretty definite. He wanted to know if I felt as he did that, until we knew for sure, there might still be some hope. We agreed to meet outside Herb Sorrell's office again and try one more time.

When we got into the office, we found about twenty people there. All of the leaders of the Conference of Studio Unions. There were several bottles of booze on the table and desk. There were general and cordial greetings. Herb knew that there was something on our minds and asked us what it was. Irv spoke up and told them that we had heard that a strike might be called for the next Monday. Someone broke in with 'What d' ya mean, might be? It's already called!' Both of us muttered a four-letter word, under our breath. Herb offered us drinks, which we accepted. We started to look for a place to sit down. We somehow could not join in the general enthusiasm.

A few minutes later the phone rang and Herb answered it. The call was from Pat Casey from the producers' office. Herb asked for quiet and the room became silent. Herb answered, 'Hello, Mr Casey.' Personally they were on a first name basis. Herb was silent for a few seconds (Casey asking the big question), and then confirmed to Casey that the strike was called for the following Monday, the 12 March. He was silent for a few seconds, then said, 'Thanks, Pat. I am too. Goodbye, Pat.'

The room remained silent for a bit. Then the fact seemed to sink in that there was actually going to be a strike; the strike that had been talked about for so long was now a reality. The talk started to come up again. There were a few voices speaking disjointedly. There was a realization that they should be starting to do something – to get down to business.

Irv and I looked around the office to see who was there. These were all fine, decent, intelligent men whom we liked and admired. The thing that we noticed was that there were no members of the Communist Party there. There was no reason for us to stay, so we had another drink and left, wishing them good luck. We did feel that if the CSU won their objective, maybe we would get some leverage to use in the direction of sanity, as we saw it, in any settlement.

We stopped down on the sidewalk, and stood there for a while. Then we sat down on the curb, between two cars, for over an hour. We were very depressed. We talked about their chances. Herb had plenty of experience, taking part in one prolonged strike, the FMPC strike in 1937, as picket captain, and as the leader of a couple of quickie strikes and a strike against Walt Disney, which lasted nine weeks. We were silent at one point and we could hear the sound of voices and laughter from the office above us. It reminded me of the lines '...there was the sound of revelry by night', the night before the Battle of Waterloo.

So often Irv had said, 'The Party should have stayed close to Herb. They should have taken his crap. That was their job. They should not have isolated him, they should not have let him isolate himself.' He said it again that night. We went over the idea of the drive in unionism toward 'centralism' of power in the AFL unions and its relationship to the CSU's drive for local control of everything that the CSU tried to accomplish. We could feel the opposition to that in the AFL parent organizations of the members of the CSU. We couldn't see a single ray of hope. We did recognize that Herb's personality was an unknown factor; he might just 'luck out', but we really had nothing to hang the idea on.

After the producers refused to abide by the Tongue decision, the CSU concluded that the producers were not acting in good faith and decided to strike the major studios. The CSU local unions made this decision in violation of the no-strike pledge signed by their own International unions at the beginning of the war. The strike began on 12 March and initially involved 7,000 workers. The CSU unions that originally walked out were the four Painters locals, Local 1185 International Alliance of Machinists (IAM), Building Service Employees (BSE), IBEW Local 40, blacksmiths, molders, plumbers and sheetmetal workers. Carpenters Local 946, which was not at the time a member of CSU, walked out in sympathy with the strikers. IA Local 683 (film lab technicians) had by this time withdrawn from the CSU under pressure from IA President Walsh. But Local 683 and thousands of rank and file members of other IA locals did not cross the CSU lines for the first three days of the strike. The major studios were shut down for varying periods of time.[8]

The question of getting down to business in the organization of a strike follows certain general lines, if the strike is controlled by the local membership. At this point the membership takes over, totally, the control of the union and functions through the formation of the strike committee. The daily meetings of this committee are open to any of the membership who wish to attend. Irv and I went to several meetings of the CSU strike committee. Any member of the unions involved was recognized by the chair but could not vote, except at general membership meetings. The input by the members was very valuable.

The regular officers continue to be responsible for the conduct of their regular business, subject to the will of the strike committee, i.e. the rent of the building where the office of the union is located and such business as is sent to them by the strike committee, in addition to such routine business as payment of regular bills. The book-keeping becomes a bit complicated in these conditions, so the strike committee has a separate bank account and establishes other accounts for the welfare fund, the food supply committee and other such committees as necessary. All the paid local officials go off the payroll (not the International officials, of course!). The office workers in the union office still get paid, but if they belong to an office workers' union, then their pay is negotiated, perhaps reduced for a time. Usually the office workers stay, despite the pay cuts, on the strength of their loyalty.

The strike committee then forms the various sub-committees necessary for the conduct of the strike. There is the picket captain and the picket committee. These are some of the same people who are on the strike committee. The picket captain forms the picket roster for each place to be picketed. The picket captain also appoints the safety committee, which tries to control the picketing at each point, sees that the members do their fair share of picketing, and makes sure that the pickets are protected. Also there is the food committee which supplies the pickets with the all-important coffee and sandwiches.

There are often two committees working to get contributions. One is the welfare committee, which takes care of hardship cases relating to such things as rent and food for families in need. The finance committee looks for contributions for the general strike fund. This committee canvases the local merchants, churches, lawyers, doctors and other individuals for people who might be sympathetic and willing to help. These two committees might also get help from the International unions, depending on the circumstances of the internal politics of the unions involved.

In Hollywood there was a 'Hollywood Welfare Association'. The charter for this organization was such that it covered not only striking workers and their families but also people indirectly affected by the strike. That meant anybody, and was therefore tax-exempt. The key to this was that, for instance, a shoemaker was helped by them if he had repaired picket shoes worn out picketing. Others were helped if they had been laid off because of the strike.

Then there was the negotiation committee, with the final responsibility, again, in the hands of the strike committee. This committee is usually elected from the floor by the general membership. There is no ironbound way of forming or conducting these committees; they all grow out of the immediate needs. The important thing is that they are run by the membership, out in the open and subject to a vote on any action by any committee.

The national and International unions can sometimes be of real help, and sometimes not. During this strike the Painters Union sent out to Hollywood a man who was to try to negotiate behind the negotiation committee's back. I witnessed the attempt to 'explain' it to a mass meeting assembled in the American Legion Stadium. Herb Sorrell broke in on him and he explained that he was just trying to find out what the membership would accept in order to end the strike. Herb then told him, publicly, that if he wanted to know what the Conference of Studio Unions would accept, to ask him. The membership roared their approval. The guy was sent home.

The key to all this organizing is to have the members run the strike, and to help the membership learn how to get the job done. Education is the basic idea. I attended some of the strike committee meetings at which as many as 125 members of various committees were attending, and that was just the regular delegates. The other 150 were just active members. A lot of these people got a great education in grass-roots organizing, but then again most of them ended up blacklisted by the studios, too.

These strike procedures were built up over a period of many years, as long ago as the strikes in the 1600s among the textile workers in England. Not all strikes have been run this way. The 1933 IA strike in the studios was run by the International officers. The result was a disaster. That strike was lost within a very few weeks. The CSU strikes of 1945 and 1946 went well into 1947. You could fault Herb for underestimating his enemies, but you could not fault him for lacking the stamina and know-how to carry out a protracted strike.

The Roots of the Hollywood Blacklist
The members of IA Local 44 were caught in the middle of the struggle. Their own union leaders and studio executives ordered them to do the

work of the striking carpenters, painters and set decorators. The centrifugal force of the IA–CSU struggle began spinning off the first of its several hundred victims. The remnants of the old Local 37 IA Progressives were, of course, the first to go. They were the 'premature fascists' of the studio labor scene, the people who had tried to resist the corruption of the Browne and Bioff regime.

Monday morning I slept late, having a noon call. When I went to work I relied on some of the things that Irv and I had talked about Friday night. We would go in across the picket line, refuse to take any job vacated by a striking worker; try to circulate a petition demanding a meeting of Local 44 to get the Local's opinion on what we should do.

We had both been called by several friends as to what we thought we all should do relative to the picket line. We told them what we were going to do, leaving it up to the individuals to decide for themselves. We had no authority to speak for anyone, we were just a committee to try to elect Jesse Sapp (one of our men) to the office then held by 'Old 2 per cent' DuVal. That afternoon, three men who worked on the MGM lot came over to ask me what they should do. Irv and I had already discussed the idea of a petition and I suggested that they circulate it at MGM and the other studios. Irv and I had separately decided to try the same thing. However, Irv had something else to deal with, so he only got to the point of talking to people on the Columbia studio lot where he worked. Of the petitions that were circulated several were invalidated because some of the signatures were on a sheet of paper stapled to the petition. It was a rough start for both sides. Even with people crossing the CSU picket lines, there was no filming done that first day.

Shortly after I got home, Irv called to ask me what had happened at Fox that day. I told him briefly, which was not much. Then he told me what he had been doing. Later several of the men who had witnessed it all told me that it was every bit as good as Irv had told me, even better. Someone called Columbia studio where Irv was working and told him to get right out to Warners, where all hell was breaking loose! He left immediately and got to Warners about ten o'clock. There he found Jesse Sapp and the whole Prop-Miniature Department, of which Jesse was the foreman, out on the street near the backlot gate having an argument with someone Irv had never seen. This man was telling Jesse Sapp and a large group around him to get their asses back into the studio and do as they were told. When Irv joined the crowd, he jumped into the argument with both feet. When he heard Jesse Sapp and the men with him being ordered into the studio, he asked the stranger who he was. When this man said that he was an International representative of President Walsh, Irv asked him to show his card. Irv read it and accepted the fact that he was Roy M. Brewer and was in fact an International representative of the IA. When Brewer saw Irv's card he told Irv, 'I've heard about you. You're expelled!' Just like that, Irv was kicked out of the IA again. It became clear a while later that it had been a mistake to try to handle Irv in that way.

Irv told Brewer several things right there on the street: Brewer had no right to order these men around as if they were little boys. They were quite capable of making up their minds as to what they should do. The fight was not of their choosing. They had not had an opportunity to judge what was the right thing to do in this situation. They had no vote on whether Local 44 wanted the set decorators. The IA didn't even want the decorators until they had organized themselves.

Brewer responded that the IA had jurisdiction of the set decorators. This was not true. In fact, the War Labor Board had initially decided the case in favor of the CSU, but the IA, through DuVal, had appealed that decision. The studios and the IA insisted that only the National Labor Relations Board had the authority to certify a union as the bargaining agent of any workers. In order to get the board into law, Roosevelt had to agree that the decisions of the board would not be binding on the employers. In this case they wouldn't agree to recognize the decision, that Local 1421 was the bargaining agent; thus siding, again, with the IA. In short, the CSU had been forced out.

What Irv could never had known when he approached Brewer on that fateful day was that the result of the argument was that the men of the Warner Bros prop-miniature shop were not allowed to return to work. Brewer took their names and blacklisted them.

We had hoped, in vain, that there might be a groundswell of support from IA members to refuse to cross the CSU picket lines, but phone calls before the lines were set up indicated no widespread feeling toward such an action. This could well have forced a settlement very early. We had to recognize the fact that most of the IA men were crossing the CSU picket lines. If we had refused to cross, we would have been isolated, cut off from the other members of our local. We didn't want to cross the line but for the time being we had to.

Two days after the start of the strike, IA President Walsh, working against the CSU, ordered all IA projectionists to stand ready to picket the producers' theater chains if the producers agreed to the CSU's demands for recognition for the set decorators. This was all the producers needed to become the 'victims' of jurisdictional warfare.

On the third day of the strike, Walsh ordered all IA members to return to work so that the studios could continue to operate. The vast majority of IA workers did cross the lines as did members of the three studio talent guilds: the Screen Actors Guild (SAG), the Screen Writers Guild (SWG) and the Screen Directors Guild (SDG). SAG leaders polled their members by mail after making it clear that the union had a nine-year contract with the producers that contained a no-strike clause and that a vote to respect the CSU picket lines was a vote for no contract. The SWG and the SDG were initially sympathetic to the strike, but they caved in after the SAG vote and returned to work. The producers publicized the fact that they had a nine-month backlog of unreleased features. They also pressured the three white-collar unions affiliated with the Painters – the Screen Office Employees Guild (SOEG), the Screen Publicists Guild (SPG) and the Story Analysts – to return to work or face lawsuits for breech of contract.[9]

Meanwhile the War Labor Board (WLB) sent mixed signals to the strikers. WLB Chairman George W. Taylor threatened to take the Local 1421 case off the WLB docket until the strike ended, but another WLB spokesman claimed that the board had adopted a wait-and-see attitude, an attitude that was well-suited to the producers' needs. The rationale for the WLB was that unless the production of army and navy training films was curtailed the board would not intervene. However, when the producers dismissed an IA man who happened to be a veteran of the US Marine Corps for his refusal to do the work of the striking carpenters, the Veterans' Bureau began an investigation of the producers' actions. This particular case is worth noting because it is an early example of much of the rhetoric in speeches and leaflets during the strike, as both sides attempted to 'wrap themselves in the flag' wherever possible, i.e. to defend their cause based on veteran status. The War Manpower Commission also wanted to know whether the producers had brought in strikebreakers without proper availability certificates.[10]

Handling Walsh's affairs on the West coast was his newly appointed Hollywood representative Roy Brewer. Brewer had been a projectionist in Lincoln, Nebraska, before moving up in the ranks of the AFL state labor organization to become the President of the Nebraska state AFL organization at the age of 24. During the war Brewer had worked for the War Production Board in Washington, D.C., handling labor grievances for people working in defense plants. With the war coming to a close, Brewer realized that he could never again go back to being a projectionist in Nebraska. He had tasted power and responsibility and wanted more. He snapped at the chance to be Walsh's personal representative in Hollywood.[11] His impact on Hollywood labor relations can hardly be overestimated. Shortly after the strike began, Brewer began issuing daily bulletins to workers and strikers explaining the IA's position on the strike. These early bulletins were mostly informational in character. By late April, however, Brewer had changed the tone of his strike bulletins. John Cogley described Brewer's new approach in his *Report on Blacklisting*:

> The question was: 'Is This a Union Labor Strike?' The answer was 'No!' The leaflet went on to explain that the strike 'must be a result of a long-range program instituted many years ago by a certain political party for one reason: To Take Over and Control Organized Labor in the Motion Picture Industry'. The strike was described as a 'political strike.' Sorrell was charged with being 'sympathetic and definitely interested in the communistic idea.'[12]

Brewer, along with IA publicist Ed Gibbons (originally brought to Hollywood by Browne and Bioff), accused prominent members of the Hollywood liberal community of being Communists. They produced no evidence to back their claims beyond guilt by association, i.e. signing anti-fascist petitions, contributing to left-wing or merely liberal organizations, etc. Ironically, in the early days of the strike the US Communist Party agreed with Brewer that the strike was unpatriotic. The CPUSA was still committed to a policy of 'no strikes during wartime'. Brewer explained this anomaly in an interview in 1984 with the comforting thought that 'they' (meaning the 'international communist conspiracy') are not perfect, that 'they' sometimes get their signals crossed.

A couple of days after the start of the strike, Irv Hentschel heard that Lou Goldblatt had come down to Hollywood from San Francisco, to see Herb Sorrell. Lou Goldblatt was an official of the Longshoremen's Union and a

close associate of Harry Bridges. He and Herb had been friends for a long time. All sincere labor leaders as well as many of the rank and file of the unions, on the West coast especially, were concerned about the strike. The fact that Goldblatt came to see Herb was another indication of how isolated Herb had become. There were many actions that had not occurred to the CSU leadership which should have been taken. Herb and the rest of the CSU personnel had failed to take into consideration the other unions and guilds, and their feelings toward the strike.

One of the results of the Goldblatt meeting with Herb was that Herb called Irv and asked that Irv and I come to his office that night about seven o'clock. This was the night before the meeting that had been called by Walsh to try to sell Local 44 on the idea of becoming scabs. It was made plain that no business would be conducted at this meeting. We would just be allowed to hear Mr Walsh talk. As usual we met on the sidewalk by Herb's office and went up together. We found Herb there all alone. He called us to see if we would help him compose a letter to the IA membership in the studios, explaining the facts of the strike. He explained that the members of the IA should know that the CSU was not going to wreck the IA locals or do anything beyond trying to settle the whole dispute to the satisfaction of all of the rest of the studio workers. This was a terrible shock to both Irv and me: that Herb was so isolated that he had to turn to Irv and me at a time like this, when all hell was breaking around this strike, and that Lou Goldblatt had to ask him what had been done to involve the non-striking studio workers, or to explain the issues as the CSU saw them at this late date.

We started to compose a letter and worked for about a half hour. What the three of us put together was stilted and awkward. There was a pause of a few minutes. Suddenly Herb said, 'Why don't you two write this up and sign my name to it? You both know what I would say. I've seen your work on several of the letters that you two have written.' We had to admit that the three of us were getting nowhere, so we agreed to do it. We told Herb that there would be no time to change the letter if he didn't like it because Walsh had called a meeting of Local 44 for the next day at the Women's Club, on Hollywood Boulevard, near La Brea Avenue. If it was not satisfactory, there would be no time to rewrite it.

Herb said that he was quite sure that we would be OK with it. We discussed how many copies we should make. We decided that there should be about 6,000 of them run off. It was to be my job to cover deliveries to all except the Women's Club meeting. I was to take them to the studios on Monday morning and the pickets there would be expecting them and would pass them out. The next question was Herb's signature. We had him sign several times on a sheet of paper so that we could trace it onto the bottom of the stencil master.

We left Herb alone in his office and drove to Irv's home. Herb had arranged for someone to pick up the letters that would be distributed at the meeting of Local 44. With these things taken care of, we didn't have anything to do but get down to business, writing and grinding it out on Irv's mimeograph machine. It took all night. When Irv had been black-listed in 1937, he had started a small business, turning out mimeograph machines. He sold them to small businesses and to restaurants for their menus. By this he had kept his family fed and clothed. He made one for himself and for such things as we were doing. There was only one thing wrong with it – it had no motor, so we had to take turns cranking it, far into the night.

When we finally finished, I went home and got a couple of hours sleep and a quick shower. Irv picked me up in time to get to the meeting and we received our copies of the letter from Herb. We accepted them and tried to look as if we were reading it for the first time. We saw a couple of sentences that we should have rephrased, but generally we were satisfied with what we had done. This episode indicated that there was a great trust among the three of us.

The 27 March regularly scheduled meeting of Local 44 was a night to remember. It was reminiscent of Clifford Odets' play *Waiting for Lefty,* which takes place in a Teamsters meeting hall. The play calls for a large number of actors to play members of the union, sitting there in the audience. It concerns a taxicab local union ousting a group of gangsters, there in the meeting hall. It is a loud, raucous, thrilling play to witness. Irv and I had both seen it years ago. I was also reminded of Whitman's lines about the French Revolution, 'their feet in the ashes and the rags, their hands clutched to the throats of kings, half startled at themselves.'

The membership of Local 44 had fought back.

The following is a copy of the minutes of the meeting, changed by me to reflect who really made motions at the meeting. (DyVal had the minutes changed after they were recorded to provide hanging evidence against us!) Irv and I congratulated ourselves on the fact that we had not been called upon to make any motions. I seconded one motion, to keep it alive. The membership did the rest themselves. The only exception to this was when Lou Hafley turned around to me when his motion was ruled out of order, and asked me, 'What the hell do we do now?' I told him, 'Appeal the decision of the chair'. He did that and the membership was off and running again. Neither Irv, Bob Ames, Jesse Sapp nor I had to do anything else that night. The efforts of the officers of the local to reject the motions presented by the members show plainly what we were up against.

The 'approved' Minutes are as follows:

Meeting was called to order by President Goodwin at 8.30. Officers present: Goodwin, O'Connor, Hill, D. Thompson, H. Smith, Losey, J. Thompson, Dailey, Lee Arrowsmith, Clifford, Hoffman. Officers excused: DuVal, Northrop, Powers, Madigan. Also present: International Vice Presidents Cooper, Barrett, and International Representative Brewer.
The Chair announced the deaths of Brothers Wm. Douglas on 23 March 1945, and Chris Christensen on 24 March 1945. The Members stood in silence in respect for the departed Brothers.
Minutes of the Membership Meeting of 25 February 1945 were read. President stated, if there were no errors or omissions they would be approved as read. So ordered.

Moved by Brother Hafley and seconded by Brother Chadsey to suspend the regular order of business in order to discuss the present dispute in the studios between Local 44 and some of the other studio Locals. The Chair ruled the motion out of order in as much as the entire matter was in the hands of the International. Brothers Hafley and Gotten appealed the decision of the Chair.

Vice President O'Connor took the Chair and stated, 'Shall the decision of the Chair be sustained?'

Chair in doubt on a voice vote and due to the number unable to get a seat requested a hand vote, which resulted in Aye 109, No 155. The decision of the Chair was not sustained.

The President took the Chair and put the motion on suspending the order of business. Hand vote, Aye 183, No 77. Motion carried by more than the necessary two-thirds vote.

Moved by Brother Koontz and seconded by Brother Mailes that members should stay in their own department. President ruled motion out of order as such matters were now in the hands of the International and the motion conflicted with a ruling of the International President Walsh.

Discussion continued.

Moved by Brother Koontz and seconded by Brother Magginetti that members of Local 44 are not to work out of the jurisdiction of their craft. The Chair ruled motion out of order as it conflicts with orders from the International.

Brother Mailes and Koontz appealed the decision of the Chair.

Vice President O'Connor took the Chair and stated, 'Shall the decision of the Chair be sustained?' Motion lost, decision of Chair not sustained.

Moved by Brother Carruthers and seconded by Brother Kyffin that the question before the House be tabled to the next meeting. Hand vote, Aye 94, No 114.

Brother Irwin Hentschel and Brother Sapp moved the previous question. Hand vote, Aye 117, No 76. Motion lost as two-thirds vote necessary.

Discussion continued on main motion.

The President stated that if the main motion carried, he would protest to the International President.

International Vice President Cooper read Art. 7, Sec. 14 of the International constitution and by laws.

The main motion pertaining to the members working only in their own jurisdiction was put by the Chair. Hand vote, Aye 106, No 64.

When the count was announced, International Representative Brewer stated that the order of the International President supersedes any action of the body.

Regularly moved and seconded to adjourn. Meeting adjourned at 11.40 p.m. [13]

The first thing about this copy of the minutes is the continuous use of the phrase, 'in the hands of the International'; then the use of the 'hand vote'. The voice vote was never in doubt, it was overwhelming. The use of the hand vote was to make the dissenters expose themselves to the officers of the Local and International officers present. The corruption we were faced with was based on 'job fear', and the hand vote was aimed at creating this kind of fear in the members.

Several times during the meeting questions were directed to Roy Brewer. Whenever this happened, his reply was that he would answer all questions to him before the vote was taken; he always wanted to have the last word before any votes were taken.

It was quite obvious to us later that there were going to be charges filed against Irv and me and possibly also against Bob Ames. We considered it only remotely possible that charges would be filed against Jesse Sapp. Had we been allowed to see the Minutes as altered by Brewer or DuVal, we would have been sure that charges were going to be filed against the four of us. When we saw these Minutes at the time of the first session of the trial, we understood how long the expulsion had been planned. We were all, except Bob Ames, recorded in the Minutes as movers or seconders of motions, when we had not opened our mouths, except me, during the whole time of the meeting. Our names had to be in the Minutes in order to give some appearance of credence to the request by the Local officials to have the International take over Local 44 and run it by fiat.

During this early part of the strike Walsh made threats to take over as many locals as necessary to force the rank and file to become scabs. This threat was made in all seriousness and we knew that it could be done. We had learned that if we thought it was impossible that Walsh or Brewer would take a particular step, then that was just the thing they did next. They were ruthless and incredibly corrupt.

As the meeting went on, the membership became more and more sure of itself and more and more insistent on having its way. Brewer had made quite a splash when he arrived. Resentment against him and his tactics was strong. His continual use of the word 'enemies' of the Alliance when referring to the men in the striking unions offended many of the members. This 'bloodthirsty hero' had spent the war behind a desk in Washington, D.C. He was a pain in the ass to the men who had been in the service, and to the rest of the members who had the ability to think for themselves.

Finally, when the previous question on whether we should be taking the jobs of the strikers was moved, the President of Local 44 told the members that if the previous question was voted on affirmatively we would not be able to hear what Brother Brewer had to say. Someone yelled, 'We've heard enough from him already.' We knew the die had been cast! As the final business of the meeting was concluded, Vice-president Cooper was reading something from the IA constitution. As we were on our way out of the meeting room door, we saw Brewer talking earnestly to several of the local officers. We guessed that there was going to be another 'takeover'. We were right.

Brewer was calling the present members of the Executive Board into an emergency meeting. Brewer, of course, was there as International representative and so was International Vice-president Billingsley. Barrett had gone home. Local 44 President Goodwin presided.[14] The business of the meeting was recorded as follows:

> President Goodwin stated that he was very disturbed over the action of some of the members at the meeting and had prepared a telegram to be sent to International President Richard F. Walsh and requested their approval or disapproval. The secretary read the telegram as follows: 'At a meeting tonight dominated by members whom we consider to be disloyal to the I.A.T.S.E., a motion was passed that the members of Local 44 should not work out of the jurisdiction of their craft. In view of the emergency confronting Local 44 and the International, we recommend that you immediately declare a State of Emergency and place Local 44 under the supervision of the International office.'
> It was moved by Brother Dailey and seconded by Brother Hoffman that the wire be approved and be sent at once. The motion carried unanimously.
> Meeting adjourned at 1:15 A.M.
> Note: Wire in Hollywood Western Union office at 1:55 A.M. March 28, 1945.

The hearing to determine if the State of Emergency did in fact exist was held the next afternoon. Present were the Executive Board of Local 44, all of whom had requested the International officers to suspend the constitution of Local 44 and run the union. Also present were Harlow G. Cooper, Vice-president of the International, who had already approved the takeover; Floyd Billingsley, also a Vice-president of the International, who had approved the takeover the previous night; Roy M. Brewer, who had enthusiastically urged the takeover and was to conduct the hearing, and would make the decision of recommendation to the International that the local be blocked from further action, and the International's lawyer, Mike Luddy, of the law firm of Breslin, Bodkin and Luddy.

The minutes of the hearing state that the officers had tried to contact someone who had opposed the takeover, so that they could be present and speak against the Executive Board's action. It was known where we were working and that we would have been glad to appear in opposition to the action. Had one of us been there, at least the minutes would have read a little differently.

Brewer gave an opening statement to the effect that disloyal elements in Local 44 had packed a meeting and jammed through a motion that was against the wishes of the membership of Local 44. The officers of Local 44 were appearing before Brewer to allow him, as an International representative, to determine if an emergency did actually exist in Local 44. Brewer then stated:

> The Officers (of Local 44) are now given an opportunity to establish that the facts reported to the International President are not as represented and a State of Emergency does not, in fact, exist. Do the

106

Officers of Local 44 desire to present evidence to the effect that the facts creating the emergency are nonexistent, or false?
No Response.[15]

The hearing took twenty minutes. Upon hearing nothing to the contrary, as an International representative of the President of the IA and with the authority vested in him Roy Brewer declared that a State of Emergency did in fact exist and that the Local was now run by the International. Further, that as the International representative he had the authority to run Local 44. Whereupon he appointed all the officers to serve in their present capacity. In short everybody who was on the payroll of the local was to stay on the payroll of the local.

As to the legality of this, it must be remembered that the IA convention in 1936 had voted this constitution into law applicable to the International union. This was the constitution that was drafted by the mob's lawyers working to secure the position of George Browne. Brewer held a hearing as set forth in the law of the union. In that event the courts would not interfere.

Notes

1. John Cogley, *Report on Blacklisting: I, The Movies* (New York: Fund for the Republic, 1956), pp. 55-60
2. Ibid., p. 60.
3. Stephen Englund and Larry Ceplair, *The Inquisition of Hollywood* (New York: Anchor/Doubleday, 1980), pp. 212-13.
4. *Variety*, 6 January 1943, p. 52.
5. This quote and the background material to the set decorators' strike is based on archival notes in 'Hollywood Studio Strike', a set of notes and pamphlets in the archives at the UCLA Library, Los Angeles, CA.
6. Cogley, *Report on Blacklisting*, p. 55.
7. Herbert K. Sorrell, 'You don't choose your friends', Oral History collection, UCLA archives, pp. 30-1.
8. *Variety*, 14 March 1945, pp. 1, 18; 21 March 1945, pp. 2, 19.
9. *Variety*, 14 March 1945, p. 1; 21 March 1945, p. 2; see also 'Hollywood Studio Strike' files, UCLA.
10. *Variety*, 14 March 1945, p. 18; 21 March 1945, p. 19; 28 March 1945, p. 17.
11. Interview with Roy Brewer, 1984, Studio City, CA.
12. Cogley, *Report on Blacklisting*, pp. 64-5.
13. From the transcript of IATSE proceedings againt Robert Ames, *et al.*, Los Angeles, 10 March 1946, pp. 230-3.
14. Ibid., pp. 81-6.
15. Ibid., pp. 121-7

6

THE IA BLACKLIST

Firings

At Warners and other studios workers were ordered by management to work in the studios' woodmills, recently abandoned by the striking Carpenters. Bill Magginetti, who had worked at Warners, explained in a later internal IA trial that there was initially a great deal of solidarity among members of Local 44 who worked at Warners. They nearly all refused to do the work of the CSU strikers. He explained, however, that Warners' management developed special tactics for dealing with worker solidarity, starting with the most respected property workers.

> The property masters, who were men of long standing there, 18, 20, 21, and 22 years in the business, and who do nothing but executive work, very fine men, brilliant men, because of their stand [in refusing to work out of their jurisdiction and replace striking carpenters in the mills], they were penalized, and every day they went up on the floors on top of the building, four floors, a big building that contained about 80 spittoons, and those men were compelled to clean those spittoons. They put them on a dolly and pushed it through the building every day, and they cleaned those spittoons. They did all the dirty work around the studio. Wherever there were dirty boxes to be moved, they were asked to do that work, and finally, when they were asked to go in and dress sets, why, these men somewhat had their spirit broken, and they succumbed to the request, and some of them did do that.[1]

Workers who questioned the authority of the producers or the IA soon found themselves out of work: both the producers and the IA blacklisted them. The executive board of Local 44 sent letters to Irv Hentschel and Gene Mailes notifying them that they were expelled. Shortly afterwards they, along with several other members of Local 44, were fired by the studios. The rebellion in the IA studio locals spread. Set electricians of IA Local 728 demanded that their business agent cease supplying strike-breakers, and later they refused to admit the replacement electricians brought in by their business agent.

Gathering Support

The progressives in the IA fought back against Walsh and Brewer. They issued a mimeographed letter condemning forced conscription of IA workers as strike-breakers and called a mass meeting at Hollywood's American Legion Stadium on 30 March 1945.

108

A few days later Irv Hentschel went to a meeting of the CSU strike committee. He called me to say that several of the people there and on the studio lots had advised him that what we were doing was not getting enough attention and was not as well understood as it should be. He suggested that it might be a good idea to hire the American Legion Stadium and hold a public meeting to make known to all studio workers, to the public and to the press what we were trying to get across.

We didn't yet have a consensus on what should be done to settle the strike. But we did know that when one union went on strike or was forced out by a conspiracy between the employer and another union, it wasn't right to force men to take the jobs of those people out on strike. It had to stop sometime and right then seemed to be that time. We got together the next afternoon at the office of the Stadium and wrote a check to cover a public meeting the following week.

We called as many of our group in Local 44 as we could get in touch with and they all approved of the idea. Then we called a couple of reporters whom we knew and told them about the meeting. By this time the Committee to Elect Jesse Sapp to the office of Business Agent of Local 44 was growing far beyond a mere election committee. It had grown into a bit of a revolution trying to get people to stand up for basic American trade union principles. We were a going concern. People in the Lab, Costumers, Camera and Sound Locals were helping us. The possibility of a series of takeovers by the IA International of these locals also was a very real threat. Of course, some of the officers in the Sound and Camera locals were in fear of having their locals taken over and then losing their jobs in the shuffle. We drafted a handbill to be distributed at all the studios and arranged to have it distributed. The reaction from the IA and Brewer was fast and furious. We started to receive phone calls telling us we were liable to have charges filed against us. A couple of Los Angeles policemen delivered a letter from Brewer to Irv at his home, telling us not to hold the contemplated 'outlaw meeting'. As we had said so often, everyone who should have been with us was against us.

Organizing the meeting was at times difficult. We were unable to get anyone from either the Camera or Sound Locals to speak. In the Lab Locals we had several willing to talk. From the Costumers Local no one was able to make it. When it came to the IA Electricians Local, we had one, George Merhoff Jr, the son of an old miner who had been involved in the Colorado mine strikes of the early 1900s. The electricians had been one of the main sources of strength in the IA Progressives; where were they now? From the Grips Local no one came. There was a Party member who was in that local, but he kept the Party line. The group in Local 44 was the backbone of the movement against strike-breaking, although there was a great deal of support from the rank and file of most of the locals.

We got together the night before the meeting and agreed to the idea that we should tell of our anger at being expected to take the jobs of striking workers for any reason. This practice had been going on long enough; now was the time to stop it. This old AFL policy had never benefited the employees, only the employers. We knew that, in holding

109

the meeting, we were skating on thin ice. This was the first thing we did that might have been grounds for charges against us. Well, so be it. We figured that if any charges were filed it would include only Irv, Bob Ames and me. We felt that we might have real promises of help if charges were filed against us. It was an iffy assumption, but it was all we could do at the time. By this time I was Acting Secretary, without pay, of the group and was to act in this capacity for the rest of the time. We had no president.

On the night of the meeting, Brewer got several of the officers of the various locals of the IA to wait outside the stadium, identify any of their members and order them not to go in to the meeting under any circumstances. This made many of the members madder than they had been. There was a good crowd there and when it came to collection time we got a wonderful response; we had our teenage children take up the collection. There were quite a few members of the talent guilds there. We were able to get eight members of the various locals as speakers. The opposition to the actions of Walsh and Brewer was mounting. The *Hollywood Reporter* printed this story of the meeting:

> Charging that any wrecking of the IA is being done by the International heads, who insist members strike-break, instead of by IA members who disobey such orders, nine card holders climbed into the Legion ring Friday. They were Dick Holman, Sam Callen, Gene Mailes, George Stoica, Irwin Hentschel, Bob Ames, Carl Gidlund, Jesse Sapp and George Merhoff, Jr. They represented Locals 44, 728 and 683. Speaking informally, the men simply expressed personal stands. Stoica received a telephone threat before leaving for the meeting.[2]

The write-up in *Daily Variety* said:

> More than 1,500 I.A.T.S.E. members attended a rank and file mass meeting Friday night at which Bob Ames, prop maker at Republic, presided. Speakers included Carl Gidlund, Jesse Sapp, George Merhoff, Jr., Dick Holman, Gene Mailes, Sam Callen, Bert Miller, Irwin Hentschel, and George Stoica. It was stressed that the meeting was not to violate orders of the International to work in other jurisdictions, but to explore possibility of finding some way of reaching agreements on jurisdictional matters and terminate the studio walk-out. Speakers stressed there was still the basis for settlement and that it could be handled more quickly and more satisfactorily by the rank and file membership than by Walsh and the International. With tears flowing down his cheek Dick Holman, a war veteran, told of his experience in fighting for democracy, 'only to return and find this'. Many I.A.T.S.E. business agents attended the meeting in an unofficial capacity.[3]

George Stoica, a member of Local 44 who had attempted to unseat the unresponsive leaders of the local, spoke about his own feelings. He had worked, until his suspension for supporting the strike, as the head of the hardware shop at Warners.

If you folks expect high class stuff, you are going to be disappointed. I'm not going to talk separately on local autonomy, jurisdictional disputes, dictatorships, phony charters or a hundred other things that have popped up. I'm going to take the whole mess and boil it down to where we can digest it. We have made too much progress in the last ten years. We're getting too much money for our work. Our hours are too short. We have demanded and received too much in the way of working conditions. Now with all these new contracts we have asked for and got – for the first time – two weeks' vacation with pay! How do you think the producers feel about it? Do you think for one moment they are happy over the fact that we've got a few bucks in the bank, a handful of defense bonds under the mattress, or that we can put in a day's work and still come home and play with the kids for an hour or so, or that we can take a week or two and go fishing once a year? Do you think they're happy to see thousands of people walking around with their heads up and oozing with independence?

They have, no doubt, lost plenty of sleep over those questions, wondering what those guys on the back lots were going to ask for next, and how to go about blocking it. The man who is independent can't be easily handled. Therefore, that independence must be destroyed! But how? They knew that it couldn't be done as long as one man trusted another and they both stood united; they must be set against each other. Fellowship must be destroyed. Distrust and fear must take its place. An excuse must be found to tear up those new contracts. Unreasonable unions must be broken down. The old levels of pay and hours must be re-established.

It all adds up to the old struggle between capital and labor. I know that it sounds Communistic as the devil, but by God, it's the truth![4]

George Stoica was out on a limb in March 1945, but he would not be alone out there for long. As the strike progressed, increasing numbers of workers found themselves forced to choose between two unpleasant alternatives: obedience to the producers and the IA or permanent blacklisting.

We got together the next day to see where we might be in the whole picture. It was not encouraging to think about it. There was a lot of excitement about what was happening. Several others of the group dropped over to Irv's home and we pushed it around for a while. The only thing to do was to wait and see. It was obvious to Irv and me that this bunch of men was not just with us out of loyalty to Irv and Jesse. It was firmly grounded in basic trade unionism. The questions they brought up for discussion were too fundamental for anything so unsure as friendship or loyalty.

Irv and I got together the following day and talked some more. We both had been getting calls about the meeting, all of it encouraging. Irv was worried about the numbers that had been at the meeting. Brewer and his little helpers had been able to talk too many into not entering the hall Friday night. That led to a further discussion of the Communist Party on the strike. Irv felt that the Party's lack of support had been one of the reasons that the Legion Stadium was not filled to overflowing. Irv said that the Party attitude toward the no-strike pledge was right, up to a point. The idea that the strike should be ended was right up to a point. Where we differed on the question was that, war or no war, we could not see the wisdom of sacrificing the basic American trade union principle of the right to strike.

In the studios we had seen the various shop workers marched en masse to the Carpenters' mill and, with the IA officials present, the foremen ordered the men to work in the mill, to take the jobs of the strikers. Those who hesitated to do as ordered were singled out for threats, right there on the job, in front of everyone. Very few were fired immediately; they were kept on the job for a day or so, then dropped 'off till called'. It took exceptional men to stand up against their union officials and the employers, with both threatening them with what amounted to being blacklisted unless they became scabs. The threat from Brewer was that if they didn't follow orders they were charged with disloyalty to the IA.

Irv said that he had been informed that there was a hell of a fight going on in the Communist Party about this issue. He had been told that some of the members were trying to get an expanded Party meeting called to settle the question. An expanded meeting was one that would include regular Party members, ex-members and as many other people who were liberals and friends to get others views to help them to see things in perhaps a different light.

Many trade unionists of long standing were shocked at the division on the question of whether to become scabs, regardless of the war, or whether the Carpenters union had or had not scabbed during the IA's 1933 strike. They knew that there had been a history of collusion between the employers and the IA, particularly in the era of Browne and Bioff. Men like Joe Schenck, Chairman of the Board of 20th Century-Fox in the 1930s and 40s, would rather deal with the leading criminals in the country than their own employees. These studio bosses and their stooge union were clutching the flag and 100 per cent Americanism to their breasts and calling anyone who didn't agree with them Un-American.

Following the meeting at the Women's Club, many members of the IA studio locals were getting more angry at being treated like bad children. They were fed up with the way that the IA was acting to break the strike without any reference to the membership at large. It was such a typically dictatorial style, the same one used by Browne and Bioff. The Lab, Costumers, Camera and Sound Locals were being told that their locals would be taken over if they made any criticism of the way the IA was running things. Walsh said that the IA had charter applications to issue if any of them got out of line. The Lab and Costume workers were really angry about what was being done in their names.

However, two pseudo-liberals, Herb Aller, Business Agent of the Camera Local, and Harold Smith, Business Agent of the Sound Local, didn't want anything to interfere with their jobs. We were quite sure that their own members resented being told that they were supposed to be strike-breakers; however, Aller and Smith were looking out for themselves. They were using us to protect themselves. We considered that it was still the thing to do, to keep faith with the idea of democratic control of the union. Smith and Aller counted for nothing in the larger context of basic trade unionism.

After the mass meeting at the Legion Stadium, Edwin Hill, Secretary of Local 44, declared the meeting an 'outlaw gathering'. The International had control of Local 44. Brewer wanted the International to have better control of the dissidents than the local leaders could provide. Gene Mailes, Irv Hentschel, Bob Ames and others responded by forming a 'Committee of 21' to try to settle the various jurisdictional disputes without International union intervention. Gene was the secretary of this committee. A number of courageous IA members joined the protest of Brewer's tactics and demanded that local autonomy be restored to Local 44. Following the 30 March mass meeting many members of IA studio laborers' Local 727 refused to cross the CSU lines or to do the work of the strikers.[5]

On 4 April 1945, the producers distributed an unsigned mimeographed letter to the striking workers, informing them that they would be discharged unless they returned to work immediately. In the following week Walsh chartered new locals to replace striking carpenters, painters and machinists. Strike-breakers were hired to take the jobs of the CSU workers. Walsh sought to recruit returning war veterans as strike-breakers, but the Veterans' Bureau blocked this move.[6]

The CSU did not appear to be the underdog at the outset of the struggle. The CSU strike had the support of the International offices of the Carpenters and the IBEW, two of the largest AFL International unions. This numeric strength allowed their leaders to influence the AFL to act on their behalf. On 8 May, the Executive Council of the AFL voted to order Walsh to revoke the 'phony charters' issued in the previous month. Walsh initially chose to ignore the order.[7]

Beginning a few weeks after the strike started, various ideas for a formula for settling the strike were discussed. The Local 44 progressives along with leaders of the Lab and Costumers locals, were trying to come up with a formula for settling jurisdictional disputes at the local union level. Finally, Ted Ellsworth of the Costumers Local 705 brought the matter to a head by calling for a meeting at the office of Screen Office Employees Guild (SOEG). We considered this to be neutral ground, and a lot of members of the IA local unions came. Here is what we hammered out, starting at the point that we had reached with the Local 37 Board of Governors back before we were taken over and split up in 1939:

1. Each craft would elect a three-member delegation to a Jurisdiction Committee.
2. All unions and guilds working in the studios would participate in the negotiations.

3. All national union organizations would accept any agreement that was worked out by a bargaining committee of a local union and approved by members of that local. (This was the hard one.)
4. The man or woman who had been working on the job would become a member of the union to which the job was assigned.

This idea was what the Local 37 leadership had been working toward. It was quite plain that the methods that had been tried over the years by the various AFL unions were not designed to settle such disputes in favor of the men and women on the jobs. The standard practice of the old-line AFL politicians was organizing via strike-breaking – by sending in new workers to take the jobs of striking workers. This was done particularly after the Committee for Industrial Organization (CIO) was formed. This was when the AFL was so desperate for favors from the employers that they opposed unemployment insurance.

The main failure of the AFL was that they did not organize the unorganized – they tried to steal jurisdiction from each other. Or, worse, they led their members into company unions. John Lewis, the first President of the CIO, called the President of the AFL, William Green, 'Sitting Bill'. He thought the AFL was 'a loose alliance of jealous little barons'. He had it just right.

What chance did the leader local union who wanted to have some control over the right to bargain have against these 'jealous little barons?' It is no wonder that, when these gentlemen invited a man like Herb Sorrell to sit down with them, as trusting as Herb was, they slit his and his members' throats.

This plan that we had hammered out was immediately accepted by the CSU, but turned down by the IA and the studios. There was a hard core of AFL leaders who were spooked up by the phony anti-communist patriots in league with the AFL job holders who literally sold their memberships out rather than put their own jobs at risk. Make no mistake about the early leaders of the AFL – some of them were very decent, even heroic, men and women. Many of them fought well, in some cases for years. Some of them were framed, on conspiracy or even on murder charges – the legendary Joe Hill, for example. But as the AFL leaders grew older, many of them turned to outright corruption or the 'dress suit' bribe, in which union bosses get jobs or favors from the companies after selling out their rank and file.

We pointed out repeatedly to the membership of the IA that even if they won the local unions would be filled by men and women whose jobs were dependent on their having taken the jobs of striking workers. Those people who lost their jobs would probably be glad to 'return the favor'. Added to this was the fact that the IA would be surrounded by a group of unions waiting for them to go out on strike, and these hungry people would trample them to death rushing in to take their jobs.

The results have been that the IA studio workers have not gone out on a major strike for over forty years. Of course the IA leaders claim that they didn't have to go out on strike, that the threat was enough to get what they wanted. This is simply not true. Years after more militant

114

unions have gained advantages, the IA members are still thrown a few crumbs to keep them quiet. The problems we were fighting then are still faced by the current studio workers. It might even be worse today.

Week after week the strike dragged on. The tactic used by the employers and the IA was to delay a ruling by the Labor Board on the results of the election. Of course we knew that the IA could not win the election. Three of the men who went in to work after the members of Local 1421 went out on strike came to Irv before the election and told him that they would vote to affiliate with Local 1421 rather than IA Local 44. The pressure on the War Labor Board from both sides was tremendous: the IA, the employers and the AFL on one side, and the liberals in Congress, the CIO and the progressives throughout the country on the other.

The IA's Internal Trials

Roy Brewer decided that Local 44 and its more activist members should serve as examples of the price of disobedience to the parent organization.

We heard a rumble that charges were being filed against some of us. This was being heard like an obligato. Every day someone would call us about something, and then, before ending the call, we would be asked, 'Have you heard anything yet?' We wished that they would not ask.

A few days later, Irv Hentschel, Bob Ames, Jesse Sapp and I were served with identical charges. We were all served simultaneously at dinner time. Jesse was away on a fishing trip, so his wife Matilda accepted the papers. She called Irv and expressed her thoughts on what they could do with their charges. All our wives felt the same way. Bob lived quite a way from Burbank, where Irv and I lived. He called Irv and told him that he had gotten his copy of the charges. Bob said that he was going to bed at his regular time, and that he would see us in a few days.

I went over to Irv's home and we read them over and over, paragraph by paragraph, line by line, word by word. We immediately saw how vague every charge was. We had no idea how to answer any of them. We knew that we needed help, legal advice, and someone to act as our counsel at our union trial. Since it was a union trial, our counsel had to be members of the IA. Despite the fact that we had been expecting the charges for a long time, we were at a loss to know what to do next.

Irv made a couple of calls and, shortly after, calls started coming in from friends suggesting what we might do. Sam Callen called and asked a few questions and suggested that we all go to bed and get a good night's sleep. The tension was over on this question, but it brought further questions to start thinking about. There was an air of unreality about the whole thing, although we had expected that charges would come, sooner or later. The words that struck us the hardest were 'conduct unbecoming a loyal member' of a union. This was obviously an attempt to convince members of the IA working in the studios that we were being disloyal to their union and a threat to their jobs. We had been charged with disloyalty to the 'advancement of the purposes which this Alliance pursues'. What were the objects that the Alliance pursued? They were certainly not characterized by basic American trade unionism, and had not been so for many years.

The IA leadership knew that we were among those who had been active in the fight against the mobs, that we had offered plans for the settlement of jurisdictional disputes. Yes, we had pointed out that all the present members of the official family of the IA had been in office before, during and after the period of gang control and that they were pursuing the same policies that the gang had pursued relative to other unions, that they were strike-breakers for the employers, just as the gangsters had been.

We also knew that we would not be able even to have a trial under control of the local union. The only way that they could even have us charged with anything was by the takeover method. The trial before the membership of Local 44 would have been before the whole membership, not before a trial board. It would have been a very short trial. When people in the local saw how we were being railroaded by Brewer and company, they would have raised hell.

The question of 'loyalty' came up and Irv tried to trace the line of loyalty that existed from his standpoint. First came his deepest beliefs in regard to the question of life itself – his loyalty to human life in its relationship to the world, the environment, the human race, his country, his community, his neighborhood, his front yard, his house, his tools, his ability to earn a living for his family and himself – somewhere in there was his loyalty to his union. But overshadowing all else was his loyalty to his family and friends. In our conversations he had said once, 'The only thing I'm radical about is my politics.' He wanted his family around him when it came to any of the usual times for an American family to be together: birthdays, holidays, illnesses, and sometimes just for the fun of it. Sundays he usually liked to have free to get together with family or friends or to go on a trip to the mountains. The terrible part of this was the fact that all these feelings were intertwined, and it seemed to him that Brewer was charging him with disloyalty to his deepest beliefs.

We talked for several hours about where we might be able to get help of any kind. Then we got a call from Ted Ellsworth, the Business Agent of Costumers Local 705. He wanted to talk to us the next day and asked that we bring a copy of the charges with us. From what Irv gathered, Ted was willing to act as one of our counsels. We were not yet seriously thinking about legal help, we only thought in terms of the union trial.

We made an appointment with Ted for the next day. We knew that Ted had a Phi Beta Kappa key and that there had been a family history of trade unionism – good enough! We were still leafing through the charges when Irv said, 'Listen to this!' He read over the list of witnesses at the end of the charges. Only two of them were members of Local 44: DuVal, the Business Agent, and Hill, the Secretary. DuVal was also the prosecutor and had signed the charges. Both of them were on the payroll of the local. The rest of them were International officers or members of other locals of the IA. 'Not a Goddamned man who knows us! Just a bunch of stoolies and officials!'

The next day we met Ted Ellsworth at his office and threw the whole thing around for a while. Ted was as amazed as we were at how vague the charges were and he asked us if he could have his secretary run off a copy. He offered to be our counsel and also to find other counsel for us. Jesse Sapp had not returned from his fishing trip and Bob Ames was busy building his home.

We agreed to go to Ted's office again the next day. Ted had made a few phone calls and saw a few of the officers of the other locals that were not so much interested in helping their members become strike-breakers. The officials of the Sound (Smith) and Camera (Aller) locals were trying to be left alone in their jobs, so they were willing to listen to Ted. His thesis was that in order to protect themselves they should be willing to help us. Ted thought it would be good to let the International officials see what would happen if they 'took over' one local union. We hoped to protect the autonomy of the other locals in the studios.

Sam Callen called Irv back and told him that he thought we needed outside legal advice. He asked our permission to see if he could get any of the local civil rights and labor lawyers to help us. Irv told him to go ahead. We knew that we needed help from any place that we could get it. The next day, Sam called again and told Irv that Ben Margolis had said he would like to talk to us. He had made a ten o'clock appointment for the next day, could we keep it? Not just yes, but Hell, yes! Irv called Ben's office and confirmed our appointment. Ben asked that we bring three or four men with us. The next morning, Irv, George Stoica, Jesse Sapp, Bob Ames and I were there.

Ben's office was in downtown Los Angeles, convenient to the Court House. The law firm was Katz, Gallagher and Margolis. It seemed that most of their practice was in the field of labor law and civil rights. This appointment was almost too much to ask for. We knew that Ben was looked upon as one of the best lawyers in that line of cases in the state. He had started as a researcher on the Tom Mooney case. Mooney was convicted of murder in a case that the government knew was based on perjured testimony. We also knew that he had been involved in the case that ended Jim Crow local unions in California. He had defended Harry Bridges in one of the first attempts to illegally deport him. He had also taken the test cases of the unemployment insurance cases to the state Supreme Court and intervened in the other cases that were won. That is why millions of people are able to draw unemployment insurance.

He had just successfully argued 'Sleepy Lagoon' murder case on behalf of the Mexican-American Association (People vs. Zamora) to the Court of Appeal. This was the case that was made into a motion picture, *Zoot Suit*, a few years ago. Later he was Chief Counsel for the Holly-wood Ten and later still on the landmark case of Yates v US, in which the Supreme Court finally halted prosecution of communists under the Smith Act. (The Smith Act was used by the government to prosecute communists under the assumption that all communists were guilty of conspiracy to overthrow the US government. The decision in the Yates case is considered to be a triumph for political freedom in the US by most First Amendment scholars.)

When we got to Ben's office, we realized that he was already familiar with our case. He asked to see the copy of the charges, which he read carefully, and said that his firm would do whatever they could do. We left in high spirits. Neither Ben nor any of us had mentioned any fee. He said that he would call Irv in a couple of days and we would get together again soon.

On the way home, we called Ted's office. He told us to stop by his office, that he had some news. When we got there, he told us he thought he had some backing for us. President Walsh had stated that it was his intent to take over as many locals of the IA as necessary to enforce his order to make all studio members of the IA act as strike-breakers, if necessary. This was a direct threat to several IA locals and their officials. We knew that there were now several power plays going on within the Hollywood locals of the IA and that it might be dangerous to allow ourselves to be mixed up in these. However, as the days passed, we began to see a possible thread to follow in our fight to remain in the IA and to continue to be effective in the struggle that was going on in the studios.

We had no illusions about what kind of people we were dealing with. In each of these four locals there were at least two full-time, paid jobs, the Business Agent and the Secretary-Treasurer. Also there were lesser jobs which were considered stepping stones to paying jobs with either the union or even management, as was to happen with Roy Brewer. Some of the positions carried a certain amount of prestige or additional benefits, such as having the local pay for union dues or paid trips to the conventions of the International. Some union officials from the motion picture industry lifted themselves to national political office – Ronald Reagan, for example.

To recount the number of meetings these circumstances called for would be impossible. Some of them were short talks over the phone. Others were rather formal and tense. Over the next four or five days a plan began to develop. The plan was based on various advantages that were discussed and accepted or rejected. We all agreed that the Laboratory Local 683, the Camera Local 659, the Costumers Local 705 and the Sound Local 695 would all be involved in the union trial. We were aware that some of the officers of these four locals were more worried about their own jobs than what happened to us. We knew that some of these people were honorable, decent people, schooled in the give and take of union activity. We completely trusted the leadership of the Lab workers and the Costumers local. With the Camera local's Business Agent, Herb Aller, we knew we had a scared rabbit. The Sound local was run by Harold V. Smith, the man Bioff had ordered to take Irv out for a meal during the Cleveland convention. This ex-bootlegger and Chicago petty gangster had been picked up and questioned about several murders. He was sent to Hollywood to help the mobs in their pursuits. There was a big 'but' in being involved with these two men. They would help but, when the going got tough, they would choose to hold onto their jobs rather than stick up for honest, democratic union principles.

Behind all these leaders were the members of their locals; it was the rank and file that made it possible for the democratic unions to survive. No matter how the rank and file felt about specific issues at that time, most of them wanted to protect the democratic unions and guilds.

We agreed that it would be to the advantage of all the Hollywood locals if the takeover of Local 44 caused a public fight among the studio unions and guilds. By taking over one local the International would start a fight they might not be able to contain. We leaked a story that if Walsh took over one more local, all hell would break loose, in law cases and publicity. We agreed to take the IA to court on the takeover of Local 44, if the other locals would back us financially. The case would be filed shortly after the internal union trial against us began.

The Business Agents of these four locals agreed to represent us as counsel at our union trial. Further, the leaders of those four locals agreed to work towards passing motions similar to the motion that Local 44 had passed, calling for an end to members working outside of their own jurisdiction, i.e. taking the work of the strikers.

We held this meeting at Ben Margolis' home, in the Hollywood hills. Present were Harold V. Smith, Business Agent of Sound Local 695; Herb Aller, Business Agent of the Camera Local 659; John Martin, Business Agent of Local 683, with Norval Crutcher, the Secretary of that local; Ted Ellsworth, Business Agent of Costumers Local 705, with the Secretary of that local, whose name I do not remember. From our Local 44, Irv Hentschel, Bob Ames, Jesse Sapp, George Stoica and I attended.

We told Ben about what we had agreed to do. He explained to us any questions of law that he felt were involved and answered a few from us. Questions were thrown back and forth for about an hour and a half. Then Ben told us that he had no wish to take part in any decision that we might reach. He said that he would be in the kitchen working on something else. We talked for a while longer and then called Ben back into the room. We made plain to him what we had all agreed upon. Ben then verbalized the whole thing to be sure we all understood exactly what we wanted to do and what we wanted him to do for us. His only suggestion was that we get the signatures of twenty members of Local 44 to go along with us in taking the International to court to stop the internal trial and to return control of Local 44 to the membership.

Just before we broke up for the night, Ben told us that, as he had told Ted Ellsworth previously, he wanted the final decision to be made by the four of us who were facing trial. He asked the five of us to stay when the others left. When we five were alone with him, he told us that he had insisted that we were to make the final decision on this move we had all agreed on. We discussed the integrity of the men we were involved with. We were not too impressed with either Smith or Aller. Then he told us that we should be aware that we would probably be forced out of the studios for at least a while, how long he could not say, and that, further, it was possible that we might be forced to leave or be forced out of the studios for the rest of our lives. We told him that we were prepared for that. He said, 'That is all I wanted to know.' As we left, Ben told us that he would call Ted Ellsworth to pass the word.

Within a few days all the preconditions for our action had taken place. The four local unions of the IA had passed the motion regarding not working outside their jurisdiction, and we heard that the money had been allocated for our defense.

The public statement of Local 683, the Lab local, follows:

We believe that the International President should not have invoked the Emergency Clause, in the case of Local 44. The taking over of a local of the I.A. without sufficient reason endangers the autonomy of every local in the Alliance.

We further believe that the best interests of the I.A. will be served by an immediate return of Local 44 to the control of its membership. We further believe that any member charged with infraction of International or Local laws should be tried before a tribunal established within the structure of local autonomy.

Film Technicians Local 683, I.A.T.S.E.[8]

A similar stand was taken by the other three locals.

The first night of the trial we all, the defendants and counsel, met at an Italian restaurant and went over what we thought we might be able to accomplish during the trial. The only change so far was that Harold V. Smith, the Business Agent of the Sound Local, had substituted one Zeal Fairbanks, his assistant, to appear as our counsel in his place. Mr Fairbanks had been a member of Sound Local 695 and had been appointed to the office of Business Agent of the Laborers' local charted during the Bioff period, at the time of the 1937 strike. The Laborers' local had been established as a strike-breaking local. We expected something like this from Smith. The others were there: Martin of 683, Ellsworth of 705 and Aller of 659.

When we went up to the union meeting hall, there as chairman of the trial board was Pierce. I had already had a violent argument about the issues of the strike with Pierce. He had said, 'Hentschel should be expelled from the IA.' A hanging judge. Another member of the trial board thought that DuVal was the greatest man alive. One of the people appointed to the trial board took a look at the situation and refused to take part in the trial. The other man who stayed on the board was a run-of-the-mill IA member, willing to oblige the local union officials.

Also present was Mike Luddy, of the law firm Breslin, Bodkin and Luddy, the West coast attorney for the mobs, who remained the IA attorney after the conviction of the more prominent gangsters. As with all of the mob's infrastructure, the lawyers were also able to hold onto their jobs. When we saw this set-up, we decided to call Ben Margolis, who was down there with us in fifteen minutes. Ben and Mike Luddy had an argument about why Luddy was attending. Luddy declared that he was not there to guide the prosecution in the way to quickly and easily expel us from the union; he was there as a witness. They agreed to withdraw from the proceedings until they were called as witnesses. Later they were both called.

It was the first time that all the defendants and counsels were present together. I noticed Herb Aller looking at Bob, whom he had never met. Aller had not decided which of the defendants he would represent. He seemed to be looking for a 'safe' defendant – that is , a non-communist. He again looked at Bob Ames. Bob was above average height and quite slim and rather intellectual looking. He had been elected to take the whole proceeding down in shorthand, which he had used all his life. I remember him taking out of his pocket grocery lists in shorthand. I caught Aller's thought and he saw me looking Bob over. I almost laughed at him at the thought that Herb was about to offer to defend the only Communist Party member present! Herb leaned over to me and asked what was his name. When Herb was asked who he was there to represent, by the chairman of the trial board, I couldn't help laughing. Later in the trial, Bob asked Irv and me for permission to declare himself a member of the Communist Party. We told him that we thought it was the wrong thing for him to do. Bob was too disciplined to go against our opinion. It might have been exciting to let them find one Communist Party member – they were trying so hard to find one. I'm sure that Bob would have been spectacular in what he said and how he said it.

When things had sorted themselves out a bit, Brewer rose and submitted documents to support his presence. Then came the documents to support the idea that the trial was all nice and legal. Then came the papers to prove that the local officers had requested the International president to take charge of the local's affairs. Then came the document to prove that Brewer was appointed as International representative, running things for the president; then documents proving that the National Vice-presidents had approved the takeover. Then further documents were presented, showing that the president had appointed the trial board.

Here is the 'Notice of Charges' that they presented us with:

Brothers: Irwin P. Hentschel, Eugene V. H. Mailes, Jesse L. Sapp and Robert W. Ames.
You and each of you are hereby notified that charges of which the enclosed is a copy have been filed against you before Roy M. Brewer, International Representative in charge of the business, affairs, properties and assets of Local No. 44, appointed by the International President and acting under Article Seven, Section Sixteen of the Constitution of the I.A.T.S.E. & M.P.M.O. of the U.S. and C. You are further notified that at Los Angeles, on Thursday, the 10th day of May, 1945, at 7:30 P.M., has been fixed as the time for your trial before Richard F. Walsh, International President, or Roy M. Brewer, International Representative, or any person or Committee designated or appointed by him for such purpose. Said trial will be held at 6472 Santa Monica Blvd., Los Angeles....[9]

It was made very plain that if we were convicted by the trial board, which Walsh had appointed, then we could appeal to Walsh, as President. If Walsh upheld the conviction, we could appeal to the International Executive Board, of which Walsh was chairman, which had already approved the takeover. Then we could appeal to the National Grievance Committee, of which Brewer was Secretary. However, if we lost there, we could appeal to the convention, presided over by Walsh.

That is how a company union takes over the job of 'blacklisting' trouble-some employees for the employer.

The courts are interested in private, fraternal organizations' constitutions only to the point of, 'What does the constitution say? Was this constitution approved by the governing body? Did the organization follow that constitution?' If the governing body followed the constitution, then the courts will usually not interfere. It all went back to the vote to accept the new constitution that the mob's lawyers wrote up for Browne in 1936.[10] Since what Walsh and Brewer were doing was legal within the constitution, the courts would not interfere. In short, the membership must be held responsible for not seeing the danger of their actions. Of course, this did not interfere with the overwhelming majority of the members of the union, just the Hollywood locals.

It was obvious that both sides knew the trial would wind up sooner or later in the civil courts. Irv and I saw something more than this fact in the trial. We both saw that for the first time an account of what had happened in this fight was possible. We told our counsel that we had this in mind. They recognized that it might have some historical value, so they went along with us in this. We were not sure where we might be able to deposit our copy of the transcript of our trial before the IATSE officials. Later it was given to the University of California, Los Angeles.

Ben Margolis had told us and our counsel how to best defend ourselves. He had impressed on us the importance of answering questions truthfully. If we thought that something was liable to come out that might be injurious to us, we were to rely on him to rehabilitate the answer and put it in a more favorable light. He did say, however, not to give anything away; to answer the questions with as short a sentence as possible. We were not to volunteer anything. With this in mind we did in some cases withhold information that was not asked for and could have been damaging.

The general trend of the trial can be illustrated by the attitude of hostility toward those of us who had taken part in the effort to oust the mob and their infrastructure. DuVal introduced into the trial evidence that I had taken part in that fight, as though it had been a crime that we committed. He put into the record the apology that some of us had to sign in order to get our union cards back. The apology was as follows:

To the I.A.T.S.E. and M.P.M.O.

Its International Officials and Its Members:

The undersigned, a member of the International Alliance, being cognizant of the fact that charges have been filed against me for activities during the past three or four months which were detrimental to the best interests of the International Alliance, does hereby apologize to the Alliance, its members and particularly to its International officials for all derogatory statements made by me against them, for all of my said subversive activities. I admit such activities on my part and I realize that the same have caused a great deal of trouble and unrest in the affairs of the Alliance and have seriously jeopardized the future welfare of the Alliance and of its members. I have come to the conclusion that my said activities were wrong and that the policies of the Alliance are to the advantage of and for the best interests of its members.

As an indication of my sincerity in this apology I am willing to be placed in a probationary status for a period of 18 months. If, during that period, I engage in any activities subversive of or detrimental to the International Alliance, I agree voluntarily to surrender my card to the Local having jurisdiction over my craft.

I hereby waive the statute of limitations as to my past activities and agree that if at any time during my period of membership in the International Alliance I engage in further activities detrimental to the Alliance, I may also be charged and tried for my past activities, and I will not avail myself of any objection as to lapse of time in the bringing of said charges to trial.

Dated: October 20, 1939

(Signed) Eugene V. H. Mailes[11]

When this was entered into the record, I blew up and expressed my disgust at the very idea that my activities against the mob had been made into a charge against me, an act of 'disloyalty to the union'. I nailed my colors to the mast, and finished by saying, 'I am proud to have it entered.' The twenty-five or thirty members there gave me a hand of applause, bringing from the chairman of the trial board the following:

For that demonstration I want to announce right here that if there is any more this court will adjourn and the witnesses will be left by themselves and called as we need them. That's all uncalled for. We were courteous enough to allow the defendant to speak, and he has an attorney to speak for him, and I allowed him the privilege of speaking, and I don't intend again to have this court interrupted by this kind of foolishness.[12]

The trial was packed with our friends. There were almost always at least twenty of our friends in attendance. The witnesses that the prosecution had on hand always left as soon as they were dismissed, they never stayed. The chairman's response following the applause was indicative of the board's annoyance with the defense.

Several of the prosecution witnesses had testified as to what we had said at the American Legion Meeting and had lied about it. When the trial was nearing the end, we read into the record a certified transcript of what we had said, proving that these people had lied. It made no difference. We did not allow the transcript out of our hands; had we done this it might have been used against some of the speakers belonging to other locals of the IA. The trial board allowed it to be read and taken down by the reporter. None of the witnesses against us were members of Local 44 except Hill, the secretary of the local. DuVal, the prosecutor, the Business Agent of the local, repeatedly refused to take the stand against us.

After the third night of sessions the trial was stopped when Ben obtained a temporary restraining order. Mike Luddy, the IA lawyer, agreed to suspend the trial until after the strike was settled. We figured this was the best thing to do at that moment.

The Communist Party Line

The dissension within the Communist Party had reached a point where reconsideration of the 'no strikes in wartime' pledge had to take place. A rumor about an 'expanded meeting' was in the air. On the night of the meeting, Irv Hentschel told me that Bob Ames was attending and would present our views on the subject quite well.

A Party official had been sent out to Hollywood from New York to try to settle the question. I do not know who he was. Irv found out what had happened at the meeting from several different men and passed the story to me. I also heard about it from Sam Callen and Bob Ames. This is what happened. When perhaps thirty or thirty-five people had gathered, the meeting got down to business with a review of the situation, from its beginning up to that day. When several people had spoken on the subject, taking some issue with the Party line, hardline Party member Blackie Mason took the floor and was holding forth as to what he thought was the situation. Mason said that the IA was 'in the saddle' and was going to stay there, that everyone should recognize reality and get along with the idea of strike-breaking. This was spoken in patient, intellectual, fluent Partyspeak, filled with various citations of learned thoughts.

At hearing Mason's ideas, Bob Ames blew his stack and called Mason a scab, voicing his outrage at the fact that Party members were seriously discussing being strike-breakers. Bob was further outraged that a high Party official would be sent out here on such a question, to hold a meeting. He went on to tell the gentleman from New York that they didn't need anyone to come out to Hollywood to tell them how to deal with anything relating to the Party and, further, that it was the business of the local Party members to determine how the Party in Hollywood should run its business, and he suggested that the gentleman return to New York and let the Hollywood unit run its own affairs. When he finished, Bob walked out of the room and out of the Party.

The dam broke. There was an overwhelming tide of criticism voiced against the idea of scabbing on the strike any further. For an ordinarily quiet man, Bob's anger and outrage could be monumental. The Party official returned to New York. A couple of weeks later the Party line changed and they then backed the strike. It was too late. The damage had been done.

The Strike Drags on

In July, the International President of the IBPPD (Painters), L. P. Lindeloff, ordered the three rebellious white-collar unions – the Screen Publicists Guild

124

(SPG), the Story Analysts (SA), and the Screen Office Employees Guild (SOEG) – to observe the CSU picket lines. These groups had yielded to pressure from the producers during the first week of the strike to return to work or face breach of contract suits. When Lindeloff issued his order, the ranks of the white-collar unions were split. Although the leaders of the three locals did order their members out, substantial numbers of SOEG and SPG remained in the studio offices and formed new unions.[13]

The internal AFL struggle continued. In July, AFL President William Green called a conference in Chicago of the heads of the embattled unions. The CSU unions were willing to go back to work only if the strikers would be returned to the jobs they left in March. Walsh insisted that the IA replacement workers must be retained and that the CSU must be disbanded. Thus deadlocked, the issue was put off until the following month at the AFL convention. Before the convention, however, Green again called on Walsh to revoke the charters for the IA painters and carpenters. Walsh refused, claiming that if he had not chartered these locals the studios might have gone open shop. Walsh also made a point of accusing Sorrell of being a Communist, a strategy aimed at catering to the mostly conservative AFL leaders. *Variety* learned from an unnamed 'high-ranking labor chief' (Roy Brewer) that Sorrell was 'on his way out' because there was 'irrefutable evidence' that Sorrell was a Communist who worked for the Party under his mother's name, Stewart. Carpenters' President Bill Hutcheson, a dyed-in-the-wool Republican, later claimed that he supported the CSU and Sorrell only to 'break the IA'.[14]

Of course, Sorrell probably realized this all along. His motto of 'You don't choose your friends' could just as easily apply to Hutcheson as to Communists. Although Sorrell frequently claimed to be just a 'dumb painter', he was a tough negotiator and a resourceful, if occasionally unscrupulous, strike leader; his tactics ranged from brilliant to brutal. In April 1945 he accused Walsh of being 'Bioff's delivery boy', pocketing a small portion of the 2 per cent assessment leveled during the Browne–Bioff era. At the time, Sorrell was unable to substantiate the charge, but subsequent inquiries into Walsh's income tax records for this period support the idea that he may have received some of the proceeds from the 2 per cent assessment. In May, Sorrell called for a nationwide boycott of the major companies' theater chains; for reasons that are not altogether clear, the boycott never materialized. In the following month, he threatened to publicize the names of the actors who were crossing the CSU picket lines.[15]

According to his own recollections, Sorrell was never squeamish about the use of strong-arm tactics. *Variety* reported in May 1945 that there were stories of 'quiet beatings' of strike-breakers.[16] From Sorrell's oral history, one must assume that such beatings were strategically administered to men who 'should have known better'.

While the rank and file fought these physical battles, the NLRB considered arguments from attorneys for the producers and the IA on the question of which workers would be eligible to vote in the upcoming representational election for the set decorators. The central issue was which group of set decorators – the Local 1421 strikers or the IA replacements – should be counted as the appropriate bargaining unit. On 24 May, the NLRB held the election; but the producers, the unions or the NLRB challenged every ballot on the issue of the eligibility of the voters. This technicality clouded the issue of representation for the set decorators for an additional five months. Eight Californian members of the US Congress demanded that the NLRB not count the votes of the IA strike-breakers. On 13 June, the Los Angeles regional office of the NLRB, responding to the Congressional pressure, recommended counting only the ballots of the fifty-four striking CSU set decorators.[17]

The IA filed an appeal to the national NLRB office, thus prompting the three-person national board to consider the case. The IA had a good reason for seeking the decision of these three men: two of them had financial interests in the movie theater industry, and they did not want to offend the union that controlled the projectionists. One of these two men was also a former IA member and held a lifetime gold membership card in the union.[18]

On 19 September, the three men decided not to count the votes of the striking set decorators. But President Truman and other federal officials recommended to the board that such a decision would be 'foolish' in light of their conflict of interest in the case and the combined numerical strength of the Carpenters, the IBEW and the Painters. The conflict immobilized the three-member board; they claimed that the key issue in the case was whether the striking set decorators had been legally fired.[19]

In early September, Brewer faced rebellion within the ranks and leadership of the costumers' Local 705, camera Local 659, sound technicians' Local 695, and lab technicians' Local 683. These locals were angry with his unscrupulous handling of Local 44 and with his seeming inability to settle their contracts with the producers. In response, Brewer used the IA newsletter to accuse the leaders of these locals, especially Russell McKnight of Local 683 and Ted Ellsworth of Local 705, of being Communists. Although McKnight and Ellsworth jokingly referred to the building they shared for headquarters of their locals as the 'Hollywood Kremlin', Brewer's tactics certainly did not amuse them. Ellsworth responded to Brewer's charges in his local union newsletter by noting that he certainly disagreed with many actions of Brewer but if that 'makes us "traitors" or "communistic", then there are one hell of a lot of communists floating around Los Angeles.'[20]

Brewer was not content just to attack the 'Communists' in his own union and in the CSU. He sent letters to prominent liberal talent guild members asking them to publicly answer whether 'you, you as an individual, support the campaign of slander, vilification, lies and scurrility now being carried on against our officers and those loyal American workers who believe in and support the I.A.T.S.E., and who, by doing so, have incurred the enmity and hatred of the entire Communist "apparat"?'[21]

Brewer was adopting the same strategy used by Bioff and Browne in their more desperate days and by the leader of IA sound technicians Local 695, Harold V. Smith, against his enemies in the Browne–Bioff years. Brewer's red-baiting, however, was more consonant with the general swing to the right that occurred in the US throughout the Cold War. He was building a power base for right-wing politics in Hollywood that would make him one of the most powerful men in the motion picture industry within a few years. He initiated the Hollywood blacklist, starting with the long-time irritants to the leaders of the IA, namely the remnants of the old IA Progressives and their supporters.

Notes

1. Bill Maginetti, testimony given in the IATSE proceedings against Robert Ames, *et al.*, Los Angeles, 10 March 1946, pp. 1654-5.
2. *Hollywood Reporter*, 2 April 1945, p. 1.
3. *Daily Variety*, 2 April 1945, p. 1.
4. George Stoica, IATSE proceedings against Robert Ames, *et al.*, pp. 1936-7.
5. *Variety*, 28 March 1945, pp. 4, 17.
6. *Variety*, 11 April 1945, p. 18.
7. 'Hollywood Studio Strike' file, UCLA archives.
8. Ibid.
9. IATSE proceedings against Robert Ames, *et al.* p. 19.
10. Under those rules, the national leaders of the IA broadened their powers to declare a local union in a state of emergency. The IA could seize control of the local union with little recourse for the members of that local union or their elected local representatives.
11. Ibid., pp. 1083-7.
12. Ibid., p. 1087.
13. *Hollywood Sun*, 12 September 1945, pp. 6-7.
14. *Variety*, 15 August 1945, pp. 6, 16; the statement by Hutcheson is contained in testimony given to a US congressional investigation: United States House of Representatives: *Jurisdictional Disputes in the Motion Picture Industry*. 80th Congress, 1st Session, pursuant to House Resolution 111. Washington, 1948, p. 244.
15. *Variety*, 11 April 1945, pp. 5, 18; 9 May 1945, pp. 7, 18.
16. *Variety*, 28 March 1945, p. 17; 4 April 1945, p. 20.
17. *Variety*, 13 June 1945, pp. 9, 15.
18. *Hollywood Sun*, 5 December 1945, p. 1.
19. *Variety*, 3 October 1945, p. 5.
20. *Costumers' News*, 'Hollywood Studio Strike' file, UCLA archives.
21. Stephen Englund and Larry Ceplair, *The Inquisition in Hollywood* (New York: Anchor/Doubleday, 1980), p. 219.

7

WALKING THE LINE

Bloody Friday

Every day that the CSU strikers stayed out they continued to lose wages to the IA strikebreakers. Over a thousand replacements had been brought in. The local newspapers, which had been unsympathetic to the strike from its beginning, had ceased to pay any attention to it. This absence of public concern made the strikers even more desperate. They had to take drastic action or face being starved out. The CSU had considered a mass picketing of an individual studio back in May 1945, but it refrained from taking this action in hopes that less drastic measures would succeed. In the next few months the CSU made sporadic attempts at mass picketing, but the studios counter-attacked with numerous court-ordered injunctions. On Thursday, 4 October 1945, Herb Sorrell and the CSU strike committee called a special meeting at Legion Stadium to discuss the establishment of mass picket lines around Warners' studios, starting on the following morning. The siege mentality had taken hold.

Finally, when it was obvious that all the ballots had long ago been counted and all the challenged ballots had been ruled on, and that the delay was due to nothing but pressure, the strikers finally blew their tops. At a strike meeting, during a heated discussion, a member of the Carpenters' Union, Tony Schavione, a remarkably good street fighter, got to his feet and yelled, 'Give me a thousand men and we'll close down Warner Bros studio tomorrow morning.' This was greeted with wild cheers by the whole crowd. The place was filled and immediately came alive with action, as committees were formed for the necessary work. Some people were up all night organizing the closing of the studio, over the hill in Burbank, in the San Fernando Valley.

Here is how *Variety* reported the next morning's scene at Warners, alternately termed the 'Battle of Warner Bros' or 'Bloody Friday':

> Strikers and studio police lined up for battle before sunup Friday morning and the skirmishing began when non-strikers reported for work at six o'clock and tried to pass the picket line. Strikers deployed from their barricades, halted the non-strikers and rolled three automobiles [which attempted to crash through a mass of people] over on their sides. By noon reinforcements arrived for both sides. Squads of police arrived from Glendale and Los Angeles to aid the Burbank cops, while the strikers increased to about 1,000, led by Herb Sorrell,

prexy of the Conference of Studio Unions. When more non-strikers attempted to crash the gate, there was a general melee in which various implements of war were used, including tear gas bombs, fire hoses, knuckles, clubs, brickbats, and beer bottles. After two hours of strife, 300 police and deputy sheriffs dispersed the pickets and counted about 40 casualties, none serious.[1]

Cappy DuVal, Business Agent for IA Local 44, distributed blue walking canes to IA flying squads, whose job it was to threaten the pickets to move aside to let the strike-breakers pass.

The picket lines were attacked by a combination of Los Angeles Sheriff's Department deputies and goons hired by the IA from Main Street Gym (the hangout for training boxers). Church groups were contacted by the CSU to witness the violence that was sure to come from this move, so they wanted witnesses to see when the violence started and who started it. Groups from several of the more prominent churches – Catholic, Unitarian, Quakers – and several small independent groups came and saw the whole thing. The public reaction was instant. They saw automobiles suddenly turn and run into the picket lines and go into the studio. This happened five or six times and several people were hurt and neither the police nor the Sheriff's Department took any notice or offered help. Finally, in self-protection, Tony Schavione and his helpers, seeing cars prepare to ram the lines, tipped three cars over. And at last some of the Burbank police refused to let cars ram the lines. The drivers who hesitated before ramming the people picketing were flagged on by the police. In one case a driver was scared stiff when the crowd lifted his car and were about to tip it over. He had no traction on his wheels and a angry crowd was yelling at him. It was a frightening sight. Not one of the car drivers who had rammed the lines was prosecuted for this, or even cited. The climax of the violence was on the third day. The day before there had been an attack on the line from inside the studio by studio police, coordinated with an attack by studio goons outside the gates, all backed up by L.A. County sheriff's deputies behind them. The street had been cleared but the IA, the studio bosses and the police had overstepped the bounds of decency.

The mass of pickets showed up again on the following morning with gas masks, an injunction from a Superior Court judge barring both the studio police and the municipal and county police from interfering with the strike. Warners retaliated by obtaining a new injunction limiting the number of pickets to no more than three at any gate.[2]

Sunday was a day of regrouping forces. At Hollywood Legion Stadium, several thousand citizens joined the strikers at their weekly meeting, co-sponsored by number of liberal/progressive Los Angeles citizen groups. As a group, they condemned the 'unprincipled violence committed by the riot squads of Los Angeles and the county of Los Angeles and the further use of these riot squads as strike breaking agencies.' They also adopted a resolution demanding that the NLRB hand down a decision in the set decorators' case. Screenwriter Dalton Trumbo labeled the events of Bloody Friday as 'fascism in action'. Russell McKnight, President of IA Local 683, pledged to the assembly that his local would refuse to go through the picket lines. On that same day, Local 683 elected an 'anti-Walsh' slate of delegates to the 1946 IA convention. Since the convention would not take place for another eight months, it was clear that Local 683 was using the delegates as a means of objecting to the policies of Brewer and Walsh.[3]

IA forces also regrouped over the weekend, although their meetings were more clandestine. Brewer laid plans for dealing with mass picketing by the CSU. The next morning, the IA and the producers seized the initiative. *Variety* reported that

> Rioting started when, shortly before 6 a.m., the American flag was hoisted atop Warners. Non-strikers rushed the mass picket lines in front of the entrance gates to be joined shortly by police and deputy sheriffs, swinging clubs, groups finally clearing a path. Non-strikers employed battery cables, chains, clubs, etc., and Herb Sorrell, Conference of Studio Unions prexy, was struck in the face with chain.
>
> Total of 39 injured were treated at the studio hospital, while others were carried away by friends without seeking medical aid.[4]

That day I was across the street from the Olive Avenue gate of Warners. We had been told by Ben Margolis to stay off the picket lines, when the massive attack on the picket line took place. It started when people inside the studio began dropping half-inch-by-six-inch bolts on the pickets from the top of five-storey sound stages. Then the private Warner Bros' fire department turned the fire hoses full-force on the pickets. The Warners' private police force hurled gas grenades at the pickets. Finally, a quiet period came and the sheriff in charge started to read the 'riot act' through a bullhorn from the top of the studio. My heart leapt at what I was seeing and hearing! The 'riot act' should have been read *before* the violent action by the fire department and the deputies had been turned loose on the pickets. The gathering should have been first declared an 'unlawful assembly' and been ordered to disperse. This should have been done at least twice, since the picketing had been peaceful until that point. Only after the order of the Sheriff should the street have been cleared, using only what force was necessary. Instead the bolts were dropped and the fire hoses had been turned on first. I realized that the blunder by the Sheriff had given the strikers a victory. A victory that would be costly. The injury to dozens of people was legally and morally unforgivable. The reaction by the public when the unimpeachable witnesses told their story was the final end of the delay in the Labor Board's decision. The set decorators had won the election by six votes! Take three votes from one side and add them to the other side and you have a difference of six votes! The three men that we had to go in as scabs made that possible.

Nine pickets were hospitalized. The *Evening Herald Express* reported that over seventy people were injured at the Warners' gate. The partisan strike newsletter, the *Hollywood Atom*, presented a far more graphic portrayal of the violence, telling of 'goons' from 20th Century-Fox who knocked people unconscious with monkey wrenches and then jumped onto trucks. As the 'goon squad' drove away they 'waved $50 bills they had received for their morning's work, and yelled "sucker" at the pickets.'[5]

Many Warners' workers who managed to get through the mass picket line stayed inside the studios after Monday's violence and slept there to avoid having to run the gauntlet on the following morning. Brewer arranged for other workers to enter the studios in the middle of the night, while the pickets were off duty. The violence at Warners continued throughout the week, but on a somewhat reduced scale. The Los Angeles County Sheriff was clearly supporting the studios. One newspaper report noted that the sheriff's deputies were armed with sub-machine guns.[6] Many IA workers simply refused to cross the picket lines.

Carey McWilliams formed a Citizens' Committee of prominent Los Angeles citizens to serve as a committee of observers; they hoped that their presence would prevent the police and studio security forces from committing violent acts against the strikers. On Wednesday, 10 October, Burbank police arrested 307 pickets at Warners, dragged them inside the studio gates and fingerprinted them. Buses arrived to transport those arrested to the Burbank jail. When the city bus drivers, who were Teamsters, realized the nature of their cargo, they refused to drive the buses; thus the Burbank police were forced to transport their own prisoners. Among those arrested were machinists from the Lockheed Lodge of International Association of Machinists (IAM), who were showing their support for IAM studio machinists Local 1185. On the following day nearly 2,000 workers joined the CSU pickets, waving a huge American flag.[7]

IAM members came with a marching band and IAM banners as well as the American flag. They then took the places of the pickets, so that the CSU pickets could go down to MGM in Culver City to shut it down. This was supposed to be the big fight to close down the principal enemy, MGM. Just before this was scheduled to happen, Herb Sorrell had a meeting with MGM and agreed to hold off on closing them down with mass picketing. He had gone into this meeting with the backing of the CIO, the Longshoremen and the IAM. People in these groups were coming by train, bus and cars from up and down the West coast. Herb knew this and chose instead to rely on his Painters, assuming that he had already won the strike and that it was just a matter of time before the studios threw out the scabs and put his people back to work. At this point he had won the strike, but he gave it away.

A large number of women joined the CSU picket lines on Wednesday, 10 October, and were hauled off along with the other pickets. When they were booked, they began singing songs together and visibly improved the public image of the strikers. Public apathy was changing into public sympathy in Los Angeles. The Los Angeles newspapers, with the notable exception of the *Times*, were swinging to the CSU side.[8]

Meanwhile Roy Brewer was continuing his theme of anti-communism in public statements which were also amplified by the local press:

The law is being openly flouted, and no real effort is being made to stop it. We believe it is in the interests of good Americanism that this situation be handled in a lawful manner by the proper law enforcement agencies. We do, however, demand the right for our people to work to earn a living, whether Sorrell and his Communist hoodlums approve of it or not.[9]

The IA studio locals held meetings during the week to discuss how they might best cope with such a very dangerous situation. On 10 October, Local 683 voted not to cross the lines. While the meeting was in progress, Brewer gathered the lab workers who had been working on temporary permits (and who were thus not permitted to participate in Local 683's affairs) and promised them permanent employment if they would cross the CSU lines.[10] The permit workers balked at this suggestion, but the exercise was a useful rehearsal for Brewer; in the following year, he would have his revenge against the recalcitrant leaders of the lab workers' local.

By the end of the week, pressure from prominent Los Angeles and California public figures forced the NLRB to render a decision on the set decorators' case: both the strikers' votes and the replacements' votes would be counted in the election to determine representation of the set decorators. But even with this seeming victory for the IA, Local 1421 received the larger vote total; the final tally was 55 to 45. (Exactly why there were only 100 men voting when there were a total of 154 striking and replacement set decorators is not clear. Gene Mailes' recollection of the vote was that it was 81 for Local 1421 and 73 for the IA. Assuming that an equal number of strikers and replacement workers had voted, it seems that a few IA strike-breakers had voted against the IA and in favor of Local 1421.)[11]

This was only a small moral boost, however, since neither the strike nor the violence ended. Flying squads of IA workers formed wedges to open corridors through the mass of pickets to allow the more genteel members of Local 659 (camerapersons) and Local 695 (sound technicians) to enter the studios unmolested. At Columbia studios, a car was driven through a picket line and injured four pickets as well as the head of the Columbia security police. Both the CSU and the IA issued claims that the other organization had imported thugs to do their dirty work. There were also reports of youths who joined the various battles simply to 'crack heads'. Actors, writers and directors who were opposed to the strike expressed indignation at being jostled and verbally abused by the strikers. Although progressive factions within the talent guilds were pushing for resolution of the conflict, the vast majority of actors and writers continued to cross the picket lines.[12]

The producers issued a statement saying that they still refused to bargain with the set decorators until the NLRB certified the results of the election and not until a large number of troublesome jurisdictional issues were worked out with the striking and non-striking unions. At this point, the hypocrisy of the producers' position became all too visible. The produces had encouraged a large number of these disputes by using the IA to obtain replacement workers during the strike. The CSU answered the producers' statement by filing an Unfair Labor Practice charge with the NLRB, claiming that the IA and the producers were colluding to oust the CSU from the studios. The IA insisted that the producers must retain the replacements hired during the strike, but the pressure was on all parties concerned to reach some sort of settlement. On 15 October, the SWG finally issued a public statement supporting the CSU and calling on the producers to reinstate the strikers to their former jobs. Two days later, SAG issued a similar statement. In between the issuance of those two statements, under pressure from AFL President Green, Walsh revoked the charters for the IA painters and carpenters locals which he had set up at the beginning of the strike; this indicated a major break in the struggle.[13]

Yet Roy Brewer was the 'bad cop' in this period, going after Sorrell with a vengance in the press. The *Evening Herald Examiner* quoted Brewer on 20 October: "'We are convinced,' Brewer charged, "that our nation's future and the future of world peace and security is directly threatened by a Communist party plot against the American film industry.'"[14] Brewer was working hard to get the Los Angeles Central Labor Council to turn against the CSU. His red-baiting was in harmony with a larger anti-communist sentiment growing in the US mainstream culture.

Eric Johnston, former head of the US Chamber of Commerce and newly appointed director of the Motion Picture Association of America (MPAA), called a meeting of the union leaders in Cincinnati. The meeting was convened on 22 October to attempt to arrive at a workable settlement to the six-month strike. While the producers' and International unions' representatives met in Cincinnati, the mass picketing continued and the protest spread to several other studios, including RKO, Paramount, and Republic, one of the largest independent studios. At Paramount, police used clubs to break up the pickets: fifty people were hurt and thirteen were arrested. Paul L. Brown, Mayor of Burbank, requested that California Governor Earl Warren declare martial law in his city. Warren apparently ignored this request.[15]

On 24 October, Eric Johnston sent word from Cincinnati that the unions and the producers had reached an agreement. The terms of the settlement were: 1) an immediate end to the strike; 2) local inter-union negotiations for a period of thirty days on jurisdictional questions; 3) the return of all strikers to their former jobs – replacement workers to be given sixty days severance pay; and 4) final disposition of all disputes left unsettled after the thirty-day period to be determined by a three-person committee drawn from the AFL Executive Council.[16]

Sorrell returned from Cincinnati and pleaded with the assembled crowd of strikers at their weekly meeting in Hollywood Legion Stadium for a two-day truce in the picketing to allow time for Johnston to implement the terms of the agreement. On the following day, the NLRB handed down its certification of the results of the set decorators' representational election, thereby forcing the producers, after fifteen months of struggle, to finally bargain with Painters' set decorators Local 1421. The producers agreed to recognize Local 1421 as the bargaining agent for the set decorators, but they asserted that the NLRB decision in this minor case did not settle the numerous jurisdictional disputes that existed between the contending unions. The producers insisted that all such disputes be settled before any wage negotiations could begin.[17]

On 30 October, a day on which an unknown assailant took a shot at Herb Sorrell as he backed out of his driveway, the studio executives informed the managers in the studios to clear the lots of some 3,000 replacement workers by noon the following day. Among these workers were some 1,200 regular IA members who would be retained in their old classifications. From that point on, according to the pro-CSU weekly *Hollywood Sun*, the strike 'moved inside the studios'. For reasons that are difficult to discern, the 3,000 replacement workers were required to report for work every day during a sixty-day severance period, despite the fact that, as *Variety* put it, they had nothing better to do than exchange unpleasantries with the returned strikers. For their part, the CSU strikers were quite embittered by the fact that not only had they lost a total of $16 million in wages during the strike, but they were also now forced to confront their picket line adversaries in the studios every day. The tension between the two groups became so great at one of the studios that the lot manager had to put the replacement workers in a studio bomb shelter to prevent violent confrontations.[18]

During the thirty-day period of local negotiations, only studio Carpenters Local 946 and IA grips Local 80 were able to reach a settlement on their key jurisdictional disagreement – that of set erection. On 13 November 1945, representatives of Local 80 and Local 946, together with International Representatives from both unions, including Richard Walsh and Roy Brewer, signed an agreement granting the job of set erection to the Carpenters.[19]

All other jurisdictional disputes between the Carpenters, the IBEW, the IA, Painters, Plumbers, Machinists and Building Service Employees were forwarded to the AFL three-person committee. The committee rendered its decisions on 26 December 1945. The most controversial decision of the committee was that they granted set erection to the IA grips Local 80, basing this decision on a settlement worked out on 5 February 1925 between the Carpenters and the IA. This 1925 agreement temporarily ended the practice of strike-breaking among the various studio unions and led to the signing of the first Studio Basic Agreement in 1926. But in the succeeding decades the IA had conceded the work of set erection to the Carpenters. By awarding that work to the IA, the committee had effectively taken away 300–350 jobs from the Carpenters and had apparently abrogated the inter-union agreement reached on 13 November 1945.[20] This set the stage for the next and final CSU strike, what Roy Brewer referred to as 'the Communists' last stand in Hollywood'.

The Aftermath of the 1945 Strike

From the first day of his arrival in Hollywood, Roy Brewer had been busily building ideological bridges between the IA and the radical right community in Hollywood. Brewer managed to get the Los Angeles Central Labor Council (CLC) to pass a resolution on 30 October 1945, calling for a ban on 'Communists and CIO collaborators' in the ranks of organized labor.

Parallel to Brewer's actions, an investigative committee of the California Assembly initiated hearings on the riots at the studios, noting that there seemed to be a connection between certain UCLA professors and radical students and the 'left winger' John Howard Lawson. The Assemblymen also wanted to find out why the riots had been allowed to continue without police intervention. Through several days of public hearings, charges and counter-charges were hurled from both sides of the strike. In particular, Herb Sorrell was attacked for his alleged strong connections to the Communist Party and the Glendale police chief implied that Sorrell faked the attempt on his life to gain sympathy for the CSU. Assemblyman Jack Tenney joined in the chorus of the right-wing counterattack by promising further investigations into the riots, which he termed a 'small, but full dress rehearsal to test the efficacy of the new Communist Party line for widespread disorders, racial agitation, bloodshed and violence with the aim of ultimate revolution.'[21]

Brewer widened the net of his hunt for enemies and 'subversives'. He blocked reinstatement of forty IA members who had been laid off in the midst of the strike for failing to follow orders to do the work of striking CSU carpenters and painters. Then, on 19 November 1945, he re-initiated disciplinary proceedings against the twenty 'disloyal' IA members who resisted his handling of the strike, setting a trial date of 4 December. Some of these were old IA Progressives (the formal organization of IA Progressives had dissolved after the 1939 USTG defeat) and their friends who had dared to fight Brewer. This internal trial, which took several months to complete, was something of a farce, as Gene Mailes points out, in that the verdict was a foregone conclusion. The judge was one of Brewer's own men. A number of the defendants in the trial were permanently blacklisted from the industry, among them Gene Mailes.[22]

After the truce and the unsatisfactory agreement at the end of the 1945 strike-lockout, the trial against the four of us was started up again. Also charged with us were the sixteen men who had signed the letter protesting the International takeover of Local 44. The charges against them were identical with the charges against us.

Irv and I were more convinced than ever that we should get it all on the record. Ben Margolis thought it would be a good thing to have as well. It would only cost us our time and the extra money for additional pages of the trial transcript. The new defense team included Jean Caya and Paul Jaffe, from the Lab Local, with John Martin, Business Agent of the Lab Local, Bill Magginetti of Local 44 and Ted Ellsworth of the Wardrobe Local. Both Herb Aller of the Camera Local and Zeal Fairbanks of the Sound Local were pressured by Brewer to withdraw their support for us. Brewer put it this way in later testimony:

> During that period [the delay in the trial] it became clear to us that the disaffection of the two of these Locals [the Camera and Sound] was not Communist influence, basically. We analyzed it that it was political. They had some difference politically with the International Alliance, so that during the period between May of 1945 and when the trial resumed, this whole situation had clarified itself. So that when the trial resumed, only two locals which were obviously under the influence of Communist forces renewed their participation in the trial.[23]

The gentlemen in question were Herb Aller of the Camera Local and Harold V. Smith of the Sound Local. Smith never did appear with us at the trial. His assistant, Zeal Fairbanks, appeared in his place.

These two local unions that pulled out on us were expected to do something like that. We knew that we were being used by these two

135

business agents for their own purpose, which was to strengthen their own position in studio union politics. These two men were the perfect examples of the 'jealous little barons'. But we didn't let their defections stop us from keeping faith with the idea of democratic unions. We stuck to our guns, even though nothing that we could have done would have prevented our expulsion from the IA and consequent blacklisting from the studios.

The trial went on for a total of twenty-two sessions and finally ended with each of the counsels presenting arguments summing up what we had done and had tried to do. The rest of the time was given over to each of the defendants having their last say. We started with the less involved activists, working up to Jesse Sapp, Bob Ames, and me and finishing with Irv. We all spoke as if we had a chance of being acquitted, as if it had been a fair trial. We all finished up nailing our colors to the mast, in our own ways. Some of the defendants who had not done anything else but sign the letter agreeing that their names be added to the petition for legal relief did not attend any of the trial sessions. We had reason to believe that one or two of them had been in touch with the local officials, trying to make some sort of deal for themselves to allow them to remain in the IA and continue working. In fairness to all of them, it must be noted that the only one to accuse any of us of being Communists was Roy Brewer. A couple of the people on trial with us were very pathetic in their denials of any wrongdoing. It is a sad thing to see men beg. When the session was over we tried to be sympathetic in talking with them. We shook their hands and wished them luck.

As usual, Irv and I stopped in for a couple of beers, then stayed until the place closed. We were down at the mouth.

Brewer's Witch-hunt

During the time of the trial against Gene Mailes and his friends, Brewer also actively worked at discrediting Herb Sorrell; Brewer had begun this process at the 1945 AFL Convention. In May 1946, Brewer and his red-baiting ally J. W. Buzzell, President of the Los Angeles CLC, maneuvered the CLC into a full-scale trial of Sorrell on charges of being a Communist. The star witness for the prosecution was Jack Tenney, a California State Assembly Representative as well as an embittered, deposed labor leader, who had taken upon himself the job of 'sanitizing' the labor unions in California. He headed a California Assembly fact-finding committee on un-American activities that investigated the influence of Communists in the California labor movement. In February 1946, Tenney's committee issued a report claiming that Herb Sorrell was a 'secret member' of the Communist Party. The claim was that he was registered on the Party's records as 'Herbert Stewart' – Stewart was Sorrell's mother's family name. This kind of linkage seems rather weak in that a Party member trying to come up with a pseudonym would probably not use any name that could be directly connected to them. In June 1946, eight representatives to the California state AFL convention put forward a resolution labeling Sorrell 'an important stooge and tool of the Communist Party design for the destruction of AFL unions in Hollywood.'[24] The resolution was later amended to eliminate the specific name of Sorrell, calling instead for a general investigation of 'alleged Communist domination of some American Federation of Labor unions in the motion picture industry.'[25] The Los Angeles CLC trial against Sorrell dragged on for months with quite inconclusive results. This kind of harassment and red-baiting, however, effectively served to isolate Sorrell from support in the labor movement as a whole and to keep him busy denying his alleged affiliation with the Communist Party; thus he was less able to cope with a worsening situation for the CSU in the studios. Roy Brewer's leadership of the campaign to rid the studio unions of Communists thus served the purposes of the IA and the producers quite well.

In the broader political milieu of postwar Hollywood, Brewer expanded his influence by becoming a zealous member of the Motion Picture Alliance for the Preservation of American Ideals (MPA), a right-wing organization of motion picture industry writers, actors and producers. This organization actively campaigned for congressional investigations into the Communist Party's activities in the motion picture industry. Prominent members of this organization, including Brewer, later acted as agents of 'rehabilitation' for actors, writers and directors who were accused during the McCarthy era of being Communists or fellow travelers. In this rehabilitation process, allegedly subversive members of the motion picture community were 'allowed' to confess their sins, typically by giving the MPA executives lists of names and also by emphatically admitting their 'guilt' and subsequent 'enlightenment'. In *Report on Blacklisting*, John Cogley summarized Brewer's tactics in dealing with Sorrell and the CSU:

> Brewer was working with the producers now, trying to convince them that it was to their interest to deal with him rather than Sorrell. He was lining up support within the AFL. He had become active in community work and Democratic Party politics. He was gaining influence and prestige in the MPA; the anti-Communists were full of admiration for his success in whittling away at Sorrell's prestige.[26]

While Brewer conducted his smear campaign against Sorrell, the three-person AFL committee's decision to grant set erection to the IA grips served to fuel the fires of resentment and hostility among the studio workers and the contending unions. On 21 January 1946, members of Carpenters Local 946 and Painters Local 644 staged one-day sit-in strikes at Universal and Columbia studios to protest the decision to grant set erection to the grips. Sorrell publicly questioned the committee's right to render judgment over a jurisdictional question that had been resolved by the locals involved; the International offices of the Carpenters and the IA had approved these agreements. At the urging of Carpenters' International President Hutcheson, AFL President William Green issued a statement calling for a 'clarification' of the committee's decision regarding set erection.[27]

In the meantime, the IAM (Machinists) had withdrawn from the AFL, prompting the AFL to issue a federal charter to a separate organization to handle machinists' work in the sound editing and projection booths in the studios. In early February 1946, Carpenters Local 946 formally joined the CSU, thus swelling the ranks of the organization to some 10,000 members, in comparison to the IA's 16,000 studio workers.[28] At that time, Sorrell served an ultimatum to the producers calling for substantial increases in pay and an adjustment in hours to accommodate the returning veterans seeking their old jobs in the studios. Here is Sorrell's version of his demands as recorded in his testimony before a Congressional Subcommittee on jurisdictional disputes in the motion picture industry:

> We had a 6-hour day, and 36-hour week in the studios. We had been work-ing 48 hours and being paid for 54 hours all during the war period. Now, that was perfectly all right, but the boys began to come back; the boys who had worked in there, who had left their jobs; my son, for instance, he was an apprentice painter, and he came back, and there had to be a place made for him, and we figured the best way to make a place for those boys was to go back to the 36-hour week, but we didn't like to take a cut in pay, so if we got a raise in pay to compensate for the difference in hours, everybody would make a living, and why not? The producers were making plenty of profit. They said so in the trade papers.[29]

Sorrell set 16 February 1946, as the deadline for the producers to respond to the CSU demands. Meanwhile *Variety* astutely observed that the producers hoped that the CSU would strike, since the producers could then call the walk-out a 'jurisdictional strike' by the unions involved over the machinists and the set erectors issues. Sorrell wisely chose not to call for a strike on the date of the deadline, publicly stating that the producers were still 'bargaining in good faith'. He pledged to the producers that the 'Conference [of Studio Unions] will assure the producers that we will not participate in any strike against the directive of the three-man Committee.'[30] Producers' representa-tive B. B. Kahane replied to Sorrell's pledge with the characteristically blasé style that indicated that the producers could wait forever for the settlement of the jurisdictional disputes:

> We have asked for a definite agreement on the part of each union that it will carry out the terms of that directive irrespective of the outcome of any negotiations in which we now engage. We are compelled to ask a direct agreement by each union as to this matter, as we feel that any action by, or resolution of, the Conference of Studio Unions is ineffective for this pur-pose.[31]

MPAA President Eric Johnston wrote an article for the 24 February 1946 edition of the *New York Times*, titled 'Labor Should Have a Stake in Capital-ism'. Without specifically referring to the motion picture industry, Johnston called for workers to share in both profits and management. Clearly Johnston was speaking for himself and not for the producers when he wrote this article. On the surface, the producers seemed to be genuinely interested in setting up effective arbitration machinery to handle current and future jurisdictional disputes in the motion picture industry. In late February 1946, the producers and the studio labor union leaders discussed the possibility of the appoint-ment of a studio labor 'czar' who would be empowered to arbitrate jurisdic-tional disputes within twenty-four hours of their occurrence. Unions would be bound to the czar's decisions and those decisions would have the force of legal precedent; such decisions would thus set jurisdictional patterns for the entire industry over the course of time. At the end of March 1946, Byron Price, Vice-president of the Association of Motion Picture Producers (the producers' labor relations organization), presented a five-year plan that followed the same sort of labor-czar plan.[32]

But even as Eric Johnston and Byron Price spoke publicly of cooperation and industrial peace, B. B. Kahane, the producers' chief negotiator, informed CSU negotiators that the contract for the Story Analysts Guild would be an open shop contract. The producers claimed that they were no longer bound to hire from the Story Analysts Guild because of disciplinary fines levied by the guild against those story analysts who crossed the CSU picket lines in March 1945.[33]

And at the bargaining table, the producers were still 'playing hard ball'. Labor unions throughout the country were demanding substantial wage increases to cope with the sudden leaps in the cost of living that accompanied the removal of wage and price controls imposed by the federal government during the war. Manufacturers in all industries were equally determined to hold wages down. Wartime after-tax profits in the motion picture industry had increased at a far greater rate than had the wages of motion picture craft workers. Of course, the net profits also included operating capital, but it seems clear that the producers had no intention of sharing their astronomical postwar profits with the studio craft workers.

On 17 April, several IA locals walked out of negotiations with the producers when the producers offered the locals a flat 18 cents wage increase. Both IA and CSU locals concluded that the producers were stalling for time. The more rebellious IA locals began questioning whether their chief negotiator, Roy Brewer, was sincerely bargaining for the best deal he could get for them. Members of the Painters, Carpenters and Machinists studio locals authorized strikes if the CSU negotiators felt that the producers were not bargaining in good faith. Billy Wilkerson, editor and publisher of the *Hollywood Reporter*, took his usual pro-management stand in mid-April, editorializing that there should be a long strike so that the studio craft workers would 'wake up'. Eric Johnston promised in the first week of April that he would get talks moving within one week, but this turned out to be an empty promise.[34]

On 22 May 1946, the machinists' issue came to a head when the Los Angeles CLC ordered the producers to replace the IAM Local 1185 machinists with members of the federally chartered AFL machinists local. By the following week, the CLC issued orders to the members of its affiliated studio locals to refuse to handle any equipment serviced by IAM machinists. By the middle of June, members of the Painters and Carpenters studio locals were refusing to handle sets constructed by IA grips. From 19 June 1946 the managers of the various studios began laying off hundreds of painters and carpenters for refusing to handle the 'hot sets'. On 26 June, the NLRB intervened in the machinists' dispute, demanding that the producers rehire the IAM machinists for the time being, pending further consideration of a petition filed with the NLRB by the producers regarding the machinists. Four days later, Sorrell presented a set of demands to the producers. These included substantial wage increases for members of CSU locals and a cessation of the producers' hiring of non-IAM machinists, pending the decision of the NLRB. On the next day, 1 July 1946, 7,000 CSU members walked out of the studios. IA lab technicians Local 683 refused to cross the picket lines, thus stopping the production of release prints.[35]

For once, the producers responded quickly, indicating the significance of the lab workers to the financial well-being of the industry. On 2 July, B. B. Kahane called a mass meeting of representatives from the CSU, the IA, SAG and the producers. The meeting produced an agreement that came to be called the 'Treaty of Beverly Hills'. The strikers returned to work under the conditions that all workers be granted a 25 per cent wage increase and a 36-hour work week. The machinists' issue was to be handled by an NLRB election; in the interim, the producers were free to obtain machinists from any source as they saw fit. The 'treaty' also called for the establishment of arbitration machinery to handle various jurisdictional disputes, but this arbitration process between the CSU and the IA was never established.[36]

Notes

1. *Variety*, 10 October 1945, p. 18; *Daily Variety*, 8 October, 1945, p. 11. Note how the Los Angeles-based *Daily Variety* editor chose to explain the events in contrast to the New York-based *Variety*. The deletion of the words about the cars trying to run over the pickets totally alters the tone of the story.
2. *Variety*, 10 October 1945, p. 18.
3. *Daily Variety*, 8 October 1945, pp. 1, 8.
4. *Variety*, 10 October 1945, p. 18.
5. Los Angeles *Evening Herald Express*; *Hollywood Atom*, 9 October 1945, p. 1.
6. Los Angeles *Evening Herald Express*.
7. Conrad Seiler, 'Hollywood rebellion', *New Republic*, 5 November 1945, p. 599.
8. Los Angeles *Evening Herald Express*, 10 October 1945, p. 3.
9. Ibid., p. 2.
10. *Daily Variety*, 12 October 1945, pp. 1, 6.
11. The primary source for the figures on the election count is the report in the Los Angeles *Evening Herald Express*, 12 October 1945, p. 1. The same figure was reported in *Daily Variety*, 12 October 1945, pp. 1, 6.
12. Los Angeles *Evening Herald Express*, 15 October 1945, pp. 1, 6; *Variety*, 17 October 1945, p. 5.
13. Los Angeles *Evening Herald Express*, 16 October 1945, p. 6; 18 October 1945, pp. 1, 11; 17 October 1945, p. 6; *Variety*, 24 October 1945, p. 29.
14. Los Angeles *Evening Herald Express*, 20 October 1945, p. 4.
15. Los Angeles *Evening Herald Express*, 19 October 1945, pp. 1, 8.
16. Los Angeles *Evening Herald Express*, 25 October 1945, p. 3.
17. *Daily Variety*, 30 October 1945, p. 10.
18. Los Angeles *Evening Herald Express*, 30 October 1945, p. 1; *Hollywood Sun*, 14 November 1945, p. 10; *Variety*, 14 November 1945, p. 7; see also 'Hollywood Studio Strike' files, UCLA archives.
19. United States House of Representatives, *Jurisdictional Disputes in the Motion Picture Industry*, Washington, 1948, p. 463.
20. *New York Times*, 17 February 1946, p. 4.
21. Los Angeles *Evening Herald Express*, 2 November 1945, pp. 1, 6; 8 November 1945, pp. 1, 2; 10 November 1945, p. 2.
22. Los Angeles *Evening Herald Express*, 19 November 1945, p. 7.
23. *Jurisdictional Disputes in the Motion Picture Industry*, p. 1777.

24. *New York Times*, 2 June 1946, p. 9.

25. *New York Times*, 19 June 1946, p. 18.

26. John Cogley, *Report on Blacklisting: I, The Movies* (New York: Fund for the Republic, 1956), p. 67.

27. *Variety*, 10 January 1946, p. 22; 30 January 1946, pp. 3, 20.

28. *Variety*, 6 February 1946, pp. 3, 12; 13 February 1946, p. 3.

29. *Jurisdictional Disputes in the Motion Picture Industry*, p. 772.

30. *Variety*, 20 February 1946, p. 38.

31. Ibid.

32. The *New York Times* article on Johnston's speech was cited in *Variety*, 27 February 1946, p. 3; *Variety*, 20 March 1946, p. 20.

33. *Hollywood Sun*, 10 April 1946, p. 1.

34. The *Hollywood Reporter* quote is in the *Hollywood Sun*, 10 April 1946 p. 1; 17 April 1946, p. 1.

35. *Jurisdictional Disputes in the Motion Picture Industry*, pp. 15-18.

36. Ibid., p. 18.

8

THE FINAL BATTLE

The 1946 IA Convention: Bringing the War Back Home
We knew that nothing would be final until the IA National Convention
the following July, 1946, in Chicago. The trial board had to finish their
decision, write it up, and send it back to the union headquarters in the
East. In the spring of 1946, an election for delegates to the convention
was held and we took part in the elections. None of us ran in the election but we certainly put forward a progressive ticket for the members
to consider. To our joy, none of the trial board were elected, nor was
Cappy DuVal. DuVal had to be appointed by Brewer as a delegate from
one of the scab locals, so that he could be in Chicago for the convention
and attend the Grievance Committee hearings when our case came up.
This was a clear indication of our strength within the local. Under local
control we would have been acquitted

We received notice of our conviction and sentence. Twelve of us were
convicted on all counts and the sentence was expulsion from the IA. The
findings of the trial board had to be sent through regular channels, so we
knew that we would remain as members until after the convention. We
knew that the IA was living up to the letter of the union's constitution in
order to avoid making any mistakes. They knew that we had legal talent
every bit as good as theirs. A collection was taken up on the various lots to
send George Stoica and me to the Chicago convention. Eighteen hundred
dollars were raised. They would have given us the shirts off their backs if it
came to that. Then Jesse Sapp and some of his friends on the lots suggested that he should also be a member of our appeal committee. We
didn't want to make an issue out of it, so we went along with the idea and
the eighteen hundred was split three ways. It was further agreed that the
three of us would get together and write up the appeal. But we never did.
One week before we were to leave for Chicago, I sat down and worked
around the clock for almost three days. When I finished, I showed it to
George and Jesse. At their advice, I changed a few words in the summary.
Then I took it down to Ben Margolis' office to see if it looked OK to him.
He made no corrections and said it was an excellent job. All the work had
been worth it. I then took it to the office of Local 683, the Lab Local, and
one of the secretaries there typed it up and had fifty copies of it run off on
the mimeograph machine. It was finished the day before we had to leave.

The last several days before leaving for the convention, my wife
Thelma and I had no time whatever to spend together. We left the baby

with a friend and went down to the Los Angeles Railway Station, a busy place in those days, and had a late lunch at the Fred Harvey Restaurant. This was the only time that we were able to have alone with each other for a couple of weeks. During the lunch I asked her, 'How in the hell did I get myself into this?' We laughed at the hectic life we had lived for the last several years. We talked about how we had often discussed the idea of having a sailboat. How wonderful it would be to go out on the water and drift with the wind. And rest. And rest. And play. And play. How we wished that we were going to Chicago together!

Our little committee was on the same train as the Local 683 delegation, the Super Chief. We had a stateroom and we took turns on the upper berth. I slept in the upper berth the first night and didn't wake until about nine o'clock the next day. I spent the rest of the day going over the transcript of the trial and our appeal. Over and over and over.

An attorney, Bill Esterman, was going with the Local 683 delegation. He offered to help us any way that he could. We didn't ask him for help – he looked us up and offered his services. We found that we needed him several times and he was always very generous with his time.

In late July 1946, IA President Walsh presided over the Thirty-Eighth Convention of the IA in Chicago. Eric Johnston of the MPAA gave the keynote address, in which he solemnly declared that 'Utopia *is* production!' Johnston was determined to convert the motion picture industry from a jurisdictional battleground to a productive utopia:

> This motion picture industry of ours pays the highest wages in all industry. It wants to pay even higher wages. It looks ahead to steady employment – to two things – higher wages and steady employment.
>
> But both must come out of production. If we on the management end and you on the labor end work hand in glove together, it will assure us all good jobs for all our times. That is, if we ask for more and more production. After all, it is not the hourly standard which determines a man's real pay – it's what he produces.
>
> We'll get full production only as we maintain good relations. They ought to be better than good. They ought to be the best of all industries. If we make the best pictures in the world, and if we pay the best wages in all the world, then we ought to have the best internal relations of any industry. And there's no reason why we can't.[1]

Johnston's analysis, which in places sounded a bit like a Stalinist manifesto, overlooked the fact that the producers had welcomed and encouraged jurisdictional fights since 1918 to maintain the open shop and to hold down wages. Productivity was never an issue for the major vertically integrated companies as long as they maintained their oligopolistic dominance over the three branches of the industry.

President Walsh addressed the convention at length on his personal involvement in the 1945 strike and its subsequent settlement. He also reserved a section of his address to warn the delegates about the 'very real threat' to 'our way of life' by any 'ism' that 'seeks to tear down or destroy our

God, our way of life or the Trade Unionism which has made us great and in which I devoutly believe'. Ironically, Walsh emphatically denied being a red-baiter even as he was in the process of blatant red-baiting. He managed to vilify the more progressive element in the IA by citing US Attorney General Tom Clark as an authority on the red menace. Walsh told the delegates:

> He [Clark] grouped Communists and Fascists in the same category and said, 'In the black bible of their faith they seek to capture the important offices in Labor Unions, to create strikes and dissensions, and to raise barriers to efforts to maintain civil peace'.
>
> When such statements are made and such language used by Attorney General Clark it behooves us to heed the warning while there is yet time. Look with suspicion upon those in your midst who create discord within the ranks of your Local Union. Dedicate yourselves to combating with all legitimate means at your command those among you who sow the seeds of dissension in your Local Union in order to gain control. Do it now before it is too late.[2]

Later in his address, Walsh, without mentioning specific persons, referred to the studio dissidents who sought to regain a measure of autonomy in their dealings with the producers and the other studio unions:

> A certain element in order to attack me, for the ostensible purpose of strengthening the transmission belt to Moscow, or for other vile reasons, saw fit to prostitute the Alliance by continually keeping before our employers, Labor and the general public the incident [Browne and Bioff] which had almost proved disastrous to our Organization's future.[3]

Linking his own prestige with the fate of the 'free world', Walsh reminded the delegates that the 15 million Americans and Canadians who fought in the recent war did not fight to 'change our way of life'.

> Rather, they saw fit to shed their own lives' blood to preserve our democratic principles. Can we conscientiously do less at this Convention than to make certain that their glorious deeds have not been made in vain?
>
> I have tried to make this challenge as clear and as simple as the English language will permit. In the interests of unity and harmony during the war years I purposely refrained from making this an issue at our Conventions. I now feel, however, that the time has come for plain talk and concrete action on the part of the Delegates to this Convention to either welcome and adopt the 'party line' as a definite plan of this Organization or to take positive action that will now and all time rid the Alliance of this growing, insidious menace.[4]

To make certain that the delegates fully understood the 'clear and present danger', Walsh turned the microphone over to California state Senator Jack Tenney, who, according to the convention report, delivered 'a most interesting and enlightening discourse covering his ten years of service as a member of the California Legislature', which included his work with the California

Senate's un-American activities committee. Tenney briefly alluded to the efforts of Jeff Kibre and the Progressives to secure control of IA Local 37 back in the late 1930s. Tenney inexplicably took personal credit for the defeat of the United Studio Technicians Guild in 1939, and warned the delegates: 'One thing about these people is that they are never discouraged. . . . If they lose today, they organize their forces for tomorrow'. In a crazy-quilt fashion, Tenney tried to link anti-Semitism, the German-American Bund and the Ku Klux Klan with Herb Sorrell and the CSU.[5]

We had sent the appeal to the International office, so our first job was to make sure that it had arrived. We found they had received it, so all we had to do for the time being was to make sure that it went along where it was supposed to go. Before I had left for the convention, I went to see Ben Margolis. He told me not be concerned about anything but the job at hand, which was to make sure that the appeal was acted on by the Grievance Committee, then by the International Executive Board, and finally by the convention assembled. He reminded us of the importance of exhausting the internal remedies. Unless we did that, we might as well stay home.

At Bill Esterman's suggestion, we sent telegrams from the Western Union desk in the lobby of the hotel to the ninth floor, where the International officers were headquartered. We never received an answer, so we had to go around and ask when our case was coming up. It was frustrating, but we made it to every place that we should go. Nobody ever seemed glad to see us. We were not, as my father used to say, 'seeking fame at the cannon's mouth'. We just had a job to do and we did it.

At the Grievance Committee hearing we realized that they didn't have to put up any arguments against us. They just had to sit tight and we would lose the case. It was that simple. We went to a session of the International Executive Board and the same thing was apparent there. However, we made both bodies listen to us for over an hour.

When we got to the floor of the convention, we realized what we were really up against. The President's Report was full of anti-communist charges slanted toward those of us who had been fighting for local control of the studio locals, for so many years. To see and hear a political machine roaring approval of a corrupt leadership is a terrible thing to witness. The three of us, Jesse Sapp, George Stoica and I, were by then more or less detached from what we were watching. We knew that our job would be finished as soon as the convention accepted the recommendation of the Grievance Committee and the International Executive Board. We would have then exhausted the internal remedies of the organization and were therefore free to pursue our own civil court case against the International. A weight seemed to be falling away from us; our job was about over.

We were sitting in the gallery around the convention hall looking down on what was happening. We knew that any floor debate on our behalf would be useless and we quickly agreed that our friends there as delegates would take an unnecessary beating. So we signaled down to Ted Ellsworth on the floor to come to the door of hall. I met him there and told him that we knew the fight was over and that our friends would suffer a needless defeat if they tried to say anything in our favor; further, it would be a meaningless gesture, since we had accomplished what we had set out to do in coming to the convention. Ted protested mildly, so I told him that was our decision and to let it go at that. Following the vote of the convention on our case, a motion was passed giving the International President of the IA authority to suspend the union constitution if he considered it necessary. This tied nicely to their plan to force another lockout of the Conference of Studio Unions as soon as it could be arranged.

At this same convention, New Jersey District 14 of the IA presented a resolution calling for the IA President and the Executive Board to 'take immediate steps to rid the International of any subversive, radical or communistic groups'. In a wonderful rebuttal of the wording of this resolution, representatives from the two lab technicians' locals, Local 702 New York and Local 683 Los Angeles, strenuously objected to the use of the term 'radical'. John Martin of Local 683 posed the question:

'What is a radical? Depending on how reactionary a person happens to be in a particular local, someone else may have an opposite viewpoint and then would be called a radical. If we are going to put in radical, let's put in reactionary, too, because, believe me, we have plenty of reactionaries in this country'.[6]

Speaking in favor of the resolution and against objections by Martin and Herb Aller of Camerapersons Local 659, delegate Jack Hauser of Local 96 (Worcester, Massachusetts) offered the following revealing analogy:

I know how the resolution will be taken by this group but I want to answer the previous speaker who demanded the right of local unions to try their own members. I hope that your memories are not so short that you don't remember the mistake the allies made in 1918 and 1919 when they permitted Germany to try their war criminals.

I believe that locals should have the right to exercise local autonomy, but I wonder what kind of trial we would get for the benefit of our International Alliance if we permitted Local 44 to try their own war criminals.[7]

Hauser was simply continuing the whole theme of the 1946 IA Convention, the theme underscored by Walsh's address and the 'interesting discourse' of Jack Tenney. The reactionaries in various US institutions, labor unions included, were bringing the war back home. The most repressive actions were cloaked in red, white and blue banners. Although there was perhaps some need, in light of the 'unpatriotic' wartime strikes, for US labor unions to clean up their image with the US public, conservative labor union leaders attacked the progressive fringes of their organizations primarily for the opportunistic reason of solidifying their own administrations. The techniques of repression – such as smearing reputations and silencing opposition voices – that Walsh used at the 1946 IA convention were being applied in

Brewer now had the power to keep the studio locals in line. If he could pro-voke the CSU members to walk off their jobs, he could make a clean sweep of Sorrell and the CSU.

On 16 August 1946, the three-person AFL committee issued its much anticipated 'clarification' on the issue of set erection. Although the wording of the clarification was not noteworthy for its clarity, Carpenters International President William Hutcheson quickly claimed that the new statement clearly ceded to the Carpenters jurisdiction over set erection. According to labor relations researchers Lovell and Carter:

> The clarification was worded so that the jurisdiction of the IA was limited to assembly work, while jurisdiction over all jobs involving construction was returned to the Carpenters. It thus reversed those parts of the 1945 award that favored the IA. This action came in response to an official re-port in which AFL West Coast Director Daniel F. Flanagan indicated that the IA had been violating the 1945 directives and that a serious work stop-page was threatened.[11]

On 31 August, IA International President Walsh responded by declaring that the three-person committee had no right to issue any clarifications that altered the substance of the 26 December 1945 decision. At that time, the producers had a backlog of 129 features to be used in the event of a pro-tracted strike.

Brewer began meeting behind the scenes with the producers to devise a strategy to eliminate the CSU from the studios. The strategy was quite sim-ple. Brewer was consulted repeatedly during these meetings, and he assured the producers that IA members would take the place of striking CSU work-ers. Such collusive meetings were brought to light in a later congressional in-vestigation. Pat Casey, the producers' long-time labor negotiator, who had been shunned by the producers through much of the negotiations in 1945-6, provided detailed notes of the meetings. The notes give an accurate picture of the way in which the producers conspired with the IA to force CSU workers out of the studios. Ironically, after three decades of 'back room' deals between producers and labor leaders, one disgruntled executive shed light on the whole miserable process of selling the legitimate bargaining rights of motion picture craft workers for cash or power. All of the 'business as usual' for the producers came to light in an instant.[12]

Casey's notes indicate that on 11 September 1946 the producers found just the tool they needed to wreck the CSU when the West coast International Representative of the Carpenters, Joseph Cambiano, told the producers that, as of the following day, the CSU would label 'hot' all sets constructed by IA grips; no CSU members would work on those sets. On the following day, the producers held a meeting that was attended by representatives from all the major studios as well as from several smaller studios and the Technicolor company. The minutes of the meeting included the following remarks and instructions:

> Mr Kahane reported the recent conversations with the presidents [of the producing companies] and Eric Johnston which contained the following

recommendations: 'Lay off carpenters if they refuse to perform the services to which they are assigned. Do not be in any hurry – take as much time as you can before crossing jurisdictional lines. Work with the IA to get a sufficient number of carpenters, electricians, painters, etc'.

INSTRUCTIONS TO DEPARTMENT HEADS

1. Any employee who refuses to perform the work properly assigned to him in accordance with his regular classification of work should be requested to leave the premises.

2. In the event that such employee asks whether he is being discharged he should be told 'no'.

3. In the event that any such employee asks whether or not he is being laid off he should be told that he is not being laid off, but that he is not wanted on the premises as long as he refuses to perform his customary duties.

4. In the event that any such employee further asks what is his status he should be told that he is requested to leave because of his refusal to perform services requested.

5. He should be paid off to time of leaving.[13]

The minutes also included Brewer's response when Kahane asked him if the IA would furnish the studios with strike-breakers.

Brewer replied that they [the IA] will do everything to keep the studios open – and will supply the necessary help.

However, there are a few unions such as actors, teamsters, culinary workers, etc., about which there is some question.

Kahane inquired if Brewer thought the laboratory technicians would pass a picket line – he replied he doesn't know but he will use the full power of the IATSE to force them to [do so]. He is sure the grips and sound can be depended upon.[14]

The way these 'informal minutes' came to be revealed is interesting. Pat Casey, the Chief Negotiator for the Motion Picture Producers' Association, in spite of his job, was a fairly decent man. He was also a very devout Catholic. The Archbishop of Los Angeles had involved himself in the dispute because of the privation the strikes caused for so many people. He appointed a committee of two of his highest aids to investigate the problem. The report was critical of the studios' and the IA's role in the strike. Some of the collaboration of the IA and the producers was outlined in the report and the authors also noted that both the IA and the producers over-stated the participation of the Communist Party in the strikes.

The producers' Labor Committee summarily dismissed the report as inadequate and biased. It was well known that Pat Casey was angered with that action and the implied insult to the Archbishop of Los Angeles. At the time, many people felt that this was probably the underlying reason that these secret committee minutes were released. The minutes showed clearly that the IA officials were in on the meetings at which the studios and the IA planned to force the CSU out and break the strike resulting from the combined actions of the employers and the IA

149

Strikers and non-strikers are not fighting over a question of wages and hours. They are fighting because two International presidents of AFL unions cannot agree on which union should have jurisdiction over 350 jobs. The livelihood of 30,000 American workers, all members of the AFL, is endangered and an entire industry has been thrown into chaos and confusion.[22]

The national press lapped up Montgomery's statement and spread it around the country as the 'last word' on the CSU strike/lockout. The strike had attracted national attention, but the story was cast in terms of the juris-dictional issues between AFL unions. *Life* rounded out its coverage of the strike with a posed shot of an actress facing a costumer and a make-up artist. The headline caption above the photo reads 'MOST DELICATE JURISDIC-TIONAL QUESTION: WHICH UNION MAKES THE "FALSIES"?' The text caption reads, in part, 'This picture, of an actress caught between cloth falsies and rubber falsies, symbolizes Hollywood's complicated labor troubles'.[23] Sorrell was never really given a chance to present the CSU position to the American public. *Time*, *Life* and *Newsweek* all failed to point out that Montgomery himself was a producer of his own movies. Also the national press failed to mention that it was the solidarity of the CSU that had gotten all workers in the industry the long-awaited 25 per cent wage increase back in July. But most critically, the related issues of the producers' stalling tactics and their encouragement of jurisdictional disputes were never given the attention they deserved. Industry and union people were well aware that the producers were out to break the CSU. The story was on the streets in Holly-wood, but the magazines preferred to quote the actors and trivialize the des-peration of the craft workers.

A contingent of SAG members went to the AFL convention in Chicago on 7 October to put a resolution calling for the IA and the CSU unions to enter into binding arbitration. Although the resolutions committee approved the resolution for concurrence by the convention, they added an additional clause, calling for approval of the arbitration procedure by the unions involved in the dispute. *Variety* noted that the insertion of this clause changed the resolution from a plan of action to mere 'moral pressure' on the CSU and the IA.[24]

After two weeks of picketing, the CSU had sustained substantial casual-ties, including 55 arrested, 23 hospitalized and 104 injured sufficiently to be taken off picket duty. The producers had managed to take up the slack in their labor force by hiring IA strike-breakers and by assigning IA workers already in the studios to new jobs.[25]

However, on 13 October 1946, a major break occurred in the IA's ranks when IA lab technicians Local 683 voted to support the strike. The local had recently rejected a contract negotiated for them by Roy Brewer, and they demanded that the local leaders be given the right to bargain for Local 683. When the lab technicians walked off their jobs, they effectively froze the final stage of production: the making of release prints for theaters. Technicolor was especially hard-hit since this primary facility for color print production had already been hard-pressed to meet the growing demand for release prints. At the time the lab technicians walked out, the major and independent compa-nies had a total of forty-seven feature films in production; nine of them being filmed in the Technicolor process. *Variety* detailed the complications produced by a strike at the Technicolor plant:

> Processing tie-up was bad enough before the strike, according to one industry spokesman, when Technicolor was forced to limit each company to 40 prints a month. Under the consent decree proviso that each film must be tradeshown before selling, the majors, with their average of 32 exchanges, were just about able to round up enough prints during the first month after a picture's completion for the screenings. If the majors now find themselves unable to get even those 40 prints for the nine Technicolor films, they'll be forced to spread out the product already finished in order to keep their distribution setup in operation until after the strike is settled.[26]

Roy Brewer wasted little time in solving this problem for the producers. On 15 October, IA President Walsh declared Local 683 in a state of emergency. He authorized Brewer to appoint new officers for the local. The members and leaders of Local 683 dubbed this new organization 'Local 683 and one-half'. The real officers of Local 683 mounted a steel barrier at the entrance to their offices and posted armed guards with automatic weapons. Local 683 Business Agent John Martin ran up the flag in a public statement deeply critical of the Brewer/Walsh team: 'We are tired of being used as strikebreakers against union men with whom we have worked for years, tired of collusion between top employers and top union leaders and tired of being told without proper local autonomy what kind of a contract we must work under'.[27] Brewer immediately began placing strike-breaking workers in the labs, but it was clear from reports in the trade press that as late as December 1946 the strike-breakers were unable to perform at the level of the strikers. Brewer was eventually able, however, to get a sufficient number of striking Local 683 members to return to work to train the new personnel.

Brewer had saved the day for the producers. The price of resisting Brewer's invitation to cross the picket lines was steep for striking 683 members. Their specialized skills, which made them so indispensable to the producers, also made them unemployable outside of the industry. One lab technician I interviewed in 1984 told me that he spent his time during the strike working as a clerk in a downtown Los Angeles clothing store for substantially less money than he had been earning in the 20th Century-Fox labs. He explained that he felt trapped by the events:

> I got caught in the strike and I was out two years. It was a wildcat strike and I had no business going out. They [the other striking members of 683] kept coming to me, they'd call me at 12 o'clock at night and tell me, 'Don't you go back to work. We're married, and we've got children. There's no reason for you to go back to work'. I was never in a strike before. I didn't even know what a union was.
>
> [The company] kept my job open for six months. The president of the company told me, 'I can only hold your job so long'. I was assistant [film] vault clerk at that time. They gave my job to a [man who used to be] a shoe salesman. That fellow stayed in. He has his own office now and has eight people working for him. If I had stayed in, I'd be high up today.

The next day I went up to see him. I thought it best to come out immediately and ask if he would give us a copy of the note that we had seen the previous day. He frowned and was silent for a few seconds and slowly shook his head and told me that he couldn't do that, but he would think for a while and see if there was anything he could do to help. He seemed to want to talk and asked me about George Stoica, and then Irv. Then he asked me who was our attorney. When I told him that Ben Margolis was our attorney, he raised his voice and said, 'Oh, he's tops! You couldn't have a better one!' I had the feeling that I should tell Ben Margolis about the meetings with Mr Nelson, so I called him. Ben asked me if I could come to his office and see him. Recognizing that it might be more important than I realized, I told Ben that I would be right down.

When I got to Ben's office, he told me to think over what I had said to Mr Nelson and what he had said to me, as exactly as I could remember. I went over it carefully. Ben nodded his head and thanked me for coming. We talked about how our 'army' was holding up. A few minutes later as I was going down in the elevator it struck me that I might have unknowingly carried a message. It turned out that I was right.

In talking to Mike Kommoroff, I asked him if he had been able to get the letter. He patted the right side of his breast over his inside pocket. I was talking with a reporter several weeks later and he told me that Fred Meyers, the studio manager at Fox studio, had gone to his office at 2.30 in the morning to remove his copy of the letter from his files. He knew that he had been sent a blacklist. This, of course, was after it became known that we had known of the blacklist and probably had a copy of it. Fred Meyers was not called as a witness, but other studio managers were called and we knew that they lied about this document.

Mike Kommoroff was the field examiner for these cases. He had to sift through all these cases and turn down all except the most obvious. Then Bob Rissman took over as our NLRB attorney. This examination took several months. Stewart Meecham was the Trial Examiner (Judge). We were assured by Bob Rissman that complainants were encouraged to have their own attorneys. We held back on asking Ben Margolis to represent us until the first day of the hearing, then we understood what Bob Rissman meant when he suggested that we might want Ben there. Two of us, George Stoica and I, left the hearing and went to Ben's office and told him what was happening and Ben dropped what he was doing and went with us back to the hearing.

As soon as the proceedings started, the attitude of Homer Mitchell, of the law firm of O'Melveny and Meyers, shocked all of us who were connected with the hearing. He was just within the boundary of formal courtesy toward the Trial Examiner; toward Mr Rissman and Mr Kommoroff he was downright discourteous; toward the complainants he was unbelievably discourteous. Based on other motion picture cases he was involved with, it seemed that when he represented the motion picture studios he had a 'go-for-the-throat' attitude. When he represented other companies, such as Lockheed Aircraft Company, he acted with proper courtroom decorum. We were all shocked. What was behind this we never found out. The IA was represented by Mike Luddy, of the firm Breslin, Bodkin and Luddy. They sided, of course, with the employers. They maintained that we had no rights regarding our jobs. The case and the appeals that followed dragged on for years.

There were renewed indications that there was to be another lockout before long. The first of these was the vote by the IA convention to allow the President to have the authority to suspend the constitution. Then there were rumors that an actual plot was being conducted by the studios and the IA. We were aware that the producers' labor committee was holding meetings at which a further attack on the CSU was being discussed. It was not known for quite a while what was being planned.

The expulsion letters were finally received. On Ben's advice, we ignored the letters and went to work as usual, knowing that sooner or later the employers would let us know all about it. This happened about a week after we had received our copies of the letter. I went to the 20th Century-Fox lot, just west of Beverly Hills, on the afternoon shift. Ben had advised us that when we were told that we could no longer work at whichever studio we were working, we should go up to the studio Personnel Manager's office and demand to know why we were being fired. On the Fox lot, which sprawled over several acres, there was a free bus that took anyone anywhere on the lot. It went a regular route. While I was waiting for the bus I sat down on the curb and started to go over in my head just what I would say to Mr Fred Meyers, in whose office I had been several times. As I sat there, the idea of asking why I was being fired suddenly became very funny to me. I knew damned well why I was being fired. I began to laugh. I had worked very hard giving them reasons to want me out of the business. I suddenly felt very tired and decided not to go to Mr Meyers' office. I didn't even worry about having checked in on the time clock. I went home. The drive home was lonely and depressing. Thelma and I left the baby with a friend and took a long ride up the coast, and then came back and had dinner on the Santa Monica pier and got home very late. We later were surprised that not once during that time had we talked about what had happened that day, or what we were going to do next.

I did go down and apply for unemployment insurance and drew all I could; after all, I was a landscape set dresser and I could not find a job working at that. That wasn't my fault.

The immediate problem was to get on the payroll somewhere. I had not worked for quite a while. I went to the Painters union and asked if it would be possible to work as a painter for a while. We knew that this situation was going to be a long time before any settlement, and we had to have some money coming in.

After the strike of 1946 was forced on the Conference of Studio workers we all realized that this was a very real effort by the studios to break the democratic unions in the business. It was finally decided that a way to attract public attention was to fill up the jails of Los Angeles. Columbia studio, on Gower Street, was selected as being the studio most apt to be seen by the most people. The lockout was so rotten and illegal we felt that if the story was known by enough people it might help to bring it to a stop. We were wrong.

Before returning to Washington, after the first series of hearings, Congressman Kearns stated:

A careful analysis of the testimony, heretofore received, indicates that the jurisdictional strife in September, 1946, which has continued to the present time, in the Hollywood studios is probably the result of collusion between the producers and the I.A.T.S.E. Therefore, gentlemen, unless you have evidence to the contrary to present to submit [sic] to my subcommittee it is my intention to make a finding of fact that the present labor dispute in Hollywood is the result of a lockout by the employers after having conspired with certain officials of the I.A.T.S.E. to create incidents which would make it impossible for the members of those unions affiliated with the Conference of Studio Unions to continue to work in the studios.

There is substantial evidence in the record that this conspiracy was aided by certain of the officers and employees of the Teamsters union and the actors guild, for the lockout could not have succeeded without the co-operation of both of these organizations. The incidents arranged for in conference between the producers and the I.A.T.S.E. were deferred until they had secured the assurance of cooperation and support from the teamsters and the actors.[31]

When Kearns publicly committed himself to the side of the CSU, the producers began working behind the scenes to force Congressman Fred Hartley, Chairman of the Education and Labor Committee of the Congress, to expand the subcommittee to a point where Congressman Kearns would be outvoted and his actions nullified. This led to the appointment of Gerald W. Landis, Thomas L. Owens, D. C. Fisher and John S. Wood to the subcommittee headed by Mr Kearns. Upon the appointment of these new members, the subcommittee then allowed the question of Communism to be entered into the record. The tactic of the producers and IA officials and their lawyers was to equate any opposition to criminal rule with disloyalty to the country and all that it stood for. It was a sickening and cynical abuse of patriotism, reminiscent of Samuel Johnson's remark, 'Patriotism, the last refuge of a scoundrel'. Or, to paraphrase Oriana Fallaci: 'They were a leadership who loudly proclaimed themselves as masters of courage and freedom, but the minute the mob took over the union they bedded with them like whores, and to save their jobs they slandered anyone who did or tried to do what they themselves should have been doing'.[32]

When the Kearns committee returned to Washington, the tone of the inquiry changed substantially. Congressman Fred Hartley demanded that the committee look into the alleged Communist Party affiliation of Herb Sorrell. The well-worn photostats of the party card of 'Herbert Stewart' were dragged out again, just as they had been in the Los Angeles CLC, in the California state AFL convention and at the 1947 House Un-American Activities Committee hearings into alleged subversive activity in the motion picture industry. When the Kearns committee issued its final report in January 1949, it absolved the leaders of the IA and the producers of any wrongdoing in the strikes of

1945-8. The fact that the committee overlooked the hundreds of blacklistings of craft workers – people who were neither 'Communists' nor 'fascists' but simply caught 'out of bounds' during a very confusing period – is a strong indication of just how far to the right the US had moved in the post war period.[33]

On 3 October 1947, shortly after the Kearns committee had returned to Washington, the original officers of Local 683 – John Martin, Russell McKnight and Norval Crutcher – surrendered the books and assets of the local to Roy Brewer. These three men, along with 125 other Local 683 members, were permanently expelled from the local. At least another 150 members were suspended from membership for varying periods of time. Later in that same month, Sorrell's own local, Painters 644, voted to allow members to cross the picket lines without penalty, signaling the eventual collapse of the CSU. The painters who chose to return to the studios joined the IA motion picture set painters Local 729. At that time, there were still 2,000 carpenters, 1,000 painters and 300 machinists out on strike. The picket lines continued throughout 1947 and 1948, but the lines grew smaller and smaller as the strikers were forced either to cross the lines or to seek employment out of the motion picture industry.[34]

Notes

1. IATSE, *Combined Convention Proceedings*, vol. 2, p. 637.
2. Ibid., p. 640.
3. Ibid., p. 644.
4. Ibid.
5. Ibid., pp. 680-1.
6. Ibid., p. 713.
7. Ibid.
8. Ibid.
9. Ibid., p. 718.
10. Ibid., p. 783.
11. Hugh Lovell and Tasile Carter, *Collective Bargaining in the Motion Picture Industry: A Struggle for Stability* (Berkeley: University of California Press, 1955), p. 24.
12. United States House of Representatives, *Jurisdictional Disputes in the Motion Picture Industry*, Washington, 1948, p. 909.
13. Ibid., pp. 909-10.
14. Ibid.
15. *Variety*, 25 September 1946, pp. 1, 20.
16. Ibid, p. 20.
17. Stephen Englund and Larry Ceplair, *The Inquisition in Hollywood* (New York: Anchor/Doubleday, 1980), p. 223; *Wall Street Journal*, 30 June 1945.
18. *Variety*, 2 October 1946, p. 26.
19. *Jurisdictional Disputes in the Motion Picture Industry*, p. 913.
20. George H. Dunne, *Hollywood Labor Dispute: A Study in Immorality* (Los Angeles: Conference Publishing, 1950), p. 37.
21. *Jurisdictional Disputes in the Motion Picture Industry*, p. 914.
22. *Variety*, 9 October 1946, p. 7.
23. 'Hollywood puts on a strike thriller', *Life*, 14 October 1946, p. 35.
24. *Variety*, 16 October 1946, pp. 1, 23.
25. *Variety*, 9 October 1946, p. 31.
26. *Variety*, 16 October 1946, p. 4.

because their leaders were either misinformed or failed to keep their members informed as to what was actually going on in the strike. We at [Local] 705 put out a newsletter to our members to let them know who had done what in the past week and where things stood. For people who were afraid, information really helped; it clarified issues. Many members were afraid of being blackballed by either the studio or the union. There had been a lot of this in the past, and the studio workers were well aware that they had to tow the line or leave the business.

Certainly, the leadership of the Painters union had a big influence on their radicalism. The new studio painters local which the IA established during the strike has seldom, if ever, gone on strike. Yet Ellsworth also believed that the radicalism of certain groups or individuals in the studios was directly tied to their place in the larger economic sphere:

Irv Hentschel, for example, was a particularly good cabinet-maker and had no trouble keeping busy. But a lot of less resourceful people lost good-paying jobs in the studios as a result of the strike and had to go to work in lower paying jobs outside the studios. The survival factor was whether or not your skill was salable on the outside. The grips, for example, had a tough time making the same wage on the outside as a common laborer. Many of them were designated as carpenters on the sets but hardly had the skill to make a living in the construction business. Of course, with the painters, it was a different story. They could afford to walk out and that is what made them so militant. On the other hand, the lab workers were militant for just the opposite reason: their skills were useful only in the industry and the strike came at a time when the studios were in the earliest stages of automating the labs. This threatened people's jobs. Walsh made it clear to Local 683 that he was not going to tell the labs how to run their businesses.

Film lab worker Jerry Kraus' story about taking a job in a Los Angeles clothing store gives us some idea of what happened to people who had very specialized skills in the movie industry and who were blacklisted by Brewer. It was a prelude to the blacklisting of writers, actors and directors. It was the first death rattle of the progressive spirit in Hollywood.

The stabilization of labor relations meant also the cementing of the basic terms of employment for the workers. They would be well-paid on an hourly basis but would never overcome the problem of casualization. It was just part of the job – labor on demand. They would receive higher rates of pay for overtime work but they would be required to work overtime to meet frantic deadlines. They were seldom home during production, and yet they spent too much time there in between jobs, waiting by the phone for the next call from a studio or their union office. At the risk of over-simplification, I would say that from 1948 until the present, this is how things have been for Hollywood craft workers. But only someone such as Gene Mailes can explain to you what it meant to be blacklisted.

Standing between the criminal element and their membership is the job of labor leaders. That comes with the territory. Many of the early leaders

in the labor movement did exactly that. They would have died before they would have allowed criminals to take over the unions that they led. Of course, some of them and their kind were sent to jail and were framed into prison and execution, just as Harry Bridges almost had done to him.

What is there about a man who will try to send another man to prison whom he doesn't even know? An officer of the Los Angeles Police, named Savage, tried to do that to me. I was arrested on a mass picketing line outside one of the studios. It was shortly after the war, in 1946. The police, when testifying on the witness stand, after taking the oath to tell the truth, wore their fruit salad (the ribbons for service medals; in some cases they were given for being at a certain place). This man testified that, with about 500 other police around me, I got tough with him. I was convicted on four out of four charges. Luckily, the CSU had a lot of rather bright people on call, and these people discovered that the method of jury selection was illegal, so the convictions were all thrown out. To settle this, we plead out on the lesser charge and each paid a $20 fine. Some 1,700 pickets were arrested. We plugged up the courts in Los Angeles for several months.

Look at who was in charge of the IA during and after the period of gang control: George E. Browne was the president, put into office by the three largest gangs in the country, from Chicago, New York and New Jersey. These three mobs got together and then figured out who they knew, i.e. members of the IA, in the various parts of the country, and formed the committees to round up sufficient members to take over the IA and put Browne in as president. This turned out to be quite simple. The IA officers 'took care' of the small local unions, particularly the Motion Picture Machine Operators. They tended them like one would tend a rose garden. These small groups were the base of political power in the IA. This was similar to many of the unions in the AFL in the 20s and 30s.

The IA was controlled by the manipulation of the many local unions scattered around the country. The IA International office bought the cooperation of these small unions around the country in order to out-vote the larger Hollywood studio locals. This method of control was highlighted at the 1938 IA convention. During his address to the 1938 convention, in support of Resolution 6, Irv Hentschel pointed out that although Local 37 was entitled to have 75 delegates, only 55, out of 7,500 members, were appointed as delegates to the convention and these were people who could be depended on to side with the International officers.

The conspiracy between the IA and the producers brought out in the Kearns Committee hearings on jurisdictional disputes came out at a time when it was least expected. And it was revealed only because Pat Casey was angry at his employers and let the cat out of the bag. However, the tremendous political power of the motion picture industry was brought to bear and this evidence was simply disregarded. How high did this corruption go? Probably into Congress, certainly into the Department of Justice. Look at who paid the price for the Browne–Bioff deals – one lone studio executive, even though they all benefited financially from their deals with the mob.

This process was at the heart of McCarthyism. Congress passed a law that unions had to file affidavits ensuring that their leaders were not members of the Communist Party. This was used by the AFL and the CIO as a means of disposing of the militant unionists regardless of their political leanings. It was so simple to name any member who might in the future run for office in the union, as a liberal, a radical or anything that the officials didn't like. I know of one man who was expelled from the Teamsters motion picture local on the ground that he had a red candle on his mantle long after Christmas. In reality, his 'crime' was that he had publicly stated that the Teamsters should not drive scabs through the studio gates. His name was Al Caya, the husband of Jean Caya, one of the members of the lab workers who represented us as one of our counsel during the trial.

The treatment that Al Caya got was typical of the purges in AFL and CIO unions around the country during the blacklisting era. Then the CIO crawled back to the AFL with their tails between their legs to form the AFL-CIO. The men and women who were expelled from unions had no great trouble, provided that they were in some way able to avoid telling where they had been employed for varying periods of time. A few employers, when they found that one of their employees had been caught up in this frightful net, stood against the idea of blacklisting. They were few and far between.

The McCarthy era ended several years ago but the shadow still appears in some of the most frightful ways. I had a few jobs – temporary, day labor – until I went to work for a man whom I had gotten to know during the strike. He was a terrific street fighter. A member of the Defense Committee. He was willing to wade into any gathering of strike-breakers and would come out without a scar. He was running a small lumber yard in Burbank. I went to work with him for several months. I learned what hard work was like. When business was slack he had to let me go. I went to a nearby lumber yard and stayed there for seventeen years.

I was working there in 1951 when the Un-American Activities Committee was in Los Angeles and had scared several studio writers into becoming something less than men. The Committee was insisting on people who wanted to continue working in the picture business naming publicly people who were or had been members of the Communist Party, whose names the Committee already had. These names had been given to the Committee by professional stool pigeons or members of the FBI planted in the Party. Both Irv Hentschel and Bob Ames were named by someone and it appeared in the papers.

I was closer to these two men than I was to my own brother. I figured that I would be named any day – I had already been named as a Communist party member – so I decided to tell the manager of the yard where I worked. I told him a straight story, that the two men just named had left the Party, Irv Hentschel in 1939 and Bob Ames in 1945. It turned out that the manager's brother was a co-producer in the studios and had been named by some stool pigeon, so he knew what his brother was going through. The next day he told me that since I had told him what I had been through he felt it was incumbent upon him to tell the owner of the yard what I had told him. He told me that, Rex, I'll call him, would be over to see me about it later.

Sure enough, the next day Rex came over and talked to me briefly and told me that he and the manager had talked it over and decided that I had told the truth and that what I had done before I came to work for him was my own problem and that I would stay employed as long as I liked. He did say, however, that if I were called to testify and refused to answer any question, 'Don't come back to work here.'

What I was thinking but didn't tell him was that if I were called I would not answer these questions about my politics or those of any of my friends. I would not make it easy for him. I would not voluntarily quit. He would have to fire me, face-to-face. I was fairly sure that he would not have done it.

When I was down in the Los Angeles area a couple of years ago I called Rex's son to ask permission to tell this story and to mention his father's name. He was at home that day and his secretary relayed the message. The word from him was that he did not want me to mention his father's name. Even to this day some people are frightened at the mere thought that their relatives were not quite willing to give way to the latest hysteria and acted like human beings and men. Whatever his reasons, I was left with the impression of Rex's son as something of a coward. His father, on the other hand, was a decent human being.

The blacklisting of union and political activists in the studios ended a whole era. The weakening and corrupting of the unions and guilds made it easier to get at the leftist intellectuals. It revealed how easy it was to frighten and stampede people with the cry of 'Communism!' There were no truly locally controlled unions left standing in the motion picture business. The effort to establish locally controlled, democratic unions was crushed. Some dreams have a price. Sometimes the price is high. In this case the price was being blacklisted, loss of friends, the break-up of families, economic hardship, ostracism, suspicion, misunderstanding. It meant seeing old friends coming on the street and not knowing whether to greet them, possibly risking a rebuff from one to whom you had once been close. The risks seemed endless. On occasions the meetings of old acquaintances was painful. Perhaps the most difficult part of a fight such as we were in was the misunderstanding that we met from some members of our families – to get this from a parent, for instance: 'You had a good job, why didn't you take care of it?'

After several years I met studio workers with whom I had had differences. Upon asking them how they were getting along, first I would hear how well they were doing, then after a few minutes the truth would come out and they would end up saying that they would get out of the studios if they could but they had been in that work too long to change. On further questioning, the subject of contract advantages would come up and they would find out that the benefits from their union contracts lagged way behind those gained by more militant unions.

After working in one place for years, the fact that I had once been working in the studios would come up and I would answer the questions.

was told about this several days later by Ed Gilbert, another old friend of Irv's. I had not seen Irv for several weeks and was completely surprised by the news. On the way home (I was living in a trailer park, alone, at the time), I stopped into a bar across the street from the place I had worked for several years. I asked for a straight shot of bourbon with a water chaser. I asked for another a few minutes later. The bartender, whom I had seen before but didn't know, sensed that something was unusual about my drinking two shots in quick succession. He asked me if everything was OK. I told him briefly about what had happened. When I finished he shook his head, and after a minute or two came back and said, 'You know something? That guy beat the game?' That remark pulled me out of a terrible mood. The old joke about the fisherman wanting to die of a heart attack, hooked up to a great big fish, came to mind. All my memories of him were good. Even our arguments, in which he had the damnable habit of being right, were good. The shock of it to his wife Helen and the children was another matter.

The last time I heard from Carey McWilliams was several years ago when I started to research this whole event and I wrote to him at the office of the *Nation* magazine, of which he was the editor for many years. His letter was a delight.

Kevin Brownlow had asked me to start gathering records for a possible file on what we had done to be kept at the American Film Institute. It turned out that the AFI was not interested in this material.

The Law Firm of Margolis & McTernan is still in business in Los Angeles. Several years ago they represented me in a traffic accident. I was driving on the Hollywood Freeway toward Los Angeles and a wheel bearing of the truck I was driving gave out, causing the truck to spin out of control, spinning around after hitting a guard rail and tearing off all but one of the front wheels. The truck was loaded with steel construction braces which were scattered over the freeway blocking all but one of the lanes. While spinning around with one wheel the sparks from the truck were like a wall of fire. Had the gas tank been punctured I would have been burned up. The case was settled on the courthouse steps, so to speak.

Ben Margolis and his wife spent a summer here in the Santa Cruz area close to some other friends. Ben and I went crab fishing from the Santa Cruz pier a couple of times. On one of these fishing trips we took one of his grandsons and he was the one who caught the only crab on that day.

Once Bob Ames got the sack, he finally had enough time to devote to his wood carving and then painting in oils and watercolors. Both Irv and Bob went on location with the company that made *Salt of the Earth*. The film was written and produced by writers, directors and crew who had been blacklisted from Hollywood. Irv and Bob helped with making props. Also they both had small parts in the picture. Irv plays a disgusted jailer with a mean face and Bob plays a Catholic priest baptizing a baby. The picture is still being shown at colleges and film art groups. It was very well made in spite of the efforts of Brewer and the super-patriots to stop its being made, then developed and distributed.

Bob also worked on a eight-by-ten feet bas-relief wood carving on the subject of black history, called 'Freedom Now!'. It was given its official opening on the steps of the Massachusetts State Capitol. Mrs Martin Luther King was there as well as several leaders of the Civil Rights movement, both black and white. Bob also worked as a carpenter and cabinet maker. He also worked with a contractor, Hugh DeLacy, a former Congressman from the state of Washington. As a Congressman, DeLacy had made a speech holding the United States should not be drawn into a land war in Asia. For this speech the right wing spent several million dollars to drive him out of office at the next election. They succeeded. Also we lost the land war in Asia.

Jesse Sapp took small remodeling jobs on houses in the San Fernando Valley. Jesse died several years ago. George Stoica died about fifteen years ago. Lynn Batchelder became an artist, a painter, in the Los Angeles area. I have lost touch with the rest of these men and their wives.

Bob died in 1986 in the Unitarian Church Sunset House in Los Angeles. He was a friend for forty-eight years. He died at the age of eighty seven years. At the memorial service, one of his friends told how even-tempered Bob always was. At this I couldn't help laughing. I thought of a couple of times when Bob did get angry. The first time was when his wife Alida brought a kitchen knife out to his shop and asked him to sharpen it. He started to sharpen it and Alida said, 'No, no, not that way!' Bob turned on her and said, 'Alida, I do not need a lesson on how to sharpen a knife.' As he said this he indicated his box full of wood carving knives and chisels. Alida looked at me with a look of having put her foot in her mouth. The other time was at the expanded Party meeting when he blew up at Blackie Mason. I never knew a good radical who was worth a damn who didn't get mad, once in a while. Another time was when we had a shouting match. Both of us were truly angry. The result was that I didn't see them for about eight months. Finally, I received a letter from Bob. When I got it I was of course delighted. Upon reading it I saw, with indignation, that it was not an apology! It took about two weeks for me to realize that the son of a bitch would never apologize! He didn't seem to realize just how right I had been! After thinking it over for another couple of weeks, I called them. Alida answered the phone and I said that if they were going to be home, I'd like to come over. Alida's reply was 'Oh, Gene, I think that would be very nice!' We never spoke of the argument again. That was about twenty years before he died. A friend at the Unitarian home found him lying on the floor of his room and called for help. He died on the way to the hospital.

My wife, Thelma, had died several years before, leaving the girls and me suddenly. The girls were thirteen and ten years old. I kept them with me for about a year and slowly realized how inadequate I was in this situation. I think that part of the problem could have been that it had been such a good relationship and such a situation can, in its own way, be just as distorting as a terribly unsatisfactory marriage. Trying to find such a marriage again was to leave me extremely vulnerable.

Thelma's brother, whom we raised from twelve years of age to eighteen, and his wife offered to take the children, which I gratefully